ABOUT THE PUBLISHER
New York Institute of Finance
... more than just books.

NYIF offers practical, applied training and education in a wide range of formats and topics:

* *Classroom training:* evenings, mornings, noon-hours
* *Seminars and conferences:* one-, two-, and three-day introductory, intermediate-, and professional-level programs
* *Customized training:* need-specific programs conducted on your site or ours; in New York City, throughout the United States, anywhere in the world
* *Independent study:* self-paced learning—basic, intermediate, or advanced
* *Exam preparation:* NASD licensing (including Series 3, 6, 7, 24, 27, 63); C.F.A.; state life and health insurance

Subjects of books and training programs include the following:

* Account Executive Training
* Brokerage Operations
* Currency Trading
* Futures Trading
* International Corporate Finance
* Investment Analysis
* Options Trading
* Securities Transfer
* Selling Securities
* Technical Analysis
* Treasury Management
* Yield Curve Analysis

*When Wall Street professionals think **training**, they think NYIF.*

For further information, please call or write to us. Please specify your areas of interest—classroom training, custom programs, independent-study courses, exam preparation, or books—so that we can respond promptly to your inquiry.

New York Institute of Finance
70 Pine Street
New York, NY 10270–0003
212 / 344–2900
FAX: 212 / 514–8423
TELEX: 238790

Simon & Schuster, Inc.   A Gulf + Western Company
"Where Wall Street Goes to School" ™

THE
PROFESSIONAL'S GUIDE
TO THE
U.S. GOVERNMENT SECURITIES MARKETS:
Treasuries, Agencies, Mortgage-Backed Instruments

George M. Bollenbacher

with the assistance of
Samuel P. Peluso

New York Institute of Finance

LIBRARY OF CONGRESS
Library of Congress Cataloging-in-Publication Data

Bollenbacher, George M.
  The professional's guide to the U.S. government securities markets
  : treasuries, agencies, mortgage-backed instruments / George M.
Bollenbacher with the assistance of Samuel P. Peluso.
      p.   cm.
  Includes index.
  ISBN 0-13-725532-2 : $39.50
  1. Government securities--United States.   I. Peluso, Samuel P.
II. Title.
HG4936.B65 1988
332.63'232'0973--dc19   88-12116
                                                                  CIP

This publication is designed to provide accurate and authoritative information in regard to the subject matter covered. It is sold with the understanding that the publisher is not engaged in rendering legal, accounting, or other professional service. If legal advice or other expert assistance is required, the services of a competent professional person should be sought.

*From a Declaration of Principles Jointly Adopted by
a Committee of the American Bar Association and a
Committee of Publishers and Associations*

© 1988 by NYIF Corp.
A Division of Simon & Schuster, Inc.
70 Pine Street, New York, NY 10270-0003

All rights reserved. No part of this book may
be reproduced in any form or by any means without
permission in writing from the publisher.

Printed in the United States of America

10 9 8 7 6 5 4 3 2 1

New York Institute of Finance
(NYIF Corp.)
70 Pine Street
New York, New York 10270-0003

To Betsy, who always thought this was a crazy business, but who stuck with me anyway.

Contents

Preface .... *ix*
Acknowledgments .... *xi*
Introduction .... *xiii*

SECTION ONE: OVERVIEW OF THE MARKET

CHAPTER ONE
**Background of
the Market,** 3

Origins of the National Debt *3*
Development of the Government Bond Market *5*
Development of Federal Agency Securities *7*
Recent Changes in the Marketplace *10*

CHAPTER TWO
**Structure of
the Market,** 12

Nature of an Over-the-Counter Market *12*
Organizational Structure of the Government Bond Market *14*
Recent and Impending Changes in the Market Structure *25*

SECTION TWO: SECURITIES IN THE MARKET

CHAPTER THREE
Individual Treasury Securities, 31

U.S. Treasury Bills	33
U.S. Treasury Notes	47
U.S. Treasury Bonds	63

CHAPTER FOUR
Individual Agency Securities, 69

The "Big Three" Federal Agencies	72
Minor Agency Securities	87
Other Agency Issuers	89

CHAPTER FIVE
Mortgage-Backed Securities, 90

The Passthrough Security	92
The CMO and the REMIC	93
GNMA Passthroughs	95
Federal Home Loan Mortgage Corp (FHLMC)	102
FNMA Mortgage-Backed Securities (FNMA MBS)	103
Private Collateralized Mortgage Obligations (CMOs)	104
Agency MBS Trading	104
The Mortgage-Backed Securities Market	106
Some Concluding Observations	109

CHAPTER SIX
Money Market Instruments and Financing Transactions, 110

Money Market Instruments	111
Bank Money Market Instruments	111
Commercial Paper	114

Contents

Financing Securities 115
Repurchase and Reverse Repurchase Agreements 116
The Language of Securities Financing 120

CHAPTER SEVEN
Derivative Instruments, 123

Financial Futures 124
Options on Securities and Futures 132
Options Markets 136

SECTION THREE: INSIDE THE GOVERNMENT BOND MARKET

CHAPTER EIGHT
Inside a Primary Dealer: The Trading Desk, 145

What Is a Primary Dealer? 145
Duties of a Primary Dealer 147
Structure of a Primary Dealer 148
Who Does What 149

CHAPTER NINE
Inside a Primary Dealer: The Sales Force and the Economics Department, 161

The Sales Force 162
The Economics Department 166

CHAPTER TEN
Trading Government Securities, 172

The Key to Success 173
Trading Styles of Primary Dealers 173
Market Philosophies—Fundamental and Technical 176

Methods of Trading—Naked vs. Spread 177
The Nature of Arbitrage 179

CHAPTER ELEVEN
The Language of the Market, 183

Trading Terminology 184
Auction Terminology 187
Financing Terminology 188
Settlement Terminology 191

CHAPTER TWELVE
A Day in the Life of a Dealer, 194

The Quiet Hours 195
Trading Begins 200
First Moment of Truth 203

CHAPTER THIRTEEN
Inside the Federal Reserve, 214

The Structure of the Fed 215
The Functions of the Fed 216
The Balancing Act 225

Index 227

Preface

I have lost count of the number of times I have been asked, "Where can I find a good book about the government bond market?" Many times the question has been asked of me by young people planning to pursue a career with one of the Primary Dealers as a trader or salesperson. Recently, however, the question has come more often from people who have become customers of those Primary Dealers—people who work in bank trust departments, insurance companies, portfolio management firms, or mutual funds.

They ask the question because, for all the market's importance, it is not very visible to the public. The market is very spread out, with market makers all across the United States, and the business is done in trading rooms that are shut off from the public's eye. Many of the market's customs are strange, and its language is often arcane. Finally, the Primary Dealers are acting as principal, instead of as agent, so they are not inclined to reveal everything that they know about the market.

This book is for everyone who asks the questions. "What really happens every day in the government bond market? How does business get done? Who are the Primary Dealers, and how do they do business? What is the jargon of the market, and what are its rules of the road?" It is meant to take you inside the largest securities market in the world and give you a good look around. And it is meant to help you feel comfortable in a market that trades over $100 billion in securities a day.

There are several things that this book is *not*. It is not an exhaustive treatise on individual government securities, although it contains chapters on the various classes of securities. It is not a textbook of money-market and interest calculations. It is not about "How to make a million dollars in the bond market," although it does cover some of the more popular methods of trading government securities. It is not a data book listing all the government securities that have ever been issued.

It *is* what the title says it is, a guide to the government bond market. Like a Baedeker, it is a guidebook for the traveler in an unfamiliar land. It tells you what is happening, and what to watch out for. It explains quaint local customs, if not some of the local costumes. It translates some of the language, so you can begin to do business. Whether you plan to settle in or are just passing through, it is designed to make your stay more enjoyable, and perhaps more profitable.

I was first introduced to the government bond market in 1970. Since that time, I have seen it change and grow in ways I would never have imagined possible. It has become huge, varied, and enormously important. And its past is just a preface to its future. Those of you who read this book as a beginning to a career in the government bond market are about to embark on a journey of true adventure, and I wish you good luck and Godspeed.

George M. Bollenbacher
Tarrytown, New York

Acknowledgments

When I began in the bond business, there were no books to read; there were only people to learn from. I wish to express my gratitude to a whole list of people who answered my unending questions, and helped me along the road. In the beginning, there were Dick Smith, Peter Leonard, Larry Littig, and Steve Dunn. As the years went by there were Norman Stewart, Bill Rust, Joe Sullivan, Don Meyer, Rick Landau, John Sites, and Ken Paterson. And more recently, there were Dick MacWilliams, Bill Mulhern, Doug Robbins, and especially Ashmore Mitchell. Some of these people might be surprised to see their names here, but they all enriched my professional life.

The writing of this book was a labor of love, but a labor nonetheless. In the writing of it, I was assisted, supported, and encouraged by the people at The New York Institute of Finance. I owe a great debt to Steven Winings, Bill Rini, and especially to Fred Dahl, whose enthusiasm was all-important.

Finally, all of the time that went into writing this book was taken away from my family. My wife, Betsy, and my children, Amy and John, gave me the love, support, and understanding I needed to get the job done. To them goes the most heartfelt acknowledgment of all.

Introduction

If you were to read the financial section of the local paper in most cities in the United States, it would be easy to conclude that the only financial market in this country is the stock market—in particular, the New York Stock Exchange. The newspaper's pages would be filled with stock quotations, the pulse of the economy would be measured by the performance of the Dow Jones Industrial Index, and the paper would be filled with ads for stock selection services. It would seem as if there isn't another significant market in the country.

Nothing could be further from the truth! On a high volume day, the New York Stock Exchange trades about 200 million shares, with an average price of about $50, for a total dollar value of about $10 billion. That is surely an impressive number. However, on the same day the government bond market will trade securities with a market value of about $100 billion. For a market that is virtually unknown and hidden, the U.S. government bond market is the largest and most liquid capital market in the world.

The misunderstanding of the market extends even to the name by which it is known. Many of the securities traded in this market are *not* issued by the government. Nowadays, government bond dealers trade securities issues of various agencies (such as FNMA), as well as certificates of deposit issued by banks, not to mention a whole host of mortgage-backed instruments. Very few of these securities are actually *bonds.* Along with the notes and bills that the Treasury issues, there are capital debentures (issued by agencies), passthroughs (issued by GNMA and FNMA), participation certificates (issued by FHLMC), and stripped securities (issued by dealers and banks). And, finally, it isn't a *market*, in the same sense that the NYSE is. There is no exchange floor where buyers and sellers come to trade, and no transaction tape where all trades are reported. Long ago, it was much more a true government bond market. It was a specific location, where people came to trade bonds issued by the government. Times, and the demands of the financial system, have wrought tremendous changes.

Now, the market is enormous, diverse, and highly volatile. In addition to its sheer size, the government bond market is important for several other reasons:

○ *It is where the Treasury finances its budget deficits.* In recent years, with the growth of the budget deficits to over $100 billion per year, the market's ability to absorb and distribute large amounts of securities is crucial to the smooth functioning of the Federal government. If this market were to cease functioning, the operations of the government would quickly grind to a halt.

○ *It is where the Federal Reserve executes monetary policy.* In a free-market system, the availability and cost of credit are two of the main tools for controlling the level of economic activity. In the United States, control of the cost and availability of credit is the province of the Federal Reserve System, and the Fed acts mostly through the market. The ability of the market to function in the face of abrupt changes in interest rates is very important to the efficient implementation of the nation's monetary policy.

○ *It is the meeting place of the nation's and the world's short-term credit needs.* In the United States and world economies, short-term borrowing and lending needs are very diverse and very large. Every day, corporations and nations with a need for short-term credit seek a place to meet financial institutions and pension funds with short-term money to invest. The government bond and money markets are essential for the efficient balancing of these needs.

○ *It is the investment market for billions of dollars in foreign exchange reserves.* With the growth of international trade that has occurred since World War II, nations have accumulated large holdings of currency reserves. The smooth functioning of international trade depends upon the ability of these nations to access their foreign exchange reserves at a moment's notice. Because the government bond market is so large and so liquid, most of these reserves are kept in dollars, and the wide acceptance of dollars as foreign exchange reserves has enabled the United States to run substantial balance-of-payment deficits for many years.

All that being true, it is surprising to realize that the government bond market functions in relative obscurity, and that it used to be even more obscure. For several decades, until the 1970s, the government bond market was the private preserve of a small number of trading houses and their institutional customers. Over those decades, trading practices, complex interrelationships and methods of using securities evolved, until the market ran like a well-oiled machine. That machine began to have problems, however, when the 1970s brought with it two developments—volatile interest rates and a large supply of new debt issues.

The market has always done business *over the counter,* so that dealers necessarily act as principal instead of as agent. At the same time the Treasury has always been reluctant to pay the kind of sales commissions that sellers of corporate or municipal issues are used to paying. As a result, and because the Treasury uses competitive methods of issuing securities, no organized *marketing* of new Treasury securities ever existed. Instead, dealers bid for new issues along with all other investors, and distributed their positions after the auction, not before. This system, which worked when the Treasury had relatively few issues, and small ones, has shown signs of strain as the frequency and size of the issues has risen.

The result of these pressures has been a series of subtle but significant transformations of the marketplace. One such transformation has been the expansion of the ranks of Primary Dealers, as the market has whetted its appetite for more capital. Another transformation has been in the methods of financing government securities, allowing many more securities to be financed and with much higher leverage. One of the most important transformations has been the introduction and growth of derivative instruments—financial futures and debt options—which serve to separate the price risks from other investment considerations.

For all its importance, and for all the changes it has seen, the government bond market is still very much of a closed circle. At the center stands the *Federal Reserve System,* the nation's monetary authority, and the regulator of the market. Grouped around the Fed are the *Primary Dealers,* so designated by the Fed, and the linchpin of the market. Serving the Primary Dealers are the *government bond brokers,* who facilitate transactions between the dealers. Standing on the outside of the circle is everyone else, lumped into the classification of *customer.* Whether the customer is a very large institution, like the World Bank, a very large foreign investor, like the Japanese Postal Retirement System, or the smallest savings and loan, that customer's official status is the same: it is on the outside looking in.

Since virtually all the transactions in this market are done as principal, the line between customers and dealers is very sharply drawn. The dealers make markets, the customers trade off of them. The dealers can trade with the Fed, the customers cannot. The dealers can do business with, and see the markets of, the brokers, while customers cannot. The Primary Dealers must report their daily activity and positions to the Market Statistics Division of the Fed; the customers need not.

The last requirement, daily reporting, which applies only to Primary Dealers, has pointed up a major flaw in the present market structure. Regulation by the Fed has been a function of the history of the market, and some unscrupulous dealers have taken advantage of the "old boy" regulatory structure. Because government securities were exempt from registration under the Securities Act of 1933 and because dealers who traded only securities exempt under that act were also exempt from registration under the Securities Exchange Act of 1934, there grew up a collection of bond dealers who escaped the clear oversight of either the SEC or the Fed. Sooner or later, such people cause a scandal, and these dealers were no exception. In a period of a few years, Drysdale Government Securities, ESM Government Securities, and BBS Government Securities collapsed, taking with them the funds of many smaller financial institutions.

As a result, some form of registration and regulation is clearly in store for those people who deal in governments and are not Primary Dealers. Whether those changes make the market safer or not, any institution doing regular business in this market needs to have a clear understanding of how the securities work and how the market works. The three sections of this book answer that need.

Section One is an overview of the market, how it came to look like it does, and who participates in it. Section Two looks, in detail, at all the securities traded in the market, and all the participants in the market. Section Three looks at how business gets done in the market, the conventions and language of the market, and the Federal Reserve.

These three sections are designed to do two things: (1) to give the first-time reader a comprehensive understanding of how to do business in a large, volatile, and arcane business, and (2) to serve as a reference work, refreshing the reader's knowledge of sections of the market that he has been absent from for a while. Of course, the market itself is changing all the time, so we will prepare supplements to this book, designed to reflect those changes. In the meantime, let us embark on a voyage of discovery not unlike the epic voyages of the New World explorers of centuries past. Let us explore the government bond market.

SECTION ONE

OVERVIEW OF THE MARKET

CHAPTER ONE

Background of the Market

ORIGINS OF THE NATIONAL DEBT

The origins of our *national debt* are inextricably mixed in with the origins of the nation itself. Although the thirteen colonies were rich in natural resources, they were prohibited by England from amassing the kind of treasury that the European powers relied on to wage a war. Without a horde of gold or silver, the American Revolution was truly a bootstrap affair, and the Continental Congress depended on the willingness of the average colonist to finance it by accepting the government's debt.

In fact, there was some borrowing by individual colonies even before the nation was born. Massachusetts and Carolina, for example, borrowed significant amounts at least seventy years before the Revolutionary War, but the first national debt came into being when the Continental Congress borrowed $3,000,000 in June and July of 1775 to pay for the Revolution. By 1780 the national debt had risen to $200,000,000; but by 1785 it had gradually ceased to circulate, having effectively been repudiated.

That was hardly an auspicious beginning for a bond market, but the country had an inauspicious beginning in a lot of ways. The British regarded their loss here as a fluke, and it wasn't until they had been defeated by the "colonists" again—in the War of 1812—that they conceded we would go our own way. Even within our borders, the attempt to hammer a group of dissidents into a nation sometimes met with local resistance, such as the Whiskey Rebellion.

However, the nation got itself organized on the financial front, as well as on other fronts, and formed the *U.S. Treasury Department* on September 2, 1789. One of the Treasury's first acts, in 1790, was to consolidate all the remaining debt from the Revolution into $54,124,464 of 4% notes maturing in 1800. In a real sense, this was the first *U.S. government bond*.

This issue, and several that followed, were totally paid off, leaving the government temporarily free of debt. Each time, though, wars put the Treasury back in the red. The War of 1812 ran the debt up to $127,334,933 in 1816, but subsequent repayments brought it down to $91,015,566 by 1820. By 1830 the debt was down to $48,565,406. It was effectively extinguished by 1835. However, debt repayments, and the subsequent depositing of Treasury surpluses in the banking system, had such a stimulative effect on the nation's economy that they resulted in the crash of 1837.

The ensuing depression, and the Mexican-American War, ran the national debt to $66,199,341 by July 1, 1852. Repayments brought the debt down to $31,974,081 in 1855 and $28,699,000 in 1857. The Civil War started the debt level back up again, to $524,177,955 in June, 1862, and $2,677,929,012 by June, 1865.

Unlike the period after previous wars, the demands of the Reconstruction prevented the retirement of much debt until the 1870s. By 1880 the national debt still stood at $2,090,908,872, much of it in the form of currency like the famous "greenbacks." These got their name from the fact that they were printed on one side only, because the Government Printing Office was in such a hurry to create new money. By 1893 the debt was down to $961,431,766, and by 1910 back up to $1,146,939,969.

By the time World War I began, the national debt stood at $1,188,235,400, and by the time it ended the debt had risen to $26,596,701,000. Subsequent redemptions brought it down to $16,805,433,000 by 1929, but New Deal programs started it back up to $40,439,532,411 in 1939.

World War II had the same effect as each war before it, only on a larger scale. By the time the GIs came home from Europe and the Pacific, the Treasury owed over $275,000,000,000.

After 1945 the Treasury ran small deficits or surpluses until 1970, so that by that year the national debt was only up to $382,000,000,000. From then on, however, the deficits mounted rapidly; as a consequence the national debt reached $914,000,000,000 by 1980, and $1,841,000,000,000 by 1985. (See Figure 1-1.)

DEVELOPMENT OF THE GOVERNMENT BOND MARKET

The existence of a large national debt does not, of course, automatically imply the existence of a *bond market*. For much of our nation's history, the New York Stock Exchange was the only available market for government bonds. Since most buyers thought of these securities as a home for savings, the debt acted more like today's savings bonds than today's government bonds, and the trading volume on the NYSE was relatively low.

In fact, the evolution of today's *Primary Dealer* began with the Treasury designating distribution agents, to assist it in placing the debt it needed to sell. Originally, *commercial banks* served as both the issuing agents and the primary buyers. As agents, they were usually paid a commission of 1/8 of 1%. In 1863, the Treasury appointed a *private banker* in Philadelphia as general agent for a $500 million issue of bonds, marking the first naming of an agent from a noncommercial bank.

During this period, the placement of Treasury debt was greatly helped by the requirement that each national bank hold a certain amount of these securities as a reserve against liabilities, and as a requirement to obtain a national bank charter. Thus, institutional holders didn't really require a liquid market for Treasuries, but even so, by 1900 three *brokers* were providing execution services for institutional holders. Even here, however, the future was not rosy. By 1905, the low trading volume of Treasury debt had reduced the market to the point that the brokers were in danger of closing. Only the Panama Canal issues gave them a new lease of life.

At about the same time, the market saw the emergence of the first *dealers*, in this case dealer-banks. The dealers' ability to take positions and offer customers commission-free executions proved so attractive that by 1911 brokers were all but extinct. When the *Federal Reserve System* came into being in 1913, it swiftly took over the issuance

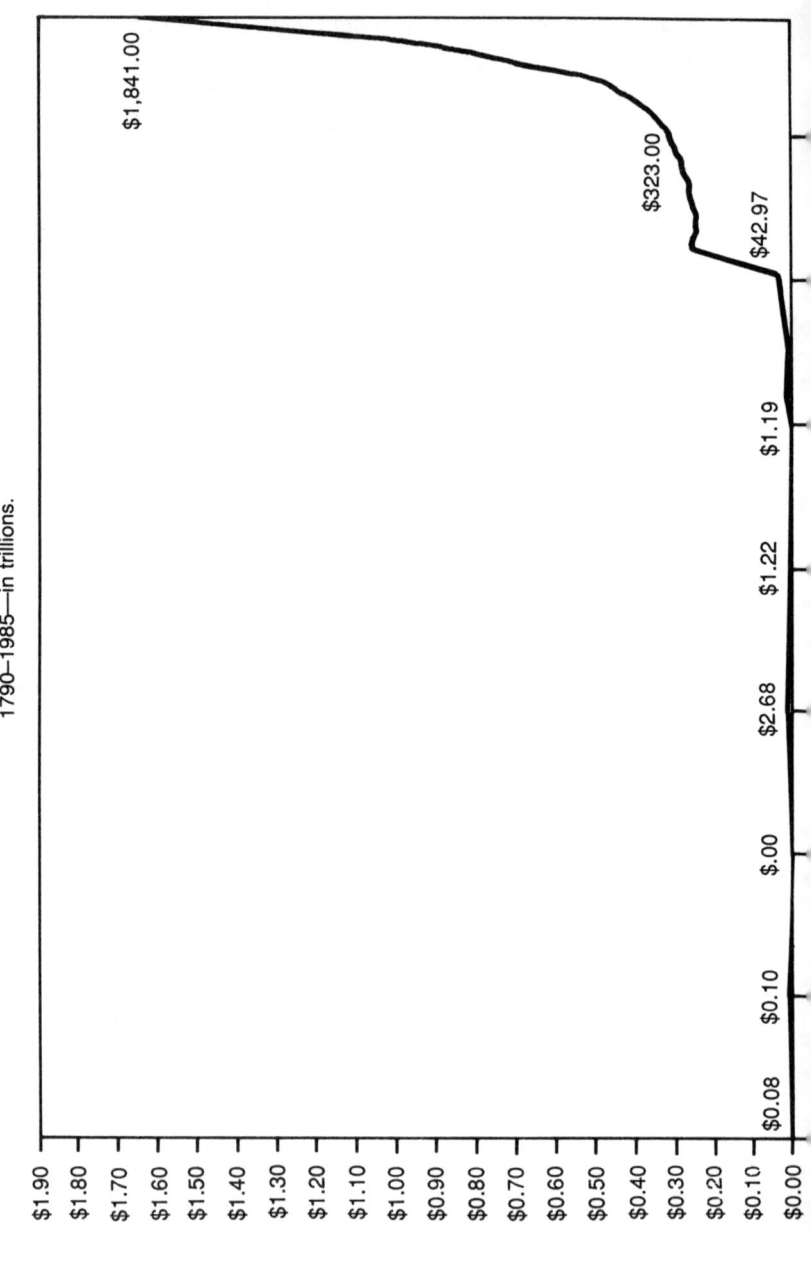

Figure 1-1
U.S. national debt
1790–1985—in trillions.

function for the Treasury, leaving the dealers to work in the secondary market and to bid on the Treasury's subscriptions. The secondary market began to grow, and the growth of the national debt during World War I brought all kinds of dealers into the fray. Some were not very scrupulous, so the Fed began to play the part of a *market regulator.*

This process took some time though. The *Federal Open Market Committee* took nine years to go from an informal concept to a formal organization. The Banking Act of 1933 brought that about, but the Fed's relationship with dealers remained rocky. There were still plenty of fly-by-night dealers in the market, quoting outrageous prices and giving the market a bad name.

By 1939, the reputable dealers and the Fed decided to do something about the situation, forming the *Government Securities Dealer Group.* Even here, progress was slow, with the first policies not set by the group until 1942. In fact, it wasn't until 1944 that the Fed restricted the Federal Open Market Committee's dealings to what have become known today as *recognized dealers.* At this time, the Fed also began the kind of informal regulation of the government bond market that reflected the relationship between the Bank of England and the London Bill Brokers. This informal regulatory approach has persisted well into the 1980s, with the Federal Reserve keeping a fatherly eye on the market through the Primary Dealers, who must report daily to the Fed in New York. The informality of this regulation has caused some problems recently, and Congress has passed legislation requiring all dealers, whether they are Primary Dealers or not, to register with some regulatory body; this subjects the government bond market to rules and regulations drawn up by the Treasury Department.

DEVELOPMENT OF FEDERAL AGENCY SECURITIES

The coexistence of our free economy with our political process has long been filled with concessions and compromises. Quite often, the economic reality and the political dream come together in conflict, and that conflict is often resolved in ways that might not make sense to someone unaware of the background. A prime example of such a process is the development of the *federal agencies* whose securities play an important role in the market.

In the case of the federal agencies, two deep-seated traditions came into conflict. First, the nation was founded on the individual farmer, who dropped his plow and scythe to take up arms in the Revolution. Ever since, the right of the individual American to work his own farm has been paramount. By extension, the right of the individual American to own his own home became a part of this sacred tenet.

Unfortunately, problems began to arise because this political belief was, and is, at odds with economic realities. As a commodity producer, the family farmer operates in a market where lowest price is everything. But the family farmer is not the most efficient producer. In the case of the homeowner, the length of time it takes to amortize the cost of a typical home exposes lenders to tremendous interest rate risk. When economic events increase interest rate volatility, those lenders cannot absorb the losses that result, and available credit for home purchases dries up.

The simplest solution to these problems was direct government intervention, in the form of low-cost loans to farmers or homeowners. Here, however, entered the other deep-seated national bias: opposition to direct government intervention in the economic process, particularly to the benefit of certain sectors of the population. Recently, for example, the government has directly guaranteed the debt of certain borrowers, such as Boeing and Chrysler, but only after a storm of protest and controversy.

In the case of the farmer and the homeowner, the compromise solution was the formation of a series of federal agencies that fall somewhere between government bodies and private corporations. In most cases, the agencies are owned by the industry they serve, but they also perform a regulatory function within that industry. This anomaly, of having an organization regulate its owners, has worked reasonably well since the first agency was formed in 1917, but the recent deregulation of the banking and thrift industry, and the credit problems of the farm and energy sectors, have put unprecedented strains on the agency structure.

The Individual Federal Agencies

- *Federal Land Banks:* Founded in 1917 to provide low-cost loans to assist farmers in acquiring and holding farmland. Their stock is owned by 400 Production Credit Associations across the United States, giving the Land Banks a collective net worth of nearly $5 billion, against which they have borrowed approximately $45 billion.

Background of the Market

- *Federal Intermediate Credit Banks:* Founded in 1923 to provide low-cost crop financing through Production Credit Associations, banks, and other agricultural finance companies. Although originally capitalized by the Treasury, the FICBs have, since 1968, been owned by about 400 Production Credit Associations, and have over $2 billion in capital and about $16 billion in liabilities.
- *Federal Home Loan Banks:* Founded in 1932 to assist the nation's thrift institutions in providing a stable source of funds to the housing industry. The FHLBs are owned by their member thrifts, but are regulated by the Federal Home Loan Bank Board, which is funded by the Treasury.
- *Banks for Cooperatives:* Founded in 1933 to provide low-cost credit for the nation's agricultural cooperatives, who own all the outstanding stock. The COOPs have a collective net worth of over $1 billion and liabilities of over $6 billion.
- *Federal National Mortgage Association:* Founded in 1938 to provide assistance to the secondary mortgage market. FNMA's stock is traded on the New York Stock Exchange; it has a net worth of over $1 billion.
- *Government National Mortgage Association:* Founded in 1968 to assist in creating a secondary market for FHA and VA mortgages, through the issuance of passthrough securities. GNMA has no outstanding stock since it is a corporate instrumentality of the U.S. government.
- *Federal Home Loan Mortgage Corporation:* Founded in 1970 to assist in creating a secondary market for conventional mortgages, through the issuance of participation certificates. All of FHLMC's stock is held by the Federal Home Loan Banks, giving FHLMC a net worth of $100 million.
- *Federal Farm Credit Banks:* Founded in 1975 to consolidate the financing needs of the FICBs, COOPs, and Land Banks. The FFCB issues both discount notes for short-term funds, and systemwide bonds for long-term funds.

Each of these agencies issues securities; some agencies issue more than one kind. Originally, all the agencies borrowed money on their own credit, and lent it out again through the existing banking system. More recently, the Housing Credit Agencies have begun to issue, and to guarantee, mortgage-backed securities. These securities, which were unknown before 1970, have become so popular that their issues now dwarf all other agency issues combined.

RECENT CHANGES IN THE MARKETPLACE

For many years, from the end of World War II until the 1970s, the issuing and trading of government securities was very bound up in tradition. The government ran small surpluses or deficits, the ownership profile of the debt remained relatively static, and the number and kind of Primary Dealers didn't change very much.

By the beginning of the 1970s, however, several forces were coming together that would change forever the face of the government bond market. First, the nation's attempt to finance both a faraway war and an agenda of ambitious social programs led to a *demand-driven inflation* that lasted for at least five years. Second, the oil-producing nations of the world, led by Saudi Arabia, grew tired of their role as commodity producers and formed a cartel. OPEC proceeded to *increase the worldwide price of crude oil* fourfold, prompting panic in the industrial nations and another round of inflation. Third, the *economic backlash* from these two bouts of inflation took hold, with banks and thrift institutions suffering widespread credit and interest rate losses. This same backlash led to a worldwide economic recession, and chronic deficits in both the federal budget and the nation's balance of payments.

All these forces have meant fifteen years of unprecedented economic turmoil, and many signs of that turmoil can be seen in the government bond market.

1. The huge budget deficits, and the resulting demand by the Treasury for credit, have tremendously increased the size of the market. By the mid-1980s, the Treasury was raising over $150 billion in new debt every year, in addition to refinancing its maturing debt issues. As a corollary, the daily trading volume in the market has mushroomed to over $100 billion a day, a number unthinkable fifteen years ago.
2. The economic turmoil has manifested itself in unprecedented interest rate volatility. Where bond prices might move a quarter of a point in the 1950s and 1960s, price movements of more than a point were commonplace in the 1970s and 1980s. Increased volatility meant increased risk, which argued for more capital in the market. That meant more bond dealers, both registered and unregistered, and whole new classes of customers, among them pension funds and foreign financial institutions.
3. Along with increased rate volatility came larger demands for capital,

Background of the Market

by industry and the housing sector as well as the Treasury. Higher risk, coupled with larger volumes of debt led to two developments. The first was derivative instruments—futures and options contracts that allowed investors and traders to separate forms of risk and pay others to take some of it. The second development was a whole world of new securities, like passthroughs, stripped issues, and asset-based securities.

Indeed, by the mid-1980s the market had become an overgrown jungle of securities, dealers, brokers, customers, regulators, futures, and options. New customers, such as the Japanese financial institutions, could overshadow a sector of the market in a matter of a few years. New securities, like multi-tranche CMOs, could grow from a minor sideline to a dominant force in the debt markets in a little over a year. A few unregistered dealers, like ESM, BBS or Drysdale, could grow like mushrooms, out of the sunlight, until their collapse could shake the very foundations of the marketplace.

From a humble beginning, the market has become a goliath—huge, powerful, and sometimes out of control. However chaotic it seems, though, there is an underlying structure which, even under the severest of strain, has managed to keep things functioning. In order to understand the market in all its complexity, we must first understand this basic structure.

CHAPTER TWO

Structure of the Market

NATURE OF AN OVER-THE-COUNTER MARKET

The typical dictionary definition of a *market* would read something like "a public gathering for buying and selling goods," or "a meeting together of people for the trading of goods." Beyond that strict denotation, the image of a market we usually get is one of a crowd gathered together to trade, either in a street (like an Arabian bazaar) or on an exchange floor. Whatever the specifics, a market is usually thought of in terms of close physical proximity and open outcry.

The government bond market, however, is utterly unlike that typical image. With the exception of the commodity exchanges, which trade futures contracts on government securities, there is no exchange floor anywhere that does a significant volume of government securities business. There is no public gathering for buying and selling, no "meeting together" of market participants, no physical proximity, and no open outcry.

Instead, there is a *telephonic network* of market participants. Spread all over the United States (and now across the world), but concentrated in New York City, are *trading rooms* devoted to the buying and selling of government securities. Some of these rooms are huge, covering an entire floor of a skyscraper, and others are small, with only enough room for a dozen people and their equipment. They all have one thing in common though: they are designed to accommodate an *over-the-counter* (OTC) market.

By its nature, an OTC market is fundamentally different from an exchange market, which it predates by hundreds of years. First of all, an OTC market is essentially a one-to-one business, with each buyer and seller dealing directly with the other. The importance of this difference cannot be overemphasized. In an auction market, with open outcry, you can be reasonably sure that each seller and buyer received the best price available at the time the trade was done. Not so in an OTC market.

Perhaps we can see this important difference by comparing the purchase of produce in a farmer's market with the purchase of produce in a supermarket. In a farmer's market, we can stroll around, compare the quality and prices, and make a choice between several vendors. In a supermarket, we have one seller, one batch of produce, and one price. To make a valid comparison, we would have to go through the checkout line and into another supermarket—not the most convenient of solutions.

In the government bond market, this OTC nature means that each dealer's offer to buy or sell securities is made directly to the customer, not in the open outcry of an exchange market. Whether that dealer's bid or offer is the best one, or worse than someone else's by a wide margin, is up to the customer to determine. Small customers, or those doing small amounts of business, or those talking to only one or two dealers, can never be sure how good an execution they are getting.

The second important feature of the government securities market is that business is invariably done as *principal*, rather than as *agent*. This is important because the flow of information is very different when one is acting as agent, as opposed to acting as principal. We can see how important this is by looking at the typical real estate broker in action. He is acting as the buyer's or seller's agent, so he is willing to reveal a fair amount about the transaction he hopes to accomplish. Buyers often come to depend upon the agent's assessment of the value of the house, the quality of the school district, and the willingness of the seller to compromise. Sellers often depend upon the agent's assessment of the firmness or softness of the market, the value of the house versus others on the market, and the willingness of buyers to pay.

Now suppose the real estate agent were buying the house as principal or selling it as such. Suddenly, the quality of his information would become much more suspect. Your willingness to sell at a lower price, or buy at a higher one, would have a direct impact on the agent's profits, so he would no longer be on your side. You might even look upon him as an adversary, and you would need to know a good deal more about his market in order to deal with him effectively.

That difference is especially true in the government bond market. With large blocks of securities trading all the time, and with a high degree of volatility in prices, each securities transaction can represent hundreds of thousands, if not millions, of dollars in profits or losses. Developing sources of reliable information, whether dealers or other sources, may be the most important job a customer does. In doing so, the customer must counteract the dealer's natural tendency, as well as his own, to regard everyone else as an adversary.

ORGANIZATIONAL STRUCTURE OF THE GOVERNMENT BOND MARKET

The best way to visualize the government bond market is to think of a giant wheel. At the center of the wheel, at the hub of the market, is the *Federal Reserve Bank of New York*. Moving out from the hub are the Primary Dealers and the government bond brokers. Around the outside of the wheel are the government securities customers, that is, anyone who does business in government securities and is not a Primary Dealer or a broker.

Federal Reserve Bank of New York

The Federal Reserve Bank is in the position of pivotal importance in the government bond market for several reasons. These are because it (1) implements monetary policy through its Open Market Trading Desk, (2) regulates the market participants, and (3) is the central clearinghouse for all government and agency trades. In Chapter 13 we will examine the Fed in detail, but for now, we should know that it is at the center of the market.

Primary Dealers

Clustered around the Fed, like spokes around the hub of a wheel, are the *Primary Dealers*. These are the firms that have entered a select circle of dealers in government securities, and have been recognized as

Primary Dealers by the Fed. They are members of the *Primary Dealer Association*, which is part of the *Public Securities Association*. The number of Primary Dealers varies from the low twenties to the forties as some dealers disappear through the merger process, while others apply for admission into the inner circle. In the mid-1980s the number stood at 36, but a large number of prospectives were knocking at the Fed's door, among them several subsidiaries of European and Japanese securities firms. The emotional issue of according Primary Dealer status to these foreign firms spilled over from the Fed and the PSA into the halls of Congress, but it became apparent that the recognition of foreign dealers was only a matter of time.

The recognition process is time consuming under the best of conditions. The first step in becoming a Primary Dealer is the formation, within a firm, of a trading and sales force devoted to government securities. As the firm's capital allows, and its sales force expands, the firm increases the volume of business it does with all participants in the market, but in particular with customers. At this point, the firm is considered a customer itself, as far as the Primary Dealers are concerned. When the firm's volume of business approaches 1% of the daily trading volume in the market (as reported weekly by the Fed), the firm contacts the Federal Reserve Bank of New York and makes known its desire to become a Primary Dealer. At this point, the Fed begins monitoring the firm's trading volume, particularly its volume with customers, as well as its record of bidding for Treasury auctions. After an appropriate period of time, the Fed concludes that this firm is a serious and stable participant in the market, and recognizes it as a Primary Dealer. The Fed then installs a direct line between the Open Market Trading Desk and the firm's trading desk. This *Fed wire* is the most prized possession in the market, for it signifies that the firm has become one of the heavyweights in the business.

Primary Dealer status carries with it a host of responsibilities. One is the responsibility to *maintain liquid markets* in all government and agency securities. Any bona fide customer for these securities can call any Primary Dealer for a bid or offering on any government security at any time of the trading day. It does not matter whether prices are falling or rising, whether a news item has just broken throwing the market into turmoil, or whether the Treasury is in the midst of auctioning a large issue; a Primary Dealer must stand ready to make markets and trade. In a highly competitive market a dealer can effectively disguise a lack of commitment by making bids slightly below the market and offerings slightly above. The Fed, however, keeps close tabs on the actual amount of business done with customers, and has stripped a few dealers of their Fed wire for not doing enough business.

In addition, a Primary Dealer must *bid on all Treasury auctions,* both for its own account and for the accounts of customers. Here again, the Fed keeps tabs on a dealer's performance and has one of its "friendly chats" with the dealer if its bids are too small or too unaggressive. Primary Dealers are also included in the selling groups for new agency issues, and each agency's fiscal agent keeps track of each dealer's performance in both new issues and secondary market trading. Because the agencies pay a selling concession on their new issues (unlike the Treasury) the dealers will, without being required, make a major effort to keep their activity in this market high, since the fiscal agent controls a source of profitable business.

Finally, Primary Dealers must *report daily* to the Federal Reserve, not only their securities positions and trading volume, but the methods they have used to finance their securities positions. This daily reporting, together with the frequent conversations between the Fed's staff and the dealer's staff, makes up the regulatory process in the government market. The reporting function, which is mandatory for Primary Dealers, may be extended to customers, but only on a voluntary basis. As a result, some customers, who do not report to the Fed and who are not registered under the Securities Exchange Act of 1934, have operated in an essentially unregulated environment. The recent collapse of several such firms prompted Congress to require registration of all dealers in governments, and to require the Treasury to set up regulations for trading in this market.

Types of Primary Dealers

Primary Dealers tend to fall into three broad classifications, each with its special characteristics. The oldest type of Primary Dealer is made up of *commercial banks,* which were the original issuing agents and purchasers of government bonds. Almost every large bank has a bond department that deals in government, agency, and municipal securities, but not all large banks are Primary Dealers.

Commercial banks have several advantages as Primary Dealers. Because they are depository institutions, they have a large supply of funds with which to finance trading positions, so capital is not nearly the constraint that it is for other types of dealers. Also, their correspondent network of smaller financial institutions gives them a ready customer base with which to trade. They are usually active in some market areas that abut government securities (such as foreign exchange and rate swaps), which gives them an advantage in executing certain cross-market transactions. Finally, their long banking relationships with many of their customers help them eliminate the adversarial relationship other dealers must contend with.

At the same time, commercial banks have some disadvantages in this market. The biggest disadvantage they have faced is the *Glass-Steagall Act*, which prohibits commercial banks from underwriting or trading corporate securities. This law, which was passed to separate the commercial and investment banking businesses, effectively keeps commercial banks out of the corporate bond market, including some of the never securities like Collateralized Mortgage Obligations. Since many of the newer participants in the government bond market also hold portfolios of corporate bonds, Glass-Steagall has restricted the ability of commercial banks to expand their customer bases.

The second type of Primary Dealer is a *full-service securities firm*. This is the newest kind of Primary Dealer, and the fastest growing, in terms of both the numbers of dealers and the volume of securities traded. In many ways a securities firm is the opposite of a bank. It cannot accept deposits, so it must finance its positions in the short-term money market. That market requires holders of securities to "haircut" their positions, meaning that the dealer cannot finance the entire market value of the position. Although the haircut may be small, often less than 1%, the resulting capital requirement can be burdensome when large positions are being traded.

Also, securities firms are often viewed by customers in a different light than banks, because they make most of their money from commissions, as opposed to earning interest on loans. Thus, although both banks and securities firms may do this business in exactly the same way, customers may be predisposed to resist the securities firm's trading ideas more than the bank's. On the other hand, securities firms are not constrained by Glass-Steagall, so they can execute transactions in corporates and governments at the same time, a distinct advantage when a pension fund, for example, wants to shift a major portion of its portfolio from one market to another.

The final type of Primary Dealer is the *special-purpose government securities* firm. This firm, which does business only in governments and agencies, is something of a throwback to the era before 1960, when the market was much smaller and less volatile. Special-purpose dealers still survive, but they are a shrinking part of the market, both in numbers and in trading volume. It is not hard to see why. They have many of the disadvantages of both banks and full-service firms, including capital limitations and a lack of capability in either corporates or foreign exchange. They compensate for these limitations by relying on their longstanding relationships with customers and fiscal agents, and by concentrating all their efforts, both trading and sales, on this market. Even so, the trend for these firms is clearly toward their being a smaller and smaller force in the market.

Government Bond Brokers

Also within the marketplace wheel are the *government securities brokers*. These firms, largely unknown outside the market, facilitate trading between the Primary Dealers. Brokers do not carry positions themselves, and make no bids or offers for their own account. Instead, they solicit bids or offers from the primary dealers, reflect them to other Primary Dealers, and execute trades between Primary Dealers for a small commission. Although it may appear that the market could get along very well without the brokers, their presence has become essential to its smooth functioning.

There are two main reasons for their importance. The first is *anonymity*. Dealers who carry large positions in individual securities often feel that they would be at the mercy of the other Primary Dealers if their positions or trades were to become widely known. Brokers never reveal whose bids or offers they are in touch with, who did which trades, or who wants to buy or sell securities. Thus a trader can execute a large trade in bonds through a broker without his competitors knowing who did the trade, why, or whether there is more of the trade to be done.

The second main reason is, oddly enough, the exact opposite: the *dissemination of information*. Without an exchange floor to go to, each Primary Dealer needs a source of information about the best bid or offer in any security at a moment's notice. The five or six brokers maintain a network of CRT terminals, called *screens,* in the offices of the Primary Dealers, showing the best bids and offers they are in touch with for each security. Traders, and some salespeople, for a Primary Dealer will have a screen from each broker on their desks, showing that broker's current markets for a particular sector of the list of securities.

Reading a Broker's Screen

These screens are loaded with information. Look, for example, at one such screen, provided by Telerate. (See Figures 1-2 and 2-2.)

Figure 2-1
Telerate screen showing market for long-term
Treasury securities at 1:10 P.M. on October 22.

```
TELERATE SYSTEMS

10/22  13:10 EDT   CANTOR FITZ (C) 86      11.125   8/03
       10.125  5/93                        10.750   8/05
        7.375  4/93                      > 9.375    2/06      112.04-     1X
        7.250  7/93      99.19-      1 X   12.750  11/10
     >   .000 10/93W*    7.27-26     1 X 2 14.000  11/11

       13.125  5/94                        10.375  11/12      122.08      X 1
       11.625 11/94                        12.000   8/13
       11.250  2/95                        12.500   8/14
       11.250  5/95     122.10-     1 X    11.750  11/14      134.19-    1 X
       10.500  8/95                        10.625   8/15      127.02-09  1 X 1
        9.500 11/95                         9.875  11/15      119.10-14  1 X 1
        8.875  2/96     108.08-     1 X     9.250   2/16      114.24     X 1
      > 7.375  5/96      99.03-04   2 X 5 > 7.250   5/16 *TAK  93.23+    X 4

2 YR.W*TAK 6.37+     X 21              FULTON-PREBON FED FUNDS
3 YR.   100.01-02   1 X 50 3MO.  5.30-28  5X  5 BID 5 15/16   OPN 5 7/8
4 YR.   TAK 99.23      X 2 6MO.  5.37+-36 5X  5 ASK 6         HGH 5 15/16
5 YR     98.05+HIT 26 X    1YR.  5.49+-48+ 5X 5 LST 6         LOW 5 7/8
```

19

Figure 2-2
Telerate screen showing market for long-term
Treasury securities one minute after previous screen.

```
TELERATE SYSTEMS

10/22     13:11 EDT   CANTOR FITZ (C) 86     11.125    8/03
  10.125    5/93                              10.750    8/05
   7.375    4/93                           >   9.375    2/06    112.04 -16      1X1
   7.250    7/93    99.19 -      1    X       12.750   11/10
>   .000   10/93W    7.27 -26    1    X 2     14.000   11/11

  13.125    5/94                              10.375   11/12    120.00 -08     1 X 1
  11.625   11/94                              12.000    8/13
  11.250    2/95                              12.500    8/14
  11.250    5/95   122.10 -      1    X       11.750   11/14    134.19 -       1 X
  10.500    8/95                              10.625    8/15    127.02 -09     1 X 1
   9.500   11/95                               9.875   11/15    119.10 -14     1 X 1
   8.875    2/96   108.08 -      1    X        9.250    2/16   *114.18 -24     1 X 1
>  7.375    5/96    99.03 -04    2    X 7    > 7.250    5/16     93.22+-23+    1 X 1

2 YR.W  6.37+-36*      X 10                              FULTON-PREBON FED FUNDS
3 YR.  100.01 -01+*   1 X  1  3MO.    5.30 -28      5X  5 BID   5 15/16    OPN  5 7/8
4 YR.   TAK 99.23      X  7  6MO.    5.37+ -36      5X  5 ASK   6          HGH  5 15/16
5 YR    98.05+-06    1 X  3  1YR.    5.49+ -48+     5X  5 LST   6          LOW  5 7/8
```

Structure of the Market

Telerate is a broker whose screens are available to all traders, not just Primary Dealers. Figure 2-1 shows the market for long-term Treasury securities at 1:10 P.M. on a typical trading day. Figure 2-2 shows the same market one minute later. From examining these two screens, we can tell a great deal about what is happening in the market.

First, let's look at how the information is organized. The first few lines are some housekeeping details, such as date and time. Below that, the screen is divided into two columns, with Treasury issues listed by maturity. The first issue in the left column has the shortest *maturity* on this screen, and it is the 10.125% notes maturing 5/15/93. There is no active market in this issue on Telerate at this time, but there is a market, of sorts, in the next issue, the 7.25% notes maturing 7/15/93. Here, someone is willing to pay 99.59375% of par for one million of the issue. But the screen shows the bid as 99.19. Have we misread it? No, because dollar prices for Treasury notes and bonds are expressed in *1/32ds of a point,* but written using decimals. Figure 2-3 translates the 32ds shown as decimals to real decimal equivalents and dollars per million par amount.

Figure 2-3
Price conversion table for Treasury notes and bonds.

32ds / Decimals /	Dollars	32ds / Decimals /	Dollars
.01 = .03125 or	$ 312.50/million	.17 = .53125 or	$ 5,312.50/million
.02 = .0625 or	$ 625.00/million	.18 = .5625 or	$ 5,625.00/million
.03 = .09375 or	$ 937.50/million	.19 = .59375 or	$ 5,937.50/million
.04 = .125 or	$1,250.00/million	.20 = .625 or	$ 6,250.00/million
.05 = .15625 or	$1,562.50/million	.21 = .65625 or	$ 6,562.50/million
.06 = .1875 or	$1,875.00/million	.22 = .6875 or	$ 6,875.00/million
.07 = .21875 or	$2,187.50/million	.23 = .71875 or	$ 7,187.50/million
.08 = .25 or	$2,500.00/million	.24 = .75 or	$ 7,500.00/million
.09 = .21825 or	$2,182.50/million	.25 = .78125 or	$ 7,812.50/million
.10 = .3125 or	$3,125.00/million	.26 = .8125 or	$ 8,125.00/million
.11 = .34375 or	$3,437.50/million	.27 = .84375 or	$ 8,437.50/million
.12 = .375 or	$3,750.00/million	.28 = .875 or	$ 8,750.00/million
.13 = .40625 or	$4,062.50/million	.29 = .90625 or	$ 9,062.50/million
.14 = .4375 or	$4,375.00/million	.30 = .9375 or	$ 9,375.00/million
.15 = .46875 or	$4,687.50/million	.31 = .96875 or	$ 9,687.50/million
.16 = .5 or	$5,000.00/million	.32 = 1.00 or	$10,000.00/million

From this table we can see that the bid price for the 9.375% bonds due 2/15/2006 (third item in the right column in Figure 2-1) looks like 112.04, but is really 112.125% of par, or $1,121,250 per million par amount. Here again, we can see that $1 million was bid for. But what about the issue below the 7.25% notes due 7/15/93, in the right column? Is there really an issue with a 0% coupon maturing 10/15/93?

No, this is a *when-issued* security—one that the Treasury has announced—to be auctioned in a few days. Such securities trade before they are issued, in fact before they are auctioned. Since no one knows the exact coupon that will result from the auction, that part is left blank (or listed as 0.00) and the prices are shown in terms of *yield to maturity,* instead of dollar terms. Thus someone is willing to pay a price for one million of the when-issued seven-year note that will yield 7.27% to maturity, and someone is willing to sell two million at a price that will yield 7.26% to maturity. If a trade is done (at a 7.26% yield, for example) the two parties will calculate the resulting dollar price as soon as the *coupon* is announced.

Now we can read most of the information on the screen. In the 7.375% notes maturing 5/15/96 the market is 99.03 to 99.04, 2 million by 5 million. What is that little arrow to the left of the coupon? It is Telerate's way of telling us that this is the current ten-year note, which was issued in May of 1986. Such issues are called *on the run* and are usually the most actively traded issues in the market.

Just to the right of the ten-year note is another on-the-run issue, the current thirty-year bond. Here the screen is telling us that someone has *taken* an offering at 99.23 +, or 99.734375. The amount showing is 4 million, but the trade could have started as 1 million, and may be completed as 10 million, as more bonds are added to the total. There is an asterisk next to the "TAK," which is flashing on the screen. What does this mean? In fact, there are other asterisks scattered around the screen; next to the when-issued seven-year, for example. These signify one of the trading rules brokers adhere to. When a bid is entered in response to an offering, it is shown on the screen at the same time it is shown to the offerer, but only the offerer can *hit* the bid at this point. Only after an offerer has been given a chance to hit the bid, and elected not to do so, does the bid become *clear* for the rest of the dealers. Thus, in the case of the when-issued seven-year, the 7.27 bid appeared in response to the 7.26 offering and is *not clear* yet.

The lower part of the screen shows securities in other sectors of the market that a bond trader will want to know about, to improve his "market feel." On the left are some shorter term note issues: the two-year, three-year, four-year, and five-year. These are all on-the-run

Structure of the Market

issues, and are carried on other screens provided by Telerate, along with surrounding issues, just like this screen. In the middle are Treasury bills, maturing in three months, six months, and one year. These markets look like the when-issued seven-year market, but the numbers represent a discount from par, not a yield. In Chapter 3 we will examine bill pricing in detail. Finally, on the right is *Fed Funds,* or the reserve deposits that member banks keep at the District Federal Reserve Bank. Some member banks have excess reserves, and some need more, so reserves are lent among banks on an overnight basis, and called Fed Funds. The Fed Funds rate is the linchpin rate in the whole market, because it is the one the Fed watches in setting monetary policy.

As much information as each screen communicates at any one time, a great deal more comes from watching the screen over time. Look at Figure 2-2. What has happened to the market in one minute?

First, there is a *following* market in the thirty-year bond. After the trade at 93.23+, the market has become 93.22+ bid for 1 million and 1 million offered at 93.23+. More bonds are offered in the ten-year note, and an offering has come in on the 9.375% bond due 2/15/2006. On the other hand, bids have come in for the 10.375% bond due 11/15/2012, and for the 9.25% bond due 2/15/2016. In other sectors of the market, after the when-issued two-year traded at a yield of 6.37+, the following market was 6.37+ to 6.36. After the five-year note traded *bid hit* at 98.05+, the following market was 98.05+ to 98.06. Bills and Fed Funds are unchanged.

We cannot get a very clear overall picture of the market from just this screen; fortunately there are more brokers than Telerate. By looking at all the screens, provided by all the brokers, a Primary Dealer can get an accurate picture of what is happening in the market at any point in time. Coupled with the information provided by his sales force about what customers are doing, the Primary Dealer is in at least as good a position as if he were on an exchange floor.

Government Securities Customers

Around the outside of the wheel, and on the outside of the Primary Dealer circle, are the government securities *customers*. These are defined as anyone who does business in government securities and is not a Primary Dealer or a broker. That general classification covers a multitude of businesses, some looking very much like Primary Dealers and some looking not at all like them. However large the customer is or however large his trading volume, if he doesn't have a Fed wire he is on the outside of the sanctum.

Customers fall into three groups, depending on their internal structure and the kind of business they do. The first kind of customer is the *non-primary dealer*. This firm has, as its main business, the execution of its own customers' orders or other kinds of trading with its own customer base. In some cases, the non-primary dealer is in direct competition with the Primary Dealers.

Non-primary dealers take two of the forms that Primary Dealers do: commercial banks and securities firms. In some cases, the non-primary dealer may be in the process of becoming a primary, but, until the Fed wire is in, he is still regarded as a customer. Other non-primaries have no intention of reporting to the Fed, or fulfilling any of the other requirements for getting a Fed wire, but all of them are actively soliciting customer business. Thus they often act as a buffer between the larger primaries and smaller, more far-flung customers.

The second type of customer is the *leveraged investor*. This customer buys and sells for his own account, not for the account of his customer, but he must finance any purchases in the money market. This class of customer includes the intermediaries (like banks and thrifts) when acting for their own account, and many of the trading firms that have sprung up in government securities.

The common denominator for leveraged investors is that their cost of funds precludes making much money from the risk-free buying and holding of governments. Whether the financing comes from issuing certificates of deposit or borrowing to carry securities, these investors pay more for their money than they can earn on a government with the same maturity. This means that they must depend upon the assumption of interest rate risk and/or trading to generate their profits. The kinds of trading they do are as varied as the institutions themselves, but most of them have to be in the market frequently. This high trading volume makes them popular customers for the primaries.

The third type of customer is the *unleveraged investor*. This customer oversees a pool of funds raised in some way other than deposits or money markets. Typical of unleveraged investors are pension plans, insurance companies, mutual funds, or corporate cash portfolios. Here the net yield of a government security becomes important, and trading is a means to increase that net yield.

Obviously, alternative yields are important to unleveraged investors, but they do not represent the out-of-pocket costs that are borne by a leveraged investor. Thus, with a cost of funds higher than the yield on a government security, a leveraged investor could experience a *negative carry*, where he ends up losing money by holding the security. An unleveraged investor would not normally face that situation, although an anemic net return of his investments could prompt people to pull money out of his fund, or cancel his insurance policy, or find another pension fund manager.

There is one common denominator running through all these customers: they are all financial institutions. As such, they all face some form of *regulation*. Whether it comes from the Comptroller of the Currency, the Federal Home Loan Bank Board, the Securities and Exchange Commission, the Department of Labor, or any one of dozens of other regulators, someone has a great deal to say about how each of these customers does business. Unfortunately, this regulation has grown into a crazy patchwork, with different regulators having different approaches to investing. In some cases, more than one regulator oversees a customer's business.

RECENT AND IMPENDING CHANGES IN THE MARKET STRUCTURE

The patchwork of regulation, combined with the mushrooming of trading volume and the increase in interest rate volatility, has led to several changes in the market in the 1980s and will probably lead to several more. First, although the Fed's unstructured method of overseeing the Primary Dealers worked in the past, Congress finally decided that the time had come for *formal regulation*. In 1986 Congress passed a law requiring all dealers in government securities to register with the Securities and Exchange Commission, unless they were already registered with another regulator. Additionally, Congress directed the Treasury Department to draw up regulations governing how business is to be done in the government market. Whether turning that task over to the Treasury, which has never had any regulatory responsibility, will improve matters or make them worse remains to be seen.

The second major change is the *introduction of new kinds of securities*. The first such security to come on the scene, in 1970, was the *mortgage passthrough*. The Government National Mortgage Association (GNMA) issued the first of these, but the Federal Home Loan Mortgage Corporation (FHLMC) soon followed, and the Federal National Mortgage Association (FNMA) rounded out the spectrum. By the mid-1980s there was about $600 billion of passthroughs outstanding. In addition, *stripped securities* have been issued, where the coupon payments of Treasury bonds and notes are "stripped" and sold separately. Finally, *multi-tranche Collateralized Mortgage Obligations (CMOs)* have recently been introduced. Here the stream of payments emanating from a passthrough is split into separate securities, each with its own coupon, maturity, average life, and attraction to a different kind of customer.

Each of these new securities has something in common with the others; they are all new *repackagings* of older instruments. Passthroughs repackage mortgages, stripped issues repackage Treasury notes and bonds, and CMOs repackage passthroughs. It is safe to say that this repackaging trend is not finished, so we can look for more and better creations in the future.

In another arena entirely, the persistent balance of payments deficit we have run for the last ten years has created a group of *foreign investors* who play a major role in the government securities market. From the German Central Bank to the Japanese Post Office Retirement System, huge blocks of Treasury and, to a lesser extent, agency debt are held by investors outside both our boundaries and our regulatory structure. These investors are as concerned with foreign exchange rates as they are with interest rates, and their holdings are so large that movements in the dollar can trigger major movements in the bond markets.

The emergence of the foreign bond holder may, in the long run, be the most significant change in the market. Already the global nature of the market has prompted several Primary Dealers to adopt a global, 24-hour trading stance. These firms maintain trading desks in Europe (usually London) and in the Far East (usually Tokyo). When the trading day is finished in New York, the trading position, or *"book"* is often passed to Tokyo, where the trading will soon start. When Tokyo is finished, the book is passed to London, and from London back to New York. With the exception of weekends, the market never closes.

Foreign holders, of course, operate under different regulations and tax codes than domestic holders, so their emergence has led to certain changes, either accomplished or anticipated, in the nature of securities.

Structure of the Market

For example, the IRS in the past has required the withholding of 30% of the interest payment on bonds held by foreigners. Recently, that stand has softened, and some securities have been issued which avoid that repressive tax treatment. Also, many European investors desire a high degree of secrecy about their debt holdings, in order to avoid their own tax man. As an accommodation, the Treasury has issued securities which have a less visible ownership form, specifically for foreign buyers.

As the foreign ownership of government debt grows and as the budget deficit raises the Treasury's need for new money, we can expect to see more adjustments, both in the way the market does business, and in the securities issued. In the meantime, however, let's look at the market in detail. First we will look at each security, then at a typical Primary Dealer, and then at the Federal Reserve.

SECTION TWO

SECURITIES IN THE MARKET

CHAPTER THREE

Individual Treasury Securities

The government securities market is made up of a tremendous variety of different securtities, each one designed to appeal to a particular kind of investor. In some cases the security was designed, and first issued, hundreds of years ago. Its form may not have changed much in all that time even though the market may have undergone tremendous changes. Other securities have come into existence within the last few years in response to some of those same market changes. Together, these securities make up a kaleidoscope of bills, notes, bonds, pass-throughs, and many others, that pass before the eyes of dealers and customers every day.

Only a portion of these securities are issued by the U.S. Treasury. Others, although issued by other entities, carry the Treasury's explicit backing, and are said to have *the full faith and credit* of the U.S. Government. Still others are issued by instrumentalities of the government, without the explicit backing of the Treasury. Some are issued by publicly held corporations, which occupy a special place in the credit markets because of the particular functions they perform. Finally, there are those securities backed solely by holdings of other instruments, such as mortgages or Treasury securities, which have all the credit characteristics of the underlying collateral.

In order to understand how each of these securities trades, both on its own and in relation to other securities, we will need to break the securities down into their individual classes, and then concentrate on each of their specific parameters.

In this chapter, the *issuer* of all securities is the U.S. Treasury Department. The ability of the Treasury to borrow money and to obligate the government (and, by implication, the taxpayers) to repay the debt, is conferred upon it by Congress, but not without limitations. Certainly, the most important limitation imposed by Congress is on the amount of money the Treasury can borrow. In recent years, the *debt ceiling* has been reached several times, as the Treasury has financed the budget deficit. Each time, Congress has increased the ceiling, but only after some dramatic brinkmanship and political posturing. It must strike observers from other countries as a little comical to see Congress spend itself up to the debt ceiling and then threaten to withhold the Treasury's ability to fund the resulting deficit.

In terms of the *method of interest payment,* the securities in this chapter fall into two classes. Notes and bonds pay interest every six months, to the holder of record. Because this process used to involve the clipping of a coupon, which was presented at a commercial bank in order to receive the interest payment, notes and bonds have come to be known as *coupon securities.* Bills, on the other hand, do not have a coupon. Instead, the Treasury sells them at a *discount,* and redeems them at par value on maturity date.

Maturity at issuance, for Treasury securities, can range from a few weeks to thirty years. Bills, by definition, can have maturities of up to one year from issuance. Notes can mature from one year to ten years from issuance, and bonds can mature from ten years out, although they are not usually issued with maturities longer than thirty years.

For the securities in this chapter, the current *method of issuance* is exclusively by *auction.* That has been true since about the mid-1970s, but the Treasury has used several other methods in the past, and may do so again in the future. For instance, the accepted method of issuance after World War II was a *rights offering* in which owners of maturing issues were given the rights to purchase the new issues. The Treasury has also used *subscription offerings* in the past.

None of the securities issued by the Treasury are collateralized, although securities issued by some of the other agencies are, and Treasury securities are often collateral for other securities. For tax purposes, the interest earned by holding Treasuries is exempt from state and municipal taxes, but not from federal taxes. Those agencies which regulate investments by financial institutions universally regard

Individual Treasury Securities

Treasuries as the highest quality investment, and put no restrictions on the volume of Treasuries held, although some restrictions have been put on the maturity of such securities held in specific accounts.

Let us look, then, at all the securities issued by the U.S. Treasury. In keeping with market tradition, we will start with the shortest securities, bills.

U.S. TREASURY BILLS

Bills are the shortest securities the Treasury issues and are regarded as the foundation of the government bond market. They are not, however, the oldest form of security issued by the Treasury. In fact, the Treasury was not even authorized to sell bills until the passage of the Second Liberty Bond Act in June, 1929. The first bill auction was held in December of that year.

Treasury bills were patterned after *bills of lading,* which had been used for hundreds of years to finance goods in shipment. The manufacturer, who had an order for his product, would load it onto some form of transportation for shipment to the buyer and would be given a bill of lading, showing the amount of the product and the final proceeds of the sale. He would take this bill to a merchant banker and sell it to the banker at a *discount*. When the goods were delivered and paid for, the banker got the full amount, and the discount, or the difference between the price he paid and the sale price, was interest on the money he had lent. During the time he held the bill, the banker could sell it in the market, at a discount of course, and recover the money he had put into it. For hundreds of years, bills have traded in the financial centers of Europe.

Treasury bills work very much the same way, except there is no finished good loaded onto a boat or truck. Instead, the Treasury borrows short-term money by issuing bills every week. The bills are issued at a discount and redeemed at par. Bills represent the largest single class of fixed income securities anywhere, both in dollar volume outstanding and in trading volume.

Treasury Bill Pricing

Because bills pay no interest, all their yield comes from price change. Bills are always issued at a discount and always mature at 100. However, the price that we see quoted for a bill is not its true dollar price, nor is it a true yield. Instead it is a *discount from par*, expressed in percentage terms. For example, a 7% price (quoted at 7.00) on a three-month bill means the bill is discounted from 100 enough to equal 93 (100 − 7) on an annual basis. But this bill has only 91 days to maturity. In order to find its true dollar price, we need to adjust the discount for the fraction of a year to maturity.

Even here, though, there is a slight aberration from reality. We would expect to adjust the discount by 91/365, since there are 365 days in a year. However, in "bill land," a year has 360 days so the adjustment is 91/360, or 0.25277. Thus, 7 × 0.25277 = 1.76944 so the 91-day bill at a discount of 7% costs 100 − 1.76944, or 98.23056. The purchase of $1 million par value of 91-day bills at 7.00 will, therefore, cost us $982,305.60. Suppose we held the bill for ten days and then sold it at 7.00; we would receive 98.425000, or $984,250.00. Our profit would be $1,944.40, or $194.44 per day. Using a 360-day year, that profit would add up to just about $70,000, or our original 7%.

But wait a minute. We earned that $70,000 (annualized) on less than $1,000,000. If we take the 7% discount and divide it by the price (as a fraction of par), we will get our *true yield*. In this case, 7/0.9823056 = 7.126%, the true yield on the bill. The 0.126 is called the *add-on* and varies with the amount of the discount. Thus the add-on for a 182-day bill would be larger than the add-on for a 91-day bill.

It makes no difference when a bill was issued, or at what price it was issued. All we need to know to determine true dollar price and true yield is the days to maturity and the discount rate. Look at Figure 3-1 showing the daily pricing of a 91-day bill at two different discount rates. See how the price line marches straight up toward 100 on the last day. That line represents the *interest component* of a bill's performance. But what happens to a bill's price when market rates change? To see that, let's look at Figure 3-2.

This graph shows us the components of a bill's price performance: the *interest component* and the *rate change component*. If we bought $1 million of a 91-day bill at 8% and sold it with 81 days to go at 7%, we would show a profit of $4,472.20 ($984,250.00 − $979,777.80). If we held the bill until it had 51 days left, and then sold it at 7%, we would show a profit of $10,305.50 ($990,083.30 − $979,777.80). Which trade was a better one? The graph shows us that the actual *trading profit* of the first trade was larger, because most of the profit in the second trade came from interest. When we sold the bill with 81 days left the

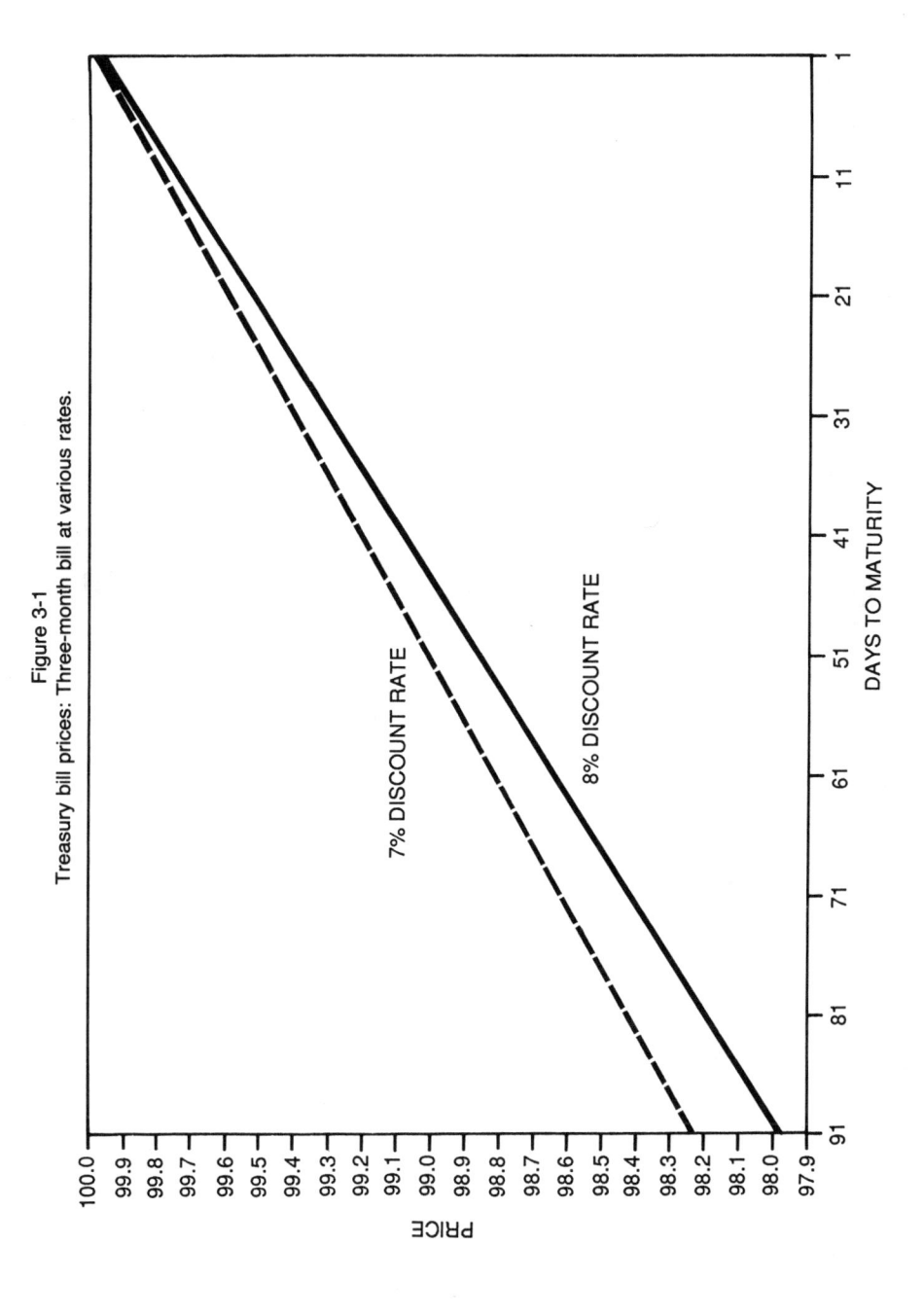

Figure 3-1
Treasury bill prices: Three-month bill at various rates.

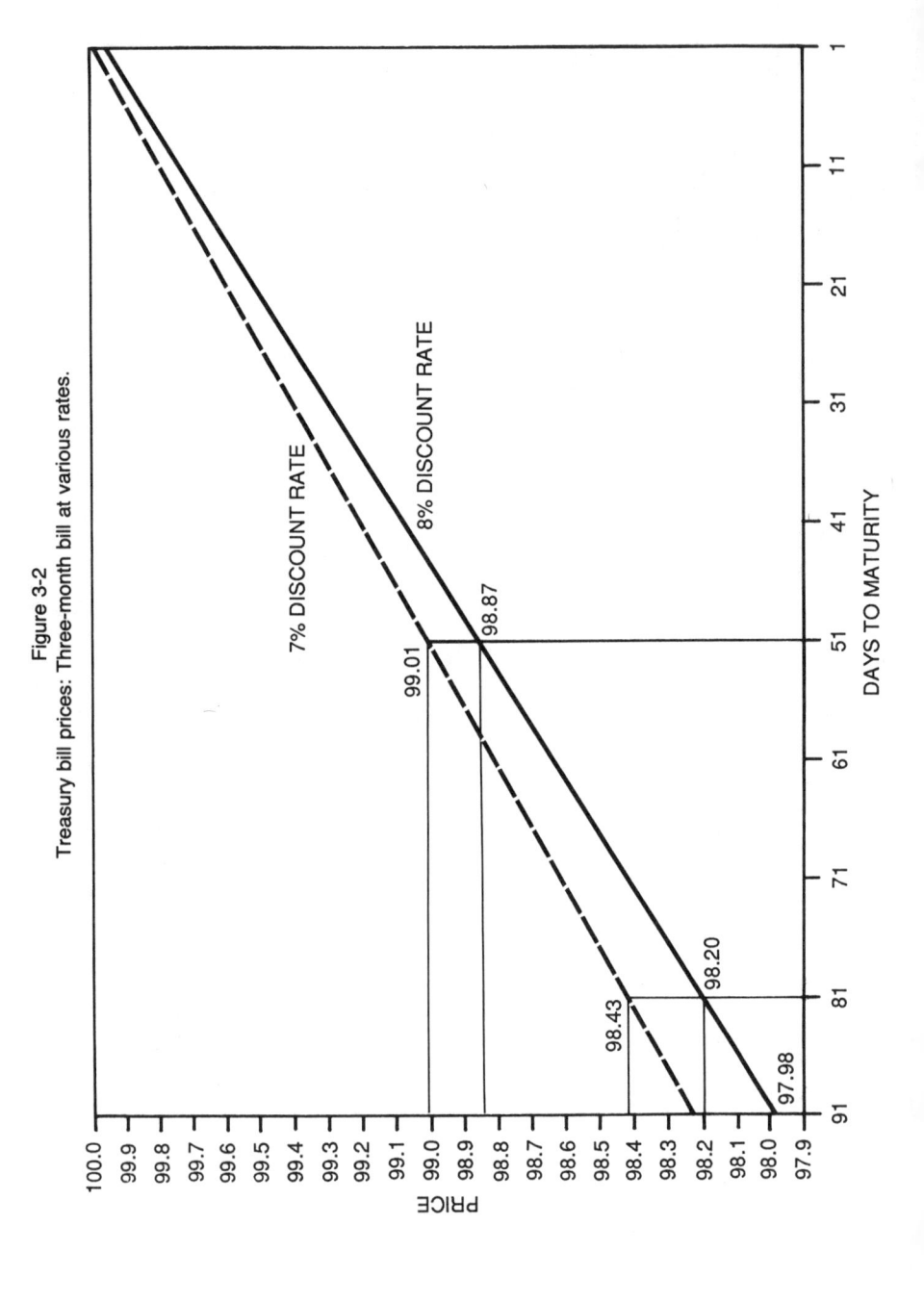

Figure 3-2
Treasury bill prices: Three-month bill at various rates.

Individual Treasury Securities

trading profit was $2,250.00, while the trading profit in the 51-day case was $1,416.60. Figure 3-2 also shows us an important fact about bills and about all fixed income securities: *the shorter the term, the less volatile the issue.*

Treasury Bill Issuance Procedures

Treasury bills are so popular in the market that they begin trading before they come into being—in fact, before they are auctioned. Every Tuesday, at 4:00 P.M., the Treasury announces the amount of 13-week and 26-week bills that will be auctioned the following Monday. From that point on, these bills can be traded in the market, even though they won't be auctioned until the next Monday, and won't be delivered and paid for until the following Thursday.

When-issued bills, like all when-issued securities, have some interesting characteristics. If you start trading them as soon as they are announced, you won't have to pay for them (or deliver them, in the case of a short sale) for over a week. On the other hand, they will not begin accruing interest for the same period of time. Thus, depending upon the margin arrangements a trader has made, when-issued bills can be a total market play, with no interest component. This fact has made when-issued bills an extremely popular trading instrument.

Inevitably, though, Monday rolls around, and the bills must be bid for. The actual process involves the filling out of a *tender form,* like the one in Figure 3-3. This is a standard three-month bill tender form, which must be delivered to a Federal Reserve Bank by 1:00 P.M. on Monday. In this case, it has been filled out by an imaginary dealer to bid for $10,000,000 in bills at a discount of 5.24%. In addition to the amount and discount, the tender contains the delivery instructions and the method of payment. Every Monday, Primary Dealers fill out hundreds of these tenders for their own account, and for the accounts of customers.

Why would a customer bid through a dealer, as opposed to bidding on his own? One reason is contained in Instruction #4 on the back of the tender. Primary Dealers need not submit any deposit with the tender, but non-bank customers must submit a deposit of 2% of the par amount bid for. That deposit earns no interest for the three days until delivery day. Another reason is that the tender must be delivered to the Fed, and many customers are not in cities with Federal Reserve Banks. Finally, Primary

Figure 3-3
Tender for three-month book-entry Treasury bills.

TB-3 (Rev. 4/84)

IMPORTANT — This is a standard form. Its terms are subject to change at any time by the Treasury. This tender will be construed as a bid to purchase the securities for which the Treasury has outstanding an invitation for tenders. *(See reverse side for further instructions.)*

TENDER FOR 3-MONTH BOOK-ENTRY TREASURY BILLS
(For Use in Subscribing Through a Financial Institution)
Do Not Use This Form for Direct Subscriptions to the Treasury

To FEDERAL RESERVE BANK OF NEW YORK
Fiscal Agent of the United States
New York, N.Y. 10045

Dated at ... NEW YORK
NOVEMBER 3, 19 86

Pursuant and subject to the provisions of Treasury Department Circulars No. 26-76 and No. 27-76, Public Debt Series, and to the provisions of the public notice issued by the Treasury Department inviting tenders for the current offering of 3-month Treasury bills, the undersigned hereby offers to purchase such currently offered Treasury bills in the amount indicated below, and agrees to make payment therefor at your Bank on or before the issue date in accordance with the provisions of the official offering circular.

COMPETITIVE TENDER	*Do not fill in both Competitive and Noncompetitive tenders on one form*	**NONCOMPETITIVE TENDER**

$ ...10,000,000...... (maturity value)
or any lesser amount that may be awarded.
Rate: ...5.24..... (Bank Discount Basis)
(Rate must be expressed in two decimal places, for example, 7.15 percent. See reverse side of form for additional explanation.)

$ .... (maturity value)
(Not to exceed $1,000,000 for one bidder through all sources)
at the average of accepted competitive bids.
A noncompetitive bidder may not have entered into an agreement, or may not make an agreement with respect to the purchase or sale or other disposition of any noncompetitive awards of this issue in this auction prior to the designated closing time for receipt of tenders.

Certification by Competitive Bidders: The Bidder's ☒ Customer's ☐ net long position in these bills (including bills acquired through "when issued" trading, and futures and forward transactions, as well as holdings of outstanding bills with the same maturity date as the new offering) as of 12:30 p.m. Eastern time on the day of this auction, was —

☒ Not in excess of $200 million.
☐ In excess of $200 million, amounting to $ .... million.

Subject to allotment, please issue and accept payment for the bills as indicated below:

Safekeeping or Delivery Instructions	**Payment Instructions**
(No changes will be accepted)	Payment will be made as follows:
Book-Entry—	☐ By charge to our reserve account
☐ 1. Hold in safekeeping at FRBNY (for member bank only) in-	☐ By credit to the Treasury Tax and Loan Note Account
☐ Investment Account (4)	☐ By check in *immediately available funds*
☐ General Account (5)	☐ By surrender of eligible maturing securities
☐ Trust Account (6)	☒ By charge to my correspondent bank
☐ 2. Hold as collateral for Treasury Tax and Loan Note Account* (7)	
☒ 3. Wire to ...CHASE NY / FIRST GOVT......(8)	CHASE MANHATTAN
(Exact Receiving Bank Wire Address / Account)	*(Name of Correspondent)*

*The undersigned certifies that the alloted securities will be owned solely by the undersigned.

Insert this tender in envelope marked "Tender for Treasury Securities"

Name of Subscriber (Please Print or Type)
FIRST GOVERNMENT SECURITIES
Address
150 WALL ST
City: NEW YORK State: NY Zip Code: 10008
Phone (Include Area Code): 212-555-1875
Signature of Subscriber or Authorized Signature: L. M. Trader
Title of Authorized Signer: Managing Director

(Banking institutions submitting tenders for customer accounts must list customers' names on lines below or on an attached rider)

_____   _____
(Name of customer)   (Name of customer)

(OVER)

PRIVACY ACT STATEMENT: The individually identifiable information required on this form is necessary to permit the bills to be issued in accordance with the General Regulations governing United States book-entry Treasury Bills (Department Circular No. 26-76, Public Debt Series). The transaction will not be completed unless all required data is furnished.

Figure 3-3
Tender for three-month book-entry Treasury bills (cont'd.).

INSTRUCTIONS:

1. No tender for less than $10,000 will be considered, and each tender must be for a multiple of $5,000 (maturity value).

2. Only banking institutions and dealers who make primary markets in Government securities and report daily to this Bank their positions with respect to Government securities and borrowings thereon, may submit tenders for customer account; in doing so, they may consolidate competitive tenders *at the same rate* (except that a separate tender must be submitted for each customer whose net long position in the bill being offered exceeds $200 million) and may consolidate noncompetitive tenders, provided a list is attached showing the name of each bidder and the amount bid for his account. Others will not be permitted to submit tenders except for their own account.

3. If the person making the tender is a corporation, the tender should be signed by an officer of the corporation authorized to make the tender, and the signing of the tender by an officer of the corporation will be construed as a representation that such officer has been so authorized. If the tender is made by a partnership, it should be signed by a member of the firm, who should sign in the form "................................., a copartnership by ...., a member of the firm".

4. Tenders will be received without deposit from incorporated banks and trust companies and from responsible and recognized dealers in investment securities. Tenders from others must be accompanied by payment of 2 percent of the face amount of Treasury bills applied for, unless the tenders are accompanied by an express guaranty of payment by an incorporated bank or trust company. All checks must be drawn to the order of the Federal Reserve Bank of New York; and personal checks must be certified. Checks endorsed to this Bank will not be accepted.

5. The Bank Discount Basis is the difference between the dollar price of a Treasury bill and the maturity value for a given number of days based on a 360-day year. (The investment return or annualized bond-equivalent yield on a Treasury bill is at a higher rate than the bank discount basis.)

6. If the language of this tender is changed in any respect, which, in the opinion of the Secretary of the Treasury, is material, the tender may be disregarded.

Dealers have good market information, which a customer may be able to utilize in deciding what to bid.

There is another way to bid for Treasury securities, called a *non-competitive* bid. The bidder can use the same tender form as in Figure 3-3 or he can use the one shown in Figure 3-4. In this case, the bidder does not specify a discount rate. Instead, he is awarded bills at the average rate for the auction. Non-competitive bids are usually submitted by smaller investors who don't want to miss buying the bills, and don't want to go through the hassle of submitting a competitive bid.

What happens at 1:00 P.M. on Monday? The Fed collects all the bids from all the Fed branches. It adds up all the non-competitive bids and subtracts that total from the amount to be awarded. Then it begins awarding bills, starting with the lowest discount first. At some point, it runs out of bills, so it *prorates* the award at that discount. Suppose that, in our imaginary case, when the Fed got to 5.24 there were $270 million to be awarded, and $643 million bid for. Each bidder would get 42% of his bid, and our dealer would be awarded $4,200,000. Then the Fed determines the average discount at which the bills were awarded, and awards all the non-competitive bids at that discount. Then they put together a press release, giving the results of the auction.

As soon as the release goes out, the auction results are flashed across the various wire systems, usually between 4:00 and 6:00 P.M. on Monday. Figures 3-5 and 3-6 show one such report, put out by Telerate. Figure 3-5 shows the results, in terms of discount and yield, for the most recent auction and for a whole string of previous ones. In the most recent auction, the *highest bid* (lowest discount) was 98.691, giving a discount of 5.18% and a yield of 5.32%. The *average bid* was at 98.678, giving a discount of 5.23% and a yield of 5.37%. The *lowest bid* was 98.675, giving a discount of 5.24% and a yield of 5.39%. The lowest bid is called the *stop,* and is important in determining how well the auction went.

During the days and hours before the auction, dealers and customers compare notes on where they expect the auction to stop, and a consensus gradually forms. This *stop talk* sets the stage for the announcement of results later. If the stop is weaker than the stop talk, the market is likely to trade down, because dealers will discover that the buyers were not as aggressive as everyone expected. Conversely, a stronger stop than expected will often move the market up, as dealers realize that the buyers were more aggressive than anticipated.

The rest of the information critical to understanding how well an

Figure 3-4
Three months (13 weeks) non-competitive tender for Treasury bills in book-entry form at the Department of the Treasury.

FEDERAL RESERVE BANK OF NEW YORK

3 MONTHS (13 weeks) NON COMPETITIVE TENDER FOR TREASURY BILLS IN BOOK-ENTRY FORM AT THE DEPARTMENT OF THE TREASURY

3

ISSUES DIVISION
For Official Use Only
ISSUE DATE
DUE DATE

Pursuant to the provisions of Department of the Treasury Circular, Public Debt Series No. 27-76, the public announcement issued by the Department of the Treasury, and the regulations set forth in Department Circular, Public Debt Series No. 26-76. I hereby submit this tender for U.S. Treasury bills.

PRIVACY ACT NOTICE
SECTION 350.7 of Department Circular, PD Series, No. 26-76, the regulations governing book-entry. Treasury bills and, in the case of Social Security numbers, section 306.10 of Department Circular 300 authorize solicitation of the requested information. The information is used to establish the Treasury bill account, and is necessary to issue the bill. The tender cannot be processed unless the essential information is provided.

- Please Read Instructions on the Reverse Side Before Completing This Form
- Please Type or Print (using ball point pen)
- This Tender will be Processed ONLY at Federal Reserve Bank of N.Y. and Buffalo Branch.

1 AMOUNT OF TENDER
$ 500,000
minimum of $10,000, over $10,000 must be in multiples of $5,000

2 ACCOUNT IDENTIFICATION

(a) INDIVIDUAL(S)
NAME JOHN DOE
TAXPAYER IDENTIFICATION NUMBER 3 6 8 5 9 2 3 0 1
OR
NAME
TAXPAYER IDENTIFICATION NUMBER

(b) COMPANIES, TRUSTS, ESTATES, GUARDIANS, ETC.
NAME
TAXPAYER IDENTIFICATION NUMBER
Employer Tax ID. No.

3 ACCOUNT MAILING ADDRESS AND TELEPHONE NUMBERS

(a) HOME ADDRESS
STREET 430 MAIN ST
CITY ELMWOOD
STATE NEW YORK
ZIP CODE 15832

(b) OPTIONAL MAILING ADDRESS FOR CHECKS ONLY
NAME OF FINANCIAL INSTITUTION
c/o
STREET
CITY
STATE
ZIP CODE
ACCOUNT NO. AT FINANCIAL INSTITUTION

Telephone Numbers
HOME NUMBER (include area code)
BUSINESS (include area code)

4 I hereby request noncompetitive reinvestment of the proceeds in a new 3 months book entry Treasury bill to be issued on the maturity date of this bill. (check box) ☐

5 PART II. – Back up Withholding on Accounts Opened After 12/31/83
Check the box if you have NOT been notified by the Internal Revenue Service that you are subject to backup withholding under the provisions of the Internal Revenue Code: section 3406 (a) (1) (c). ☐

Certification – Under the penalty of perjury, I certify my Taxpayer Identification Number shown above and other information provided on this form is true, correct, and complete.

FIRST NAMED DEPOSITOR OR AUTHORIZED AGENT
SIGNATURE John Doe
DATE November 10, 1986

6 SUBMITTER'S AUTHORIZATION
SIGNATURE John Doe
DATE 11/10/86

FOR OFFICIAL USE ONLY

TOTAL NUMBER OF CHECKS

LIST EACH CHECK SEPARATELY BELOW

CHECK NUMBER	ABA NUMBER	AMOUNT
	TOTAL	

A	CASH	
B	CHECK(S) PAYABLE TO THE FRB ONLY	
C	TREASURY CHECK(S)	
M	MATURING SECURITIES	DUE DATE
P	OTHER	
	TOTAL	

RECEIVED BY
DATE

GB 494.1 (6/84)

1 - GOVERNMENT BOND DIVISION COPY

Figure 3-5
Telerate screen showing Treasury bill auction
results in terms of discount and yield.

TELERATE SYSTEMS

11/04   12:25 EST   [U S TREASURY 3MO BILL AUCTION RESULTS]   PAGE 56
              AVGE   AVGE   HIGH   HIGH   LOW   LOW   ACCPT
              DISC   AVGE   INVEST DISC   LOW   INVEST DISC   HIGH   INVEST LOW
       DATE   RATE   PRICE YIELD RATE   PRICE   YIELD RATE   PRICE   YIELD PRICE
       11/03 5.23   98.678 5.37   5.24   98.675 5.39   5.18   98.691 5.32   42%
       10/27 5.18   98.691 5.32   5.18   98.691 5.32   5.16   98.696 5.30   74%
       10/20 5.30   98.660 5.45   5.30   98.660 5.45   5.28   98.665 5.43   85%
       10/14 5.13   98.703 5.27   5.14   98.713 5.28   5.09   98.701 5.23   31%
       10/06 5.08   98.716 5.22   5.08   98.731 5.22   5.02   98.716 5.16   85%
       09/29 5.20   98.671 5.34   5.20   98.671 5.34   5.18   98.676 5.32   65%
       09/22 5.25   98.658 5.40   5.25   98.658 5.40   5.21   98.669 5.35   77%
       09/15 5.16   98.696 5.30   5.17   98.693 5.31   5.15   98.698 5.29   26%
       09/08 5.24   98.675 5.39   5.25   98.673 5.39   5.21   98.683 5.35   67%
       09/02 5.12   98.706 5.26   5.12   98.706 5.26   5.11   98.708 5.25   77%
       08/25 5.32   98.640 5.47   5.32   98.640 5.47   5.29   98.648 5.44   58%
       08/18 5.64   98.574 5.80   5.65   98.582 5.81   5.61   98.572 5.77   9%

              U S TREASURY 6MO BILL AUCTION RESULTS AVAILABLE PAGE 57

Figure 3-6
Telerate screen showing Treasury bill auction results in terms of
volumes bid, both competitively and non-competitively.

```
TELERATE SYSTEMS

11/04  12:26 EST          [U S TREASURY BILL AUCTION RESULTS]            PAGE 58
                          TENDERS APPLIED FOR AND ACCEPTED
AUCTIONED 11/03/86        [ 3 MONTH BILLS]                  [6 MONTH BILLS]
F.R. DISTRICT    TOTAL APPLIED  TOTAL ACCEPTED    TOTAL APPLIED  TOTAL ACCEPTED
NEW YORK            23,262,265       6,774,365       22,117,675       6,945,625
CHICAGO              1,925,895         267,835        1,354,395         341,195
SAN FRANCISCO        1,486,690         343,450        1,102,035         134,905
TREASURY               320,070         320,070          344,305         344,305
**SEE PAGE 59 -  FOR ALL OTHER FFRB DISTRICTS**
  TYPE
COMPETITIVE         24,481,410       5,157,150       21,636,115       4,445,315
NONCOMPETITIVE         996,095         996,095          758,720         758,720
SUBTOTAL, PUBLIC    25,477,505       6,153,245       22,394,835       5,204,035

FED RESERVE          1,850,725       1,850,725        1,700,000       1,700,000
FOREIGN OFFICIAL        30,500          30,500        1,109,000       1,109,000
INSTITUTIONS
  TOTALS            27,358,730       8,034,470       25,203,835       8,013,035
```

43

auction went is contained in Figure 3-6. This shows the volumes bid for and awarded, both competitively and non-competitively. In this case, we can see that the Treasury sold just over $8 billion in three-month bills, and had bids for over $27 billion. That large a *cover* can be positive for the market, depending upon some other factors, one of which is the size of the non-competitive bids, in this case just under $1 billion. Non-competitive bidders are usually customers, so a larger-than-expected number in this category indicates large customer interest—good for the market. Another indication of customer interest is the size of bids in districts other than New York: because most of the Primary Dealers submit their bids to the New York Fed, out-of-town bids are assumed to be from customers. The Fed also bids for the accounts of its customers, who are usually foreign central banks or government trust funds. A big jump in Fed bids may mean a large foreign interest in an auction.

The only remaining step in the issuance is paying for and receiving the bills. Bills no longer exist in a physical form; they are carried in the Fed's computer. This *book-entry* system allows large numbers of bills to trade every day without the need for lots of certificates being passed around. On settlement day for the auction, the Fed *credits* the *clearing account* of the specified bank with the bills, and *debits* the specified bank's *reserve account* for the cash. In our case, Chase Manhattan's clearing account for First Government Securities will get the bills, and Chase's reserve account will pay the money. First Government will already have arranged for the money to be at Chase.

How Treasury Bills Trade

Since there are more Treasury bills in existence than any other security, and they are regarded as the safest investment in the world, it is not surprising that more bills trade every day than any other security. Bills are used as a temporary haven for cash by every possible investor, from money market funds to large industrial corporations. Foreign investors universally regard bills as the safest place for their dollar-denominated assets. Pension funds, insurance companies, banks, thrifts, common stock investors, and many other customers put their temporary cash in bills.

Like other sectors of the market, bills have their own page on the various brokers' screens. Figure 3-7 is the bill page on Telerate, and it give us a good idea as to how bill trading is done. Since bills have no

Figure 3-7
Telerate screen showing a Treasury bill page.

```
TELERATE SYSTEMS

11/04     14:38 EST      2/05W  5.24+-23+    5 X 5
1/29    5.23 -      5 X  5/07W  5.32 -31+   25 X 5
4/30    5.31 -30 10 X 25 10/29  5.41 -40    60 X 5

3M/ROL                  6M/ROL                      1Y/ROL
11/13                    2/19  5.24 -21    5 X 3   4/16
11/28    5.14     X 5    2/26                      4/23   5.31  -29+    5 X 5
12/04    5.02 -99 5 X 5  3/05                      5/14
12/18    5.05 -   5 X    3/12        5.21    X 5   6/11          5.31+   X 5
12/26    5.12 -   5 X    3/19  5.23  -22  5 X10    7/09
1/02     5.02+-02 5 X 4  3/26        5.18+   X 2   8/06
1/08     5.13 -11+ 5 X 5 4/02        5.20+   X 4   9/03   5.39   HIT    9 X
1/22     5.23 -22 5 X 5  4/09  5.18-        10 X  10/01   5.43  -42+*  10 X 5


2 YR.        100.09 -09+  6 X 6       FED FUNDS    5 7/8 -6    L5 15/16
```

coupon, they are identified only by their maturity date, which is always a Thursday. The date this screen carries is November 4, 1986, a Tuesday. There is very little trading in the bill maturing 11/6, so it has been taken off the screen. The shortest bill showing matures November 13 and is called the *11/13 bill.* There is no market on Telerate for this bill now, but there is an offering of the 11/28 bill. Five million are offered at a discount of 5.14%. The bills are listed one after another, a week apart, until we get to the 1/29 bill. Where is it listed? At the top of the screen, because it is the *current three-month bill,* which was delivered Thursday, October 30. The 2/05 bill, which was auctioned Monday, November 3, is listed at the top of the next column, with a "W" after the maturity, indicating that it is a *when-issued bill.*

We pick up again with the 2/19 bill and progress weekly out through 4/23. Then back to the top left for the *current six-month bill,* the 4/30 bill, and the *when-issued six month,* the 5/07 bill (top middle). After that the bills mature monthly, because year bills are auctioned monthly, out to the current year bill, the 10/29 bill. Every week the screen is updated, with bills moving into the top half as they become three-month and six-month bills, and back down to the bottom half as they go "off the run."

But wait! There are three strange items in the top half: 3M/ROL, 6M/ROL, and 1Y/ROL. What are they? They represent transactions that are extremely popular in the bill market: *bill rolls.* Every week, when the new bills are announced, many customers and dealers move from the current three- and six-month bills into the when-issued ones, and vice versa. The transaction in which you sell the current bill and buy the when-issued is called a *forward roll,* and the transaction where you sell the when-issued and buy the current is called the *reverse roll.* In this case, selling the 1/29 bill and buying the 2/05 bill is a three-month forward roll. Based on the prices on the screen, we should be able to do that to *pick up* one-half a basis point, by selling at a 5.23 and buying at a 5.23 + . In the six-month forward roll, the trade can also be done to pick up one-half a basis point, from a 5.31 to a 5.31 + .

What causes those prices to be where they are? The *net interest impact* of owning the bill for a week. In the case of the three-month bill, a 5.23 discount means a 5.30% yield. If I can own that bill for one week, and finance it at 5%, I can make .30% for one week, or $58.33 per million. In that case, since each basis point is worth $25 per million for the 91-day bill, I would be willing to do the forward roll to give up two

Individual Treasury Securities

basis points, since I would still eke out a tiny profit. Obviously, on November 4, the bill yield and the cost of financing had to be almost equal to generate the rolls we see here.

Let's look at some other prices. Between 12/26 and 6/11, the quotes seem to be in the range of 5.10 to 5.30. But what about the 1/02 bill, which seems really out of line? What is the story there? That bill has an unusual tax implication, which explains its price. Since bills do not pay interest, their income is *not taxable until they mature.* Thus a bill purchased in one year but maturing in another does not create taxable income until the second year. Financing costs, however, can be accrued for tax purposes. So it does not take a great deal of imagination to see lots of investors holding 1/02 bills in order to transfer taxable income into 1987.

There are some other reasons for price aberrations. For instance, the 3/05 bill is the one deliverable into the December *bill futures contract,* so it might trade richer than the 2/26 or 3/12 bills. The 3/12 bill itself comes right before a *corporate tax payment date,* so it might be more in demand than others. And bills that mature around the end of a calendar quarter are often in demand to be used as "window dressing" for financial statements. Other bills may just be temporarily out of line. Why, for instance, are the 1/08 and 1/22 bills 10 basis points apart? Maybe we should sell the 1/08 bills and buy the 1/22 bills for a spread of ten and wait for them to come back in line. It is trade ideas like these that keep bill traders and bill customers occupied all day long.

U.S. TREASURY NOTES

Notes are the second largest class of security the Treasury issues, both in terms of amount outstanding and trading volume. Notes, like bills, came into existence many years after the Treasury Department did, in this case under the Victory Liberty Loan Act of 1919. Before this point, the only securities issued by the Treasury were called bonds.

Actually, the first notes were issued in June of 1921, but their number grew rapidly. By the end of World War II notes represented a major part of the Treasury's debt. By the 1960s, notes represented the only marketable securities the Treasury could issue with maturities longer than a year, because Congress had put an interest ceiling of 4.25% on bonds issued by the Treasury. More recently, Congress has allowed limited issuances of bonds yielding more than 4.25%, but the Treasury regularly uses up that *bond authorization,* and must request more from Congress.

With the periodic uncertainty as to its ability to issue bonds, and with ever-increasing budget deficits to finance, the Treasury has expanded both the size of its periodic note issues, and the classes of notes issued. By the mid-1980s the Treasury had over 120 separate note issues outstanding, with maturities ranging from a few weeks to ten years, and interest rates ranging from 6.125% to 16.125%.

All notes pay interest *semiannually,* on the anniversary of the maturity date and six months later. Thus a note that matures on November 15, 1989, will pay interest each November 15 and May 15. Many years ago such securities were issued as *physical certificates,* with coupons attached for each interest payment. In order to receive your interest payment, you clipped the coupon and took it to a national bank. The bank would give you the interest in cash and then collect it from the Treasury. For this reason, all Treasury securities that pay semiannual interest are called *coupon securities.*

Nowadays, all coupon securities are issued in book entry form, and the interest payments are paid out to holders of record by the Federal Reserve. Ownership of these securities is recorded on the Fed's computer, in the name of the member bank which is the custodian. The member bank keeps records as to which of its customers own which notes. Interest payments are credited to the bank's reserve account, and the bank credits the accounts of its customers.

Treasury Note Issuance Procedures

As of the mid-1980s, all Treasury notes were issued primarily through the same kind of auction as for bills, but in the past the Treasury has also used other methods. For example, before 1932 all notes were issued by a *rights offering.* In a rights offering, owners of maturing issues are given the right to subscribe for the new issue. In most cases, subscribers can surrender the maturing issue in payment for the new one. Thus, a rights offering is a good method for issuing securities when the Treasury is merely refunding outstanding issues.

The Quarterly Refunding

For many years, Treasury debt management amounted to a series of refundings, and during that time a pattern was established, called the

Individual Treasury Securities

quarterly refunding, which the Treasury still uses. Quarterly refundings occur in the months of February, May, August, and November, and encompass the issuance of notes with initial maturities of three years and ten years, and a bond with an initial maturity of thirty years.

Although the issuance takes place in those four months, the process usually begins in the previous month. On the last Wednesday of January, April, July, and October the Treasury, after a series of meetings with Primary Dealers and customers, announces the size of each issue that it will sell. An example of such an *announcement* is shown in Figure 3-8. Currently, the sale is accomplished by *auction,* and the auctions are held the first week of the month. Three-year notes are auctioned on Tuesday, ten-year notes on Wednesday, and thirty-year bonds on Thursday. Coupled with the regular bill auctions on Monday, this makes for a very busy week on the market. All three issues are delivered and paid for on the fifteenth of the month, and mature the fifteenth of the same month the required number of years hence.

The note auction process is essentially the same as the bill auction process. Bidders submit tenders like the one in Figure 3-9. This tender is for the three-year note auctioned in the November 1986 quarterly refunding, maturing November 15, 1989. As you can see, bids are submitted in terms of *yield to maturity,* instead of price. There is no coupon rate specified for this note issue. When the results of the auction are known, the coupon rate will be set at the highest rate (to the nearest 1/8th point) that is *below* the average in the auction. This ensures that the notes awarded at the average yield will have a price *below 100.*

Just as with bills, the tender window closes at 1:00 P.M. Eastern Time. The Fed collects all the tenders and goes through the same process of netting out the non-competitive bids and making the awards. As soon as the results are known, a press release is made up, and the information appears on the various wire services. Figures 3-10 and 3-11 show the results of this auction, as reported on Telerate.

Figure 3-10, which gives the results in terms of prices and yields, covers all notes and bonds auctioned from 6/24/86 to the three-year issue, and it shows something unusual about this auction. You will notice that the high, low, and average bids were all the same—6.42%! It happened twice before 6/24, but it is still unusual. Normally such uniformity of opinion, and such a large bid at that level, means that the market is in good shape. We can also see from this page that our imaginary dealer did not win any bonds with the tender we saw. Of course, he could have submitted another tender at 6.42% and would

Figure 3-8
Federal Reserve Bank of New York
Treasury announces November quarterly financing.

**FEDERAL RESERVE BANK
OF NEW YORK**
Fiscal Agent of the United States

Circular No. **10,097**
October 30, 1986

TREASURY ANNOUNCES NOVEMBER QUARTERLY FINANCING

*To All Banking Institutions, and Others Concerned,
in the Second Federal Reserve District:*

The following statement was issued yesterday by the Treasury Department:

The Treasury will raise about $15,600 million of new cash and refund $13,407 million of securities maturing November 15, 1986, by issuing $10,000 million of 3-year notes, $9,750 million of 10-year notes, and $9,250 million of 30-year bonds. The $13,407 million of maturing securities are those held by the public, including $1,497 million held, as of today, by Federal Reserve Banks as agents for foreign and international monetary authorities.

The 10-year note and 30-year bond being offered today will be eligible for exchange in the STRIPS program and, accordingly, may be divided into their separate Interest and Principal Components and maintained on the book-entry records of the Federal Reserve Banks and Branches. Once a security is in the STRIPS form, the components may be maintained and transferred in multiples of $1,000. Financial institutions should consult their local Federal Reserve Bank or Branch for procedures for requesting securities in STRIPS form.

The three issues totaling $29,000 million are being offered to the public, and any amounts tendered by Federal Reserve Banks as agents for foreign and international monetary authorities will be added to that amount. Tenders for such accounts will be accepted at the average prices of accepted competitive tenders.

In addition to the public holdings, Government accounts and Federal Reserve Banks, for their own accounts, hold $2,114 million of the maturing securities that may be refunded by issuing additional amounts of the new securities at the average prices of accepted competitive tenders.

Printed on the reverse side is a table summarizing the highlights of the offerings.

The 10-year note and the 30-year bond will be eligible for conversion to STRIPS (Separate Trading of Registered Interest and Principal of Securities). Information about this feature is set forth in the Treasury Department's official offering circulars, copies of which will be furnished upon request directed to our Issues Division (Tel. No. 212-720-6621). Questions regarding procedures for requesting securities in STRIPS form should be directed to Daniel Bolwell, Chief, Securities Transfer Division (Tel. No. 212-720-5379).

In addition, enclosed are copies of the forms to be used in submitting tenders.

This Bank will receive tenders at the Securities Department of its Head Office and at its Buffalo Branch on the dates and times specified on the reverse side of this circular as the deadlines for receipt of tenders. *All competitive tenders,* whether transmitted by mail or by other means, must reach this Bank or its Branch by that time on the specified dates. However, for investors who wish to submit noncompetitive tenders and who find it more convenient to mail their tenders than to present them in person, the official offering circular for each offering provides that *noncompetitive* tenders will be considered timely received if they are mailed to this Bank or its Branch under a postmark no later than the date preceding the date specified for receipt of tenders.

Bidders submitting noncompetitive tenders should realize that it is possible that the average price may be above par, in which case they would have to pay more than the face value for the securities.

Payment with a tender may be made in cash, by check, in Treasury securities maturing on or before the issue date of the securities being purchased, by a charge to an institution's reserve account at this Bank, or, in the case of Treasury Tax and Loan Note Option Depositaries, by credit to a Treasury Tax and Loan Note Account. Payment by check must be in the form of an official bank check, a Federal funds check (a check drawn by a depository institution on its Federal Reserve account), or a personal check, which need not be certified. All checks must be drawn payable to the Federal Reserve Bank of New York; *checks endorsed to this Bank will not be accepted.*

Recorded messages provide information about Treasury offerings and about auction results: at the Head Office — Tel. No. 212-720-7773 (offerings) and Tel. No. 212-720-5823 (results); at the Buffalo Branch — Tel. No. 716-849-5158 (offerings) and Tel. No. 716-849-5046 (results). Additional inquiries regarding this offering may be made by calling, at the Head Office, Tel. No. 212-720-6621, or, at the Buffalo Branch, Tel. No. 716-849-5016.

E. GERALD CORRIGAN,
President.

Figure 3-8
Federal Reserve Bank of New York
Treasury announces November quarterly financing (cont'd.).

**HIGHLIGHTS OF TREASURY
OFFERINGS TO THE PUBLIC
NOVEMBER 1986 FINANCING
TO BE ISSUED NOVEMBER 17, 1986**

	3-Year Notes	10-Year Notes	30-Year Bonds
Amount Offered:			
To the public	$10,000 million	$9,750 million	$9,250 million
Description of Security:			
Term and type of security	3-year notes	10-year notes	30-year bonds
Series and CUSIP designation	Series T-1989 (CUSIP No. 912827 UE0)	Series D-1996 (CUSIP No. 912827 UF7)	Bonds of 2016 (CUSIP No. 912810 DX3)
CUSIP Nos. for STRIPS Components	Not applicable	Listed in Attachment A of offering circular	Listed in Attachment A of offering circular
Issue date	November 17, 1986	November 17, 1986 (to be dated November 15, 1986)	November 17, 1986 (to be dated November 15, 1986)
Maturity date	November 15, 1989	November 15, 1996	November 15, 2016
Interest rate	To be determined, based on the average of accepted bids	To be determined, based on the average of accepted bids	To be determined, based on the average of accepted bids
Investment yield	To be determined at auction	To be determined at auction	To be determined at auction
Premium or discount	To be determined after auction	To be determined after auction	To be determined after auction
Interest payment dates	May 15 and November 15	May 15 and November 15	May 15 and November 15
Minimum denomination available	$5,000	$1,000	$1,000
Amount required for STRIPS	Not applicable	To be determined after auction	To be determined after auction
Terms of Sale:			
Method of sale	Yield auction	Yield auction	Yield auction
Competitive tenders	Must be expressed as an annual yield, with two decimals, e.g., 7.10%	Must be expressed as an annual yield, with two decimals, e.g., 7.10%	Must be expressed as an annual yield with two decimals, e.g., 7.10%
Noncompetitive tenders	Accepted in full at the average price up to $1,000,000	Accepted in full at the average price up to $1,000,000	Accepted in full at the average price up to $1,000,000
Accrued interest payable by investor	None	To be determined after auction	To be determined after auction
Payment Terms:			
Payment through Treasury Tax and Loan (TT&L) Note Accounts	Acceptable for TT&L Note Option Depositaries	Acceptable for TT&L Note Option Depositaries	Acceptable for TT&L Note Option Depositaries
Payment by non-institutional investors	Full payment to be submitted with tender	Full payment to be submitted with tender	Full payment to be submitted with tender
Deposit guarantee by designated institutions	Acceptable	Acceptable	Acceptable
Key Dates:			
Receipt of tenders	**Tuesday, November 4, 1986,** prior to 1:00 p.m., EST	**Wednesday, November 5, 1986,** prior to 1:00 p.m., EST	**Thursday, November 6, 1986,** prior to 1:00 p.m., EST
Settlement			
a) cash for Federal funds	Monday, November 17, 1986	Monday, November 17, 1986	Monday, November 17, 1986
b) readily-collectible check	Thursday, November 13, 1986	Thursday, November 13, 1986	Thursday, November 13, 1986

Figure 3-9
Tender for three-year Treasury notes of Series T-1989.

Form N/B-Y (Rev. 9/86)

IMPORTANT — This tender must be received prior to 1:00 p.m., Tuesday, November 4, 1986
TENDER FOR 3-YEAR TREASURY NOTES OF SERIES T-1989

TO FEDERAL RESERVE BANK OF NEW YORK
Fiscal Agent of the United States
New York, N.Y. 10045

Dated at NEW YORK
NOVEMBER 4 1986

The undersigned hereby offers to purchase the above-described book-entry securities in the amount indicated below, and agrees to make payment therefor at your Bank in accordance with the provisions of the official offering circular.

COMPETITIVE TENDER	Do not fill in both Competitive and Noncompetitive tenders on one form	NONCOMPETITIVE TENDER

$ 20,000,000 ...... (maturity value)
or any lesser amount that may be awarded.

Yield: 6.43
(Yield must be expressed with two decimal places, for example, 7.10)

$ .... (maturity value)
(Not to exceed $1,000,000 for one bidder through all sources)
at the average price of accepted competitive bids.
A noncompetitive bidder may not have entered into an agreement, or may not make an agreement with respect to the purchase or sale or other disposition of any noncompetitive awards of this issue in this auction prior to the designated closing time for receipt of tenders.

Certification by Competitive Bidders: The Bidder's ☒ Customer's ☐ net long position in these securities (including those acquired through "when issued" trading, and futures and forward transactions, as well as holdings of outstanding securities of the same series as the new offering) as of 12:30 pm Eastern time on the day of this auction, was —
☒ Not in excess of $200 million.
☐ In excess of $200 million, amounting to $..................................million.

Subject to allotment, please issue and accept payment for the book-entry securities indicated below:

Safekeeping or Delivery Instructions
(No changes will be accepted)

Book-Entry—
☐ 1. Hold in safekeeping at FRBNY in-
 ☐ Investment Account (4)
 ☐ General Account (5)
 ☐ Trust Account (6)
☐ 2. Hold as collateral for Treasury Tax and Loan Note Account*(7)
☒ 3. Wire to CHASE NY/FIRST GOVT. (8)
(Exact Receiving Bank Wire Address/Account)

Payment Instructions for Institutions

Payment will be made as follows:
☐ By charge to our reserve account
☐ By credit to the Treasury Tax and Loan Note Account
☐ By check in *immediately available funds*
☐ By surrender of eligible maturing securities
☒ By charge to my correspondent bank

CHASE MANHATTAN
(Name of Correspondent)

*The undersigned certifies that the allotted securities be owned solely by the undersigned. (If a commercial bank or dealer is subscribing for its own account or for account of customers, the following certifications are made a part of this tender.)

WE HEREBY CERTIFY that we have received tenders from customers in the amounts set forth opposite their names on the list which is made a part of this tender and that we have received and are holding for the Treasury, or that we guarantee payment to the Treasury of, the payments required by the official offering circular.

WE FURTHER CERTIFY that tenders received by us, if any, from other commercial banks or primary dealers for their own account, and for the account of their customers, have been entered with us under the same conditions, agreements, and certifications set forth in this form.

Insert this tender in envelope marked "Tender for Treasury Securities"

Name of Subscriber (Please Print or Type)
FIRST GOVERNMENT SECURITIES
Address
150 WALL ST.
City: NEW YORK
State: NY
Zip Code: 10008
Phone (Include Area Code): 212-555-1875
Signature of Subscriber or Authorized Signature: I. M. Trader
Title of Authorized Signer: Managing Director

(Institutions submitting tenders for customer account must list customers' names on lines below or on an attached rider)

———————————————— ————————————————
(Name of customer) (Name of customer) (OVER)

See Reverse Side For Further Instructions

PRIVACY ACT STATEMENT — The individually identifiable information required on this form is necessary to permit the subscription to be processed and the securities to be issued. If registered securities are requested, the regulations governing United States securities (Department Circular No. 300) and the offering circular require submission of social security numbers; the numbers and other information are used in inscribing the securities and establishing and servicing the ownership and interest records. The transaction will not be completed unless all required data is furnished.

52

Figure 3-9
Tender for three-year Treasury notes of Series T-1989 (cont'd.).

INSTRUCTIONS

1. No tender for less than $5,000 will be considered; and each tender must be for a multiple $5,000 (maturity value).

2. Only banking institutions, and dealers who make primary markets in Government securities and report daily to this Bank their positions with respect to Government securities and borrowings thereon, may submit tenders for customer account; in doing so, they may consolidate competitive tenders *at the same yield* or at the same price and may consolidate noncompetitive tenders, provided a list is attached showing the name of each bidder and the amount bid for his or her account. Others will not be permitted to submit tenders except for their own amount.

3. Tenders will be received without deposit from commercial and other banks for their own account, federally insured savings and loan associations, States, political subdivisions or instrumentalities thereof, public pension and retirement and other public funds, international organizations in which the United States holds membership, foreign central banks and foreign states, dealers who make primary markets in Government securities and report daily to the Federal Reserve Bank of New York their positions with respect to Government securities and borrowings thereon, and Government accounts. Tenders from others must be accompanied by full payment of the face amount of the securities applied for.

4. Payment with a tender may be in the form of a personal check, which need not be certified, an official bank check, or a Federal funds check (a check drawn by a commercial bank on its Federal Reserve account). All checks must be drawn payable to the Federal Reserve Bank of New York; *checks endorsed to this Bank will not be accepted.* Payment may also be made in cash or Treasury securities maturing on or before the issue date of the securities being purchased. Treasury Tax and Loan Note Option Depositaries may make payment for Treasury securities by credit to their Treasury Tax and Loan Note Accounts.

5. For information on currently available Treasury *offerings,* call our 24-hour recorded message at (212) 720-7773 at the Head Office or (716) 849-5046 at the Buffalo Branch. For *results* of recent Treasury auctions, call (212) 720-5823 at the Head Office or (716) 849-5046 at the Buffalo Branch. For other information about Treasury securities, call (212) 720-6621 at the Head Office or (716) 849-5016 at the Buffalo Branch during normal business hours.

6. If the language of this tender is changed in any respect that, in the opinion of the Secretary of the Treasury, is material, the tender may be disregarded.

Figure 3-10
Telerate screen showing Treasury three-year note
auction results in terms of price and yield.

```
TELERATE SYSTEMS
11/05  11:48 EST        U S TREASURY NOTE/BOND AUCTION RESULTS        PAGE 63
   3-YEAR NOTE          AVGE   AVGE   HIGH    LOW    LOW    HIGH    AT LOW
DATE   COUPON  MATURITY YIELD  PRICE  YIELD  PRICE  YIELD  PRICE    PRICE
11/04   6.375  11/15/89  6.42  99.879  6.42  99.879  6.42  99.879    49%
10/28   7.125  10/15/93  7.21  99.542  7.23  99.434  7.18  99.703    38%
10/22   6.375  10/31/88  6.39  99.972  6.39  99.972  6.38  99.991    46%
09/24   6.75   09/30/90  6.87  99.586  6.89  99.518  6.84  99.690    27%
09/23   6.375  09/30/88  6.44  99.880  6.44  99.880  6.42  99.917    66%
08/27   6.500  11/15/91  6.51  99.916  6.52  99.873  6.48  99.047    41%
08/20   6.125  08/31/88  6.21  99.843  6.22  99.824  6.19  99.880    22%
08/07   7.250  05/15/16  7.63  95.522  7.65  95.297  7.59  95.975    58%
08/06   7.375  05/15/96  7.47  99.316  7.48  99.248  *7.44 99.521    70%
08/05   6.625  08/15/89  6.73  99.719  6.74  99.692  6.69  99.826    77%
07/23   6.625  07/31/88  6.67  99.917  6.67  99.917  6.67  99.917    76%
06/25   7.25   07/15/93  7.33  99.561  7.36  99.399  7.26  99.940    30%
06/24   7.250  06/30/90  7.26  99.966  7.26  99.966  7.26  99.966    40%

*ACCEPTING ONE TENDER OF 1,000,000.   NOTE/BOND DISTRIBUTION SEE PAGE 64
```

Figure 3-11
Telerate screen showing Treasury three-year note
auction results in terms of volume bid by district.

```
TELERATE SYSTEMS

11/05  11:48 EST      U S TREASURY NOTE/BOND AUCTION RESULTS        PAGE 64
         TENDERS APPLIED FOR AND ACCEPTED (IN THOUSANDS OF DOLLARS)
   3-YEAR NOTE     AUCTION: 11/04/86   MATURITY:11/15/89   SETTLEMENT:11/17/86
   FED DISTRICT       APPLIED           ACCEPTED
   BOSTON          $      19,305     $      16,305     -COMPETITIVE:     $9,451 MLN
   NEW YORK           38,311,740           9,593,120   -NONCOMPETITIVE: $ 608 MLN
   PHILADELPHIA           18,105              18,105
   CLEVELAND             111,885              32,885   -FEDERAL RESERVE BANKS AS
   RICHMOND               83,180              23,680    AGENTS FOR FOREIGN AND
   ATLANTA                41,815              21,815    INTERNATIONAL MONETARY
   CHICAGO             1,903,145             166,045    AUTHORITIES:     $300 MLN
   ST. LOUIS              88,715              45,715   -GOVERNMENT ACCOUNT AND FRBS
   MINNEAPOLIS           247,630              32,630    FOR THEIR OWN ACCOUNTS:
   KANSAS CITY            78,070              71,070                    $1510MLN
   DALLAS                 22,810              12,810   -MINIMUM PAR AMOUNT REQUIRED
   SAN FRANCISCO       1,184,550              22,550      FOR STRIPS TO PRODUCE
   TREASURY                1,985               1,985        MULTIPLES: $X
   TOTAL              42,112,935          10,058,715
```

55

have been awarded about half the amount he bid for. Many dealers and customers submit *multiple tenders* at different prices.

Figure 3-11 gives us the volume information about the auction. The cover here was about four times, another good sign, but there were very few bonds awarded to foreign central banks. Virtually all of the issue was awarded in New York, which may mean that most of it was purchased by dealers, as opposed to customers. Since dealers are not regarded as long-term holders of these notes, it might be said that the notes are not in *strong hands*. One additional negative is that many of the out-of-town bids were not successful. Look, for example, at Chicago, San Francisco, and Minneapolis. If these cities represent customer interest, it may be that the dealers have gotten ahead of their customers in their enthusiasm for the market.

There remain two more auctions in this refunding, and the market may be quite unsettled while they are going on. In fact, it may remain unsettled until the securities are delivered and paid for on November 15.

Note Issuance Cycles

The Treasury issues notes in cycles other than the quarterly refunding of course. As of the mid-1980s, here is the complete cycle of Treasury note issuances:

- *Two-Year Note*—Auctioned late in every month, to be delivered and mature on the last business day of the month. Thus the two-year note for July 1986 was auctioned on 7/23 for delivery 7/31, maturing on 7/31, and paying interest on 1/31 and 7/31.
- *Three-Year Note*—Auctioned in February, May, August, and November, as part of the quarterly refunding.
- *Four-Year Note*—Auctioned in March, June, September, and December as part of another group of issuances called the *consolidated financing* or the *mini-refunding*. Thus, the June 1986 four-year note was auctioned on 6/24 for delivery on 6/30, maturing on 6/30/90, and paying interest on 6/30 and 12/31.
- *Five-Year Note*—Auctioned late in February, May, August, and November, but not part of the quarterly refunding. The August 1986 five-year note was auctioned on 8/27 for delivery 9/15, maturing on 9/15/91, and paying interest on 3/15 and 9/15.
- *Seven-Year Note*—Auctioned in March, June, September, and December as part of the mini-refunding. The June 1986 seven-year note

Individual Treasury Securities 57

was auctioned on 6/25 for delivery on 7/15, maturing on 7/15/93, and paying interest on 1/15 and 7/15.

○ *Ten-Year Note*—Auctioned in February, May, August, and November as part of the quarterly refunding. The August 1986 ten-year note was auctioned 8/6 for delivery 8/15, maturing on 8/15/96, and paying interest on 2/15 and 8/15.

There are sometimes reasons why this schedule is disrupted. For example, Congress delayed raising the debt ceiling in September of 1986, so the auction of the seven-year note was delayed until October. Also, the Treasury occasionally reopens an older issue, and auctions more of it in the next cycle. This means that a reopened ten year, for example, might actually have a maturity of nine years and nine months.

Treasury Note Trading

In the meantime, all these notes that were issued in all these cycles will be trading every day. There are so many note issues that they are split up into sectors. Each dealer divides them up his own way, and each broker divides his screens into pages a little differently. Figure 3-12 shows the *short coupon* page on Telerate, covering issues maturing from May 1988 to November 1991. Not every note or bond that matures within that span is listed; only the ones that trade fairly actively. This screen shows the market on Wednesday, November 5, the day after the three-year note auction we just covered.

How has the three-year note fared? Not too well to this point. You can see it at the bottom of the left column: the 6.375% issue of 11/89W. The little arrow means that it is the current three-year note. The auction level was at 99.879 or approximately 99.28 in 1/32ds. Here, at about noon the next day, it is trading at approximately 99.26. For each million dollars of securities, 2/32ds equals $625, so a loss of that size on this issue amounts to $6,250,000. That's not a lot of money when spread among the Primary Dealers, but further erosion of the issue could prompt a wave of selling.

This screen has a lot more going on, of course, than the three-year note. There is action in the 6.375% issue of 10/88, the current two-year note. It was auctioned on 10/22 at an average price of about 99.31 and is now trading around 100.08. The current four year, the 6.75% note of 9/90 has also appreciated from the auction level of about 99.16 to

Figure 3-12
Telerate screen showing a Treasury short coupon page.

```
TELERATE SYSTEMS

11/05 11:49 EST CANTOR FITZ (C) 86            9.625    6/89
    7.125     5/88                           13.875    8/89
    7.000     6/88                            8.375   12/89   105.00 -02+   1 X 1
    6.625     7/88   100.22 -24    1 X 1     11.000    2/90
    6.125     8/88    99.27 -28   10 X 1      7.250    3/90   *101.24 -     5 X
    6.375     9/88   100.06+-08    1  X 1     7.250    6/90    101.24 -     1 X
>   6.375    10/88   100.08  -08+ 10 X 10   > 6.750    9/90   100.08 -10    3 X 30

   11.250    12/87   105.26          X 10     9.875    8/90
   11.750    11/88   110.10          X 1     10.500    1/90   110.27+-00    1 X 1
   11.750     5/89                            9.125    2/91   108.
    6.875     5/89                            8.125    5/91
    6.625     8/89   100.14          X 6      7.500    8/91   102.18         X 1
>   6.375    11/89W   99.26 -26+*   1 X 1   > 6.500   11/91    98.31+-00+   1 X 5
                                                      FULTON-PREBON FED FUNDS
7 YR.    100.10+12   1 X 2 3MO.   5.27 -24+   5X  25 BID 6           OPN 5 15/16
10YR.W    7.23 -22   2 X 1 6MO.   5.35 -34    5X   5 ASK 6 1/16      HGH 6
30YR.W    7.46 -45   1 X 8 1YR.   5.43+-42+   5X  25 LST 6           LOW 5 15/16
```

58

Individual Treasury Securities

100.08. The current five year, the 6.5% of 11/91, has not done as well, going from an auction price of 99.28 to 99.31 +.

All these prices don't mean much, however, unless we translate them into *yield to maturity (YTM)*. That number is the common denominator of the bond market and is used to compare every issue in the corporate and municipal market, as well as in this one. In order to see how all these issues interrelate, let's look at a *government quote sheet*.

Figure 3-13 is part of a typical government quote sheet, published daily by any number of banks or Primary Dealers. Most such sheets have the same information on them, although it may be arranged in a slightly different manner. This part of the sheet lists every issue that the Treasury has outstanding from November 1986 to November 1990. The first two columns show the *total size* of each issue, and the amount held by the *public*. For example, using the second issue on the list, the total issue is $7.7 billion of which $6.5 billion is held by the public. The rest is held by the Fed or Government Trust Funds. Then each issue is identified by coupon and maturity, with all maturities being the fifteenth of the month unless otherwise indicated.

Then the sheet gives the *bid* and *offered* prices as of the end of the trading day, followed by a column labeled *Yield (E)*. That number is the YTM (or To Call if the issue is above 100) at the offered price. There are two components to a security's YTM: *current yield* and *accretion*. Current yield is the security's coupon divided by its price as a fraction of 100. Accretion is the security's inexorable march to 100 at maturity. Together, they make up YTM or the yield a holder would receive if he bought the security at the offered price and held it to maturity.

Look at the last two issues on the sheet, the 9.625% of 11/90 and the 13% of 11/90. If we took their coupon rates and divided them by their prices, we could derive their current yields. For the 9.625% issue it is 9.625/1.0990625, or 8.76%. For the 13% it is 13/1.21625, or 10.69%. Does that make the 13% issue a better buy? Not necessarily, because by 11/90 it will have fallen 21.625 points in price, while the 9.625% will have fallen only 9.90625 points. In fact, the Yield column tells us that these securities will give us exactly the same yield if we bought them at the offered price and held them to maturity: 6.77%. Because it takes so many factors into consideration, YTM is the common denominator of the entire fixed income market.

The next column shows the *after-tax yield,* assuming a 46% tax rate. This column enables taxable buyers to compare these yields with those on municipal issues. The next column, *Corporate Taxable*

Figure 3-13
Quote sheet listing Treasury note and bond issues.

Amount Outstdg (D)	Publ Held (D)	Coupon	Maturity (C)	R	Bid	Asked	Yield	After Tax Yield (A)	Corp Tax Four	Change to Prev Day (32nd)	Yield Value 1/32	Days Int Equiv to 1/32nd	Range of Bids High	Range of Bids Low	Min Denom
1.20	.330	6 1/8	NOV. 86	n	99-30	100-01	4.55	2.46	4.55		1.3980	1.88	100-30	87-16	1000
7.70	6.50	11.00	NOV. 86	n	100-04	100-04	4.98	2.69	4.98	-1	1.3659	1.05	103-26	95-14	5000
3.20	3.20	13 7/8	NOV. 86	n	100-04	100-07	3.57	1.93	3.57	-1	1.3467	.83	112-12	100-04	1000
3.50	3.20	16 1/8	NOV. 86	n	100-05	100-03	4.28	2.31	4.28		1.3331	.71	119-00	100-05	1000
9.00	9.00	10 3/8	NOV. 30,86	n	100-08	100-11	4.68	2.53	4.68		.4757	1.10	103-01	99-00	5000
9.0	9.0	9 7/8	DEC. 31,86	n	100-18	100-21	5.19	2.80	5.19	-1	.2061	1.16	103-12	99-11	1000
5.90	5.60	10.00	DEC. 31,86	n	100-19	100-22	5.10	2.75	5.10	-1	.2059	1.15	102-18	93-00	5000
9.0	9.0	9 3/4	JAN. 31,87	n	100-27	101-00	5.23	2.82	5.23		.1322	1.18	102-12	98-01	1000
6.20	4.60	9	FEB. 87		100-27	101-30	5.39	2.91	5.39		.1133	1.28	102-03	90-11	5000
6.50	6.30	10 7/8	FEB. 87		101-11	101-14	5.37	2.90	5.37	-1	.1123	1.06	103-28	98-11	1000
3.40	3.30	12 3/4	FEB. 87		101-28	101-31	5.25	2.83	5.25	-1	.1112	.90	109-08	94-14	5000
9.0	9.0	9	FEB. 28,87	n	101-12	101-12	5.42	2.93	5.43		.0986	1.13	102-31	98-10	5000
6.50	6.00	10 1/4	MAR. 31,87	n	101-24	101-27	5.43	2.93	5.43	-1	.0784	1.11	103-16	92-23	1000
9.0	9.0	10 3/4	MAR. 31,87	n	101-29	102-00	5.47	2.95	5.47	-1	.0783	1.06	103-31	99-22	5000
9.0	9.0	9 3/4	APR. 30,87	n	101-12	101-13	5.44	2.94	5.44	-1	.0653	1.16	103-30	99-16	1000
2.50	2.00	12.00	MAY 87		103-10	103-13	5.29	2.86	5.29	-2	.0595	.96	107-06	96-28	5000
6.50	6.50	12 1/2	MAY 87		103-15	103-18	5.47	2.96	5.47	-1	.0594	.92	107-03	97-23	1000
3.50	3.50	14.00	MAY 87		104-12	104-15	5.20	2.81	5.20	-3	.0589	.82	113-14	101-05	5000
9.0	9.0	9 1/8	MAY 31,87	n	101-27	101-30	5.57	3.01	5.57		.0560	1.25	102-30	99-26	5000
9.25	9.25	8 1/2	JUNE 30,87	n	101-22	101-25	5.64	3.04	5.64	-2	.0489	1.35	102-23	98-29	1000
6.40	6.00	10 1/2	JUNE 30,87	n	103-01	103-01	5.64	3.04	5.64	-1	.0484	1.16	104-27	92-19	5000
6.40	6.00	8 7/8	JULY 31,87	n	102-05	102-08	5.67	3.06	5.67		.0433	1.30	103-00	99-14	1000
6.50	6.50	12 3/8	AUG. 87	n	104-31	105-02	5.55	3.00	5.55		.0400	.93	107-20	97-28	5000
4.10	4.00	13 3/4	AUG. 87		106-07	106-10	5.27	2.84	5.27		.0396	.84	160-23	100-17	1000
9.25	9.25	8 7/8	AUG. 31,87	n	102-22	102-25	5.70	3.08	5.70		.0390	1.27	103-06	99-14	5000
9.25	9.25	9	SEPT 30,87	n	102-22	102-25	5.76	3.11	5.76	-1	.0354	1.26	103-15	99-23	1000
6.50	6.50	11 1/8	SEPT 30,87	n	104-16	104-19	5.37	3.12	5.37	-1	.0349	1.02	106-13	93-26	5000
9.25	9.25	8 7/8	OCT. 31,87	n	102-28	102-28	5.81	3.14	5.81		.0325	1.27	103-13	99-23	5000
2.40	1.80	7 5/8	NOV. 87		101-20	101-26	5.77	3.12	5.77		.0315	1.51	102-18	84-28	5000
6.50	6.50	11.00	NOV. 87	n	104-28	105-00	5.88	3.18	5.88		.0308	1.05	106-23	99-16	1000
5.40	5.30	12 5/8	NOV. 87	n	106-18	106-22	5.79	3.12	5.79		.0304	.91	109-24	97-19	5000
9.5	9.5	8 1/2	NOV. 30,87	n	102-18	102-22	5.85	3.16	5.85		.0301	1.35	103-14	99-02	5000
6.00	6.00	11 1/4	DEC. 31,87	n	105-23	105-27	5.89	3.18	5.89		.0281	1.46	102-30	93-15	5000
2.70	2.70	12 3/8	JAN. 88		107-12	107-16	5.73	3.10	5.73	-1	.0271	1.02	107-18	96-16	1000
9.5	9.5	8 1/8	JAN. 31,88	n	102-13	102-17	5.95	3.21	5.95		.0261	1.42	109-09	99-02	5000
5.00	5.00	10 3/8	FEB. 88	n	105-06	105-04	5.87	3.17	5.87		.0262	1.14	103-28	99-26	1000
7.25	7.25	10 3/8	FEB. 88	n	105-06	105-10	5.96	3.22	5.96		.0249	1.11	106-19	89-26	5000
9.5	9.5	8.00	FEB. 29,88	n	102-12	102-16	5.98	3.23	5.98	-1	.0249	4-31	106-09	4-31	1000
9.5	9.5	7.125	MAR. 31,88	n	101-12	101-15	6.01	3.24	6.01	-1	.0246	1.41	103-12	99-02	5000
6.00	6.00	12	MAR. 31,88	n	107-27	107-31	5.95	3.22	5.95	+1	.0234	1.60	102-07	99-01	1000
3.20	2.80	13 1/4	APR. 88		109-29	110-03	5.82	3.14	5.82		.0224	.95	110-23	93-10	5000
9.75	9.75	6 5/8	APR. 30,88	N	100-21	100-25	6.06	3.27	6.06	-1	.0215	.86	112-14	98-24	1000
											.0223	1.71	101-18	98-05	5000

6:06 P.M. (EST) QUOTATIONS WEDNESDAY NOVEMBER 5, 1986   YIELDS FOR DELIVERY NOVEMBER 7, 1986

U.S. TREASURY NOTES AND BONDS

60

4.10	2.40	8 1/4	MAY 88	N	103-03	103-11	5.92	3.20	5.92		+3	.0213	1.39	104-04	83-26	1000
6.00	5.90	9 7/8	MAY 88	N	105-10	105-14	6.08	3.28	6.08			.0210	1.16	107-19	88-14	1000
8.0	8.0	10	MAY 88	N	105-16	105-20	6.07	3.28	6.07			.0210	1.15	107-25	4-31	5000
9.75	9.75	7 1/8	MAY 31,88	N	101-12	101-16	6.10	3.29	6.10		−1	.0210	1.61	102-13	98-19	5000
9.75	7	7	JUNE30,88	N	101-07	101-11	6.12	3.31	6.12			.0200	1.64	102-09	98-19	5000
6.0	6.0	13 5/8	JUNE 88	N	111-19	111-25	5.99	3.24	5.99			.0187	.84	114-14	99-24	1000
3.50	3.40	14.00	JULY 88	N	112-19	112-25	5.92	3.19	5.92		+2	.0182	.82	115-18	100-28	5000
6.0	0.10	6 5/8	JULY31,88	N	100-20	100-24	6.15	3.32	6.15			.0192	1.74	101-22	99-22	5000
8.5	8.5	9 1/2	AUG. 88	N	105-12	105-16	6.16	3.33	6.16		−1	.0182	1.10	107-31	4-31	5000
5.80	5.60	10 1/2	AUG. 88	N	107-01	107-07	6.13	3.31	6.13		−3	.0180	1.20	109-23	89-20	5000
		6 1/8	AUG.31,88	N	99-26	99-30	6.17	3.33	6.17			.0185	1.85	100-30	99-05	5000
6.0	6.0	11 3/8	SEPT.88	N	100-05	100-09	6.21	3.35	6.21		−2	.0177	1.78	101-13	99-05	5000
3.50	3.20	15 3/8	SEPT30,88	N	109-08	109-08	6.12	3.31	6.12		−2	.0167	1.00	112-10	98-21	1000
10	10	6 3/8	OCT. 88	N	116-13	116-21	6.20	3.30	6.12		−4	.0157	.74	121-12	105-12	1000
		6 3/8	OCT.31,88	N	100-06	100-10	6.20	3.35	6.20		−1	.0170	1.77	101-03	22-05	5000
8.75	8.75	8 5/8	NOV. 88	N	104-17	104-25	6.20	3.35	6.20			.0162	1.33	107-03	84-00	1000
3.40	3.40	8 3/4	NOV. 88	N	110-04	110-12	6.21	3.35	6.21		−1	.0162	1.31	107-08	93-00	1000
6.2	6.00	11 3/4	DEC.31,88	N	108-13	116-26	6.25	3.38	6.25		−1	.0156	.98	111-15	97-03	1000
3.50	3.40	10 5/8	JAN. 88	N	116-18	116-26	6.27	3.40	6.27		−3	.0149	1.08	120-10	102-12	1000
9.00	9.00	8	FEB. 89	N	103-11	103-15	6.33	3.42	6.33		−3	.0140	.79	104-30	4-31	5000
6.20	6.00	11 3/8	FEB. 89	N	110-15	110-18	6.30	3.40	6.30		−3	.0147	1.44	112-02	91-16	1000
6.25	6.25	11 1/4	MAR.31,89	N	117-18	117-26	6.35	3.43	6.35		−3	.0134	1.01	112-02	99-20	1000
3.30	3.20	14 1/2	APR. 89	N	106-31	106-23	6.36	3.44	6.36		−3	.0126	.79	120-07	101-16	1000
9.00	9.00	6,875	MAY 89	N	104-03	104-03	6.40	3.45	6.40		−2	.0135	1.67	104-28	4-31	5000
2.60	2.20	9 1/4	MAY 89	N	107-18	107-18	6.36	3.44	6.36		−3	.0131	1.24	107-13	83-30	1000
6.00	6.00	11 3/4	MAY 89	N	111-30	112-06	6.44	3.48	6.44		−3	.0127	.98	113-25	92-19	1000
6.5	6.5	9 5/8	JUNE30,89	N	107-13	107-17	6.48	3.50	6.48		−3	.0124	1.19	108-15	88-01	1000
4.70	4.60	14 1/2	JULY 89	N	119-09	119-17	6.44	3.49	6.44		−3	.0115	.90	121-27	101-30	1000
9.50	9.50	6 5/8	AUG. 89	N	100-10	100-14	6.57	3.55	6.57		−2	.0124	1.74	104-02	4-31	5000
	6250	13 7/8	AUG. 89	N	117-05	118-13	6.50	3.51	6.50		−2	.0112	.83	120-19	99-24	1000
6.75	6.75	9 3/8	SEPT30,89	N	107-09	107-13	6.52	3.52	6.52		−3	.0115	1.21	108-05	99-30	1000
4.20	4.20	11 7/8	OCT. 89	N	113-26	114-02	6.53	3.53	6.53		−3	.0109	.96	115-18	92-18	1000
5.80	3.80	10 3/4	NOV. 89	N	111-04	111-12	6.54	3.53	6.54		−3	.0107	1.07	112-05	88-02	1000
6.5	6.5	12 3/4	NOV. 89	N	116-16	116-24	6.55	3.54	6.55		−2	.0105	.90	118-15	99-01	1000
	7.0	8 3/8	DEC.31,89	N	104-23	105-01	6.57	3.55	6.57		−2	.0108	1.37	106-02	98-11	1000
4.80	4.80	10 1/2	JAN. 90	N	105-23	104-31	6.62	3.57	6.62		−3	.0103	1.10	112-01	86-00	500
1.60	1.60	3 1/2	FEB. 90	F	94-27	96-11	4.72	2.77	4.72			.0106	3.29	95-14	85-00	500
2.60	2.60	11	FEB. 90	N	112-24	112-20	6.64	3.58	6.64		−3	.0100	1.07	113-23	97-11	1000
6.75	6.75	7 1/4	MAR.31,90	N	101-23	101-27	6.63	3.58	6.63		−2	.0103	1.57	103-06	97-01	1000
7.00	7.00	10 1/2	APR. 90	N	111-12	111-20	6.66	3.59	6.66		−2	.0096	1.39	112-25	86-02	1000
5.10	5.00	8 1/4	MAY 90	B	104-23	105-11	6.53	3.52	6.53		−2	.0098	1.01	106-28	78-02	1000
1.20	.840	11 3/8	MAY 90	N	114-06	114-14	6.70	3.62	6.70		−2	.0093	.98	115-22	98-02	1000
7.00	7.00	7 1/4	JUNE30,90	N	101-23	101-27	6.67	3.60	6.67		−2	.0097	1.59	102-08	98-02	1000
7.25	7.25	10 3/4	JULY 90	N	112-25	113-01	6.70	3.62	6.70		−2	.0090	1.07	114-00	86-26	1000
5.00	4.90	9 7/8	AUG. 90	N	110-04	110-12	6.71	3.62	6.71		−3	.0090	1.16	111-25	95-14	1000
3.80	2.60	10 3/4	AUG. 90	N	100-00	113-08	6.71	3.62	6.71		−3	.0088	1.07	114-13	86-22	1000
7.5	7.5	6 3/4	SEPT30,90	N	115-27	116-03	6.65	3.59	6.65		−3	.0092	1.68	101-12	99-06	1000
5.00	5.00	11 1/2	OCT. 90	N	109-23	109-29	6.77	3.66	6.77		−3	.0085	.99	117-12	89-22	1000
7.25	7.25	9 5/8	NOV. 90	N	121-12	121-20	6.77	3.65	6.77		−3	.0085	1.19	110-30	98-09	1000
5.70	5.00	13.00	NOV. 90	N							−2	.0080	.88	123-10	96-02	1000

Equivalent, is a throwback to a period before the Tax Reform Act of 1986, and does not concern us here. The sheet also shows the change from the previous day's quote, and then comes a very interesting column, called *Yield Value 1/32.* This column tells us how much a security's YTM changes for a 1/32d change in its price. In fact, the yield value is the *inverse* of a security's *price volatility.*

Price volatility is a very important measure for bond traders and customers, because different securities will move different amounts in price for any unit move in yield. When a customer sells a two-year note and buys a four-year note, he wants to know how much additional *price risk* he is assuming. When a dealer is selling one issue short as a *hedge* against owning another, he needs to know how much of each to sell or hold so that his position is neutral. If you look at the yield value column, you will see that the numbers generally drop as you move down the sheet. Since volatility is the inverse of yield value, this means that volatility increases as the term to maturity increases. We can even figure out by how much.

Suppose you wanted to sell the 7% issue of 6/30/88 and buy the 6.625% of 8/15/89. How much would you increase your volatility? The quickest way to find out is to divide the yield value of the shorter issue by the yield value of the longer issue. In this case, 0.0200/0.0124 = 1.6129. That means that you would have increased your volatility by over *61%*—great if you are bullish, but not so great if you are bearish. Traders and customers make calculations like this all the time, as they move from one sector to another. Coupon and price can also affect volatility. Look at the last two issues, with the same maturity but different coupons. Their volatilities are different by about 6%.

The next column is also very valuable for traders, although less so for investors. *Days Int Equiv to 1/32d* tells you how many days of coupon interest it takes to equal 1/32d. Why is this important? Because active traders, particularly those who sell securities short, run the risk of failing to deliver on settlement date. Such a *fail* results in the loss of coupon interest for each day it exists. Thus, for the 13% issue of 11/15/90, one day's fail will more than wipe out a profit of 1/32d on a trade.

The rest of the columns contain additional information which will be of little value to us, as we look at Treasury notes in action. What is important to traders and investors is a comparison of all the various securities, in a search for those that are *undervalued* and *overvalued.* For that purpose, we will concentrate on the YTM column, looking for aberrations. Generally speaking, the YTM should increase gradually as the maturity does. Where it doesn't, or where the increase is sharp, we need to look for an explanation. One such explanation could be issue size. Smaller issues, particularly those under $2 billion, are subject to sharp price swings, because they are less liquid. With less liquidity, transactions of any size may move the market more than normal.

Generally, we would expect the YTM to increase with the dollar price, because investors usually have a bias against paying a large *premium*. In some cases, though, our sheet shows the opposite. Look, for example, at the 7% issue of 6/30/88, and the 13.625% of 6/30/88. Here the relationship is inverted, with the 7% at a YTM of 6.12% and the 13.635% at a YTM of 5.99%. Perhaps someone has sold the 13% issue short and is unable to make delivery. With such a high coupon, a fail is disastrous, so he may be willing to pay up to cover his short. This is the kind of search and reasoning that sophisticated investors and dealers work on all the time.

U.S. TREASURY BONDS

Although they are the oldest form of security issued by the Treasury, and the one by which the market is often known, Treasury bonds have become a smaller part of the market in recent years. There are two basic reasons for the decline of bonds as a factor in the market. The first is the 4.25% ceiling Congress put on the interest rate at which the Treasury could issue bonds. The rate ceiling may have made sense when it was first introduced, but it doesn't seem to make much sense now, particularly since no such ceiling exists for bills or notes.

The second reason for the decline of bonds is the rate volatility that has permeated the markets since the 1970s. With the sharp rate movements of the last ten years, many investors who were comfortable owning long-term fixed rate securities have been moving a large part of their portfolios into the shorter end of the list. There are, of course, still buyers of long bonds, enough that the Treasury still includes a thirty-year issue in the quarterly refunding. But their number has dwindled enough so that the long bond is always the smallest issue in the refunding, and the Treasury has stopped issuing a twenty-year bond in the mini-refunding.

Stripping Treasury Bond Issues

Recently, however, there has been a development which has revitalized the long bond market, and it is based on a peculiarity of the YTM calculation. Important to that calculation is the treatment of coupon payments received before maturity. The YTM calculation does not compound the coupon payments received every six months. In determining the premium or discount necessary to achieve the yield, however, the calculation assumes that you could have compounded the forgone or extra coupon, and at the same rate as the YTM. For example, in calculating the price of a 6% bond maturing in ten years to yield 8%, the formula assumes that you would have been able to compound the additional 2% of coupon at 8%.

Whenever the short-term rate is lower than the long-term rate, this peculiarity has the effect of *undervaluing* bonds at a discount, and *overvaluing* bonds at a premium. Dealers have taken advantage of that phenomenon by purchasing bonds with market-rate coupons and issuing a string of 0% coupon securities representing the coupon payments, and the final maturity payment. This has the effect of *stripping* the coupons off the bond, as if you had actually cut them off of a bond certificate and sold the coupons and the bond itself separately. In theory, the present value of all the coupon payments, plus the present value of the principal, should equal the market value of the bond, but in reality the sum of all these parts is larger than the whole.

Aside from the compounding peculiarity, one other factor makes stripped issues more valuable than straight bonds. Whenever the yield curve is positively sloped, which means short rates lower than long rates, stripping has the additional effect of turning the coupon payments into a string of short-term securities, which are valued at a lower interest rate, and thus a higher price, than the bond itself. The development of stripped bonds is another of the ways in which the market has responded to the heavy demand for savings to fund the Treasury deficit; the popularity of these bonds has greatly reduced the trading supply of some of the Treasury's older bond issues.

Treasury Bond Issuance Procedures

Since the Treasury issues only one bond each quarter, the issuance procedure is relatively simple. The announcement of the auction is contained in the regular quarterly refunding announcement. The auction

Individual Treasury Securities

itself is held on the Thursday of the following week and is the last auction of the refunding cycle. Bidders fill out a tender form like the one used for notes, turn it in to the Fed, and wait for the results to be announced. The announcement, like other auction announcements, appears on the wire services in a form similar to Figures 3-14 and 3-15. As in other auctions, traders and investors spend a substantial amount of time speculating as to the auction stop, the volume of non-competitive bids, and whether the securities are in strong or weak hands.

Treasury Bond Trading

There are, however, a few added wrinkles to the bond. One is that it is traditionally bought by investors who are not necessarily present in other sectors of the government market. In particular, bonds tend to be a favorite of *pension funds*, which have long-term commitments to provide an income for their retired workers. Until about ten years ago, pension funds, and *life insurers*, were buyers of corporate bonds almost exclusively. When the Treasury began to run large deficits in the 1970s, it stepped up the issuance of bonds, until, in the mid-1970s, it was auctioning a bond a month. Treasury bond yields rose in relation to corporate bond yields, drawing pension and insurance investors into this new market.

These new investors took up the practice of *swapping* back and forth between corporates and Treasuries, as the yield spreads swing, but not all the dealers followed along. Some, like commercial banks, were prohibited by statute from entering the corporate market. Others chose not to expand their product line to encompass new markets. As a result, some Primary Dealers have very little contact with the final buyers of Treasury bonds, although they may be well plugged in to the rest of the Treasury list.

In addition, and partly because of the limited liquidity in long bonds, there developed a *commodity futures contract* based on Treasury bonds. Traded on the Chicago Board of Trade, the *CBT bond futures contract* has proved enormously popular. It trades more dollar volume than any other single security or commodity in the world. As a result, a raft of *arbitrageurs* has sprung up, trading Treasury bonds solely in relation to the futures contract. Because of this, and because the final investor is often an institution that spends only part of its time in the government market, the bond often seems to have a life of its own—as if it were only partly a Treasury security, and partly something else.

Figure 3-14
Telerate screen showing Treasury 30-year bond auction
results in terms of yield and price.

```
TELERATE SYSTEMS

11/06    16:14 EST           U S TREASURY NOTE/BOND AUCTION RESULTS  PAGE 63
30-YEAR BOND              AVGE   AVGE    HIGH   LOW    LOW    HIGH    AT LOW
DATE   COUPON  MATURITY   YIELD  PRICE   YIELD  PRICE  YIELD  PRICE   PRICE
11/06  7.50    11/20/16   7.54   99.526  7.56   99.291  7.52  99.762  42%
11/05  7.25    11/15/96   7.25   99.999  7.25  100.210  7.22  99.999  68%
11/04  6.375   11/15/89   6.42   99.879  6.42   99.879  6.42  99.879  49%
10/28  7.125   10/15/93   7.21   99.542  7.23   99.434  7.18  99.703  38%
10/22  6.375   10/31/88   6.39   99.972  6.39   99.972  6.38  99.991  46%
09/24  6.75    09/30/90   6.87   99.586  6.89   99.518  6.84  99.690  27%
09/23  6.375   09/30/88   6.44   99.880  6.44   99.880  6.42  99.917  66%
08/27  6.500   11/15/91   6.51   99.916  6.52   99.873  6.48  99.047  41%
08/20  6.125   08/31/88   6.21   99.843  6.22   99.824  6.19  99.880  22%
08/07  7.250   05/15/16   7.63   95.522  7.65   95.297  7.59  95.975  58%
08/06  7.375   05/15/96   7.47   99.316  7.48   99.248 *7.44  99.521  70%
08/05  6.625   08/15/89   6.73   99.719  6.74   99.692  6.69  99.826  77%
07/23  6.625   07/31/88   6.67   99.917  6.67   99.917  6.67  99.917  76%

*ACCEPTING ONE TENDER OF 1,000,000.  NOTE/BOND DISTRIBUTION SEE PAGE 64
```

Figure 3-15
Telerate screen showing Treasury 30-year bond auction
results in terms of volume bid by district.

```
TELERATE SYSTEMS

11/06   16:16 EST      U S TREASURY NOTE/BOND AUCTION RESULTS       PAGE 64
             TENDERS APPLIED FOR AND ACCEPTED (IN THOUSANDS OF DOLLARS)
30-YEAR BOND     AUCTION: 11/06/86    MATURITY:11/20/16    SETTLEMENT:11/17/86
  FED DISTRICT         APPLIED            ACCEPTED
BOSTON           $     45,000        $    45,000    -COMPETITIVE:      $9.037 MLN
NEW YORK           19,409,078             8,730,758 -NONCOMPETITIVE:   $228 MLN
PHILADELPHIA          159,000               159,00
CLEVELAND              57,000                57,000 -FEDERAL RESERVE BANKS AS
RICHMOND                2,142                 2,142   AGENTS FOR FOREIGN AND
ATLANTA                 6,326                 4,326   INTERNATIONAL MONETARY
CHICAGO             1,051,481               296,721   AUTHORITIES:     $X MLN
ST. LOUIS              18,900                 6,900 -GOVERNMENT ACCOUNT AND FRBS
MINNEAPOLIS             6,607                 6,107   FOR THEIR OWN ACCOUNTS:
KANSAS CITY             4,584                 4,584                    $100 MLN
DALLAS                  3,103                 1,523 -MINIMUM PAR AMOUNT REQUIRED
SAN FRANCISCO         583,337               211,297   FOR STRIPS TO PRODUCE
TREASURY               79,000                79,000   MULTIPLES: $80,000
TOTAL              $21,085,898           $9,264,698
```

67

One last difference that some older bonds display: they can be *called* at 100 five years before they mature. What this means is that these bonds have two different maturities, depending on whether they are trading above or below 100. Government quote sheets signify such a security by displaying both dates, separated by a slash. Yields are calculated to *maturity* when the issue is below 100, and to the *call date* when the security is above 100.

There is, of course, an entire family of securities that really are from another world—partly Treasury and partly something else. They are the *federal agency securities*, and they are the subject of the next chapter.

CHAPTER FOUR

Individual Agency Securities

In Chapter 2 we discussed briefly the economic and political reasons for the foundation and continued existence of the federal agencies. It might seem, from reading that section, that the conditions leading up to the formation of those agencies and the nature of their structure and ownership, were unique to this country, and to the period in which they were formed. Instead, as we look around the industrialized world, we find countless examples of financial and industrial entities whose ownership is inextricably tied up with the government.

In Europe, for example, many industrial companies and utilities are wholly or partly owned by the government. The European steel industry is a prime source of companies that are tied to the government. Most of the railroads and airlines in Europe are either owned by or assisted by the government. In many cases, the electricity used throughout Europe is produced by government corporations. Finally, most of Europe's telephone companies are government owned and run.

The situation in the Far East is even more complicated. Although government ownership is less prevalent there than in Europe, each sector of the economy is much less autonomous in Japan and Korea. The huge banks and trading companies in Japan are totally in control of their sectors of the market. Furthermore, the Japanese Ministry of International Trade and Industry (MITI) has total control over all economic planning, private investment, and export production, as well as over many other areas of economic activity. While our corporations, unions, and regulators fight it out each day in the market, our Oriental competitors concentrate their energies on outproducing us. More than anything else, our federal agencies represent an accommodation to economic facts that Europe and the Far East dealt with long ago.

In spite of that accommodation, some of these economic facts have come home to roost in recent years. In at least two cases the result has been *substantial losses* for the federal agencies involved; other cases have seen *major changes in agency structure* in an effort to control damage done by uncontrollable economic conditions.

The first signs of trouble in the agency sector came during the early 1980s. During that period, interest rates rose to historically high levels, and many financial institutions suffered losses, as the yield on their fixed rate portfolios failed to keep up with their cost of funds. One of the more spectacular examples of this problem was the *Federal National Mortgage Association (FNMA)*, whose corporate mandate was to provide support to the secondary market for residential mortgages. During the years just prior to the early 1980s, FNMA had accomplished its mandate by buying a large portfolio of fixed-rate mortgages, much like a thrift institution might. When rates rose, their cost of funds rose too, and resulted in large *losses* for the association. During the period from 1981 through 1985 FNMA lost $277 million, or over 20% of its 1981 equity.

Because FNMA is a publicly traded corporation, with no statutory government support, these losses brought the price of its stock down to historic low levels, and widened the spread between the yield on its debt securities and those of the Treasury. By 1985, however, FNMA's program of matching the duration of its assets to its liabilities had begun to take hold. Along with falling interest rates and the introduction of FNMA's own passthrough, this program served to return FNMA to profitability in 1985, albeit in a small way.

The fall in interest rates that came in 1985 and 1986 brought with it a new, and potentially more dangerous, problem for the federal agencies. Falling rates meant a weak economy, and two areas showed special weakness. The agricultural sector of the economy had to contend with both reduced demand at home and a stronger dollar, which made exports less price competitive. At the same time, the artificially high price for oil, a result of OPEC's production restrictions, collapsed. Aside from causing widespread bank and thrift failures in the Southwest, the oil price collapse caused a collapse in the value of commercial real estate, particularly in the Southwest.

Losses due to credit problems are generally more intractable than those due to interest imbalances, and this was the case here. The *Farm Credit Agencies* felt the impact first, and perhaps worst, because they are direct lenders to the agricultural sector. Problems first surfaced in September of 1985, when the *Federal Land Bank of Omaha* indicated that it had suffered large losses. Other land banks revealed the same kinds of problems, and by late 1985, yields on issues of the Federal Farm Credit System had moved away from the yields on Treasuries by a substantial amount—from about 50 basis points to about 140 basis points. Soon after, it became clear that Congress would not let the Farm Credit Agencies default on their obligations, even though there was no statutory obligation to support them. Subsequently, the Farm Credit Agencies recouped all their lost ground, even though the land banks continued to post large losses.

By 1986, however, the situation at the Federal Savings and Loan Insurance Corporation (FSLIC) was continuing to deteriorate. As the banking/thrift industry was deregulated, many thrift institutions expanded their lending on commercial real estate, development lending in particular. The recession which began in late 1984 was particularly hard on commercial real estate development, and it prompted a wave of savings and loan failures. It became apparent in 1985 and 1986 that FSLIC did not have enough reserves to close all the thrifts that were technically insolvent, so a bailout plan was advanced.

The plan involved having the *Federal Home Loan Banks (FHLBs)*, which were in far better condition than FSLIC, use their credit to raise about $22 billion for FSLIC to use in closing down or rescuing failed thrifts. By late 1986, the FSLIC bailout was working its way through Congress, with its future and final form still uncertain. What was known, however, was that any plan based on the use of the FHLBs creditworthiness could have a significant impact on their position in the credit markets.

It has become pretty clear, then, that *being a federal agency is no protection from the vagaries of the economy*. Investors and traders who do business in agency securities have already begun to pay more attention to the underpinnings of each issuer and have begun to make some guesses as to what would happen to its credit if disaster struck. The wild card in all those calculations is Congress and the Treasury. If worst comes to worst, a bailout is always a possibility, particularly if the alternative is especially unpleasant. In the meantime, we will look carefully at all the issuers of agency securities.

THE "BIG THREE" FEDERAL AGENCIES

Farm Credit System

For investors and dealers in the market, the Farm Credit System appears as a unified financing entity, issuing securities through the *Federal Farm Credit Banks Funding Corporation (FFCB)*, in New York City. These securities are the joint and several obligations of all 37 member banks, so the FFCB is presented financially as a consolidated entity. Within that entity, there are three kinds of lenders, some of whom are in good financial shape, and some of whom are not. As long as the joint and several liability is in place, we will be concerned only with the consolidated figures.

The FFCB presents a financial picture of an institution with a substantial capital base but serious earnings problems. As of June 30, 1986, its balance sheet looked like this (in millions):

Assets	
Earning Assets	$68,643
Accrued Interest	2,224
Property Owned	1,018
Fixed and Other Assets	840
Total Assets	$72,725
Liabilities and Capital	
Notes and Bonds	$65,721
Capital	7,004
Total Liabilities and Capital	$72,725

For the six months ended June 30, 1986, the consolidated earnings looked like this (in millions):

Individual Agency Securities

Revenues	
Interest Income	$3,845
Other Income	66
Total Revenues	$3,911
Expenses	
Interest Expense	$3,389
Operating Expense	508
Loan Loss Expense	982
Total Expenses	$4,879
Net Loss	(968)

Coupled with a net loss of almost $2.7 billion for the year 1985, these figures present an institution that is rapidly eating through its capital base. As of mid-1986, the FFCB had a *capital ratio* of 10.65%, higher than many banks or thrifts, but the losses it has been running could erode that very quickly.

Within the FFCB system, certain of the 37 banks were in danger of violating capital requirements before the end of 1986. As a result, the *Farm Credit Association (FCA)* began to reallocate capital among the member banks, but encountered lawsuits from some of the Production Credit Associations which own some of the sounder banks. These lawsuits are still pending, but should the courts enjoin the FCA from reallocating capital, the credit of the FFCB may again come into doubt as it did in 1985.

In that case, Congress may have to enact legislation putting the power of the Treasury behind the FFCB, in order to enable the system to continue financing. Meanwhile, the system continues to issue securities according to a somewhat irregular schedule.

Federal Farm Credit System Issuance Procedures

The FFCB issues two kinds of securities, called *Consolidated Systemwide Bonds* and *Consolidated Systemwide Notes*. All bonds are issued with a term to maturity of over one year. All notes are issued with a maturity of six months. In both cases, the securities are the joint and several obligations of all 37 member banks.

FFCB bonds and notes are issued through a *selling group*, not by the auction procedure used by the Treasury. The selling group is made up of Primary Dealers and other bond dealers who have demonstrated to the system that they can distribute debt securities to investors. The issuance itself is handled by the *Fiscal Agent* for the system, who has a job akin to the treasurer of a corporation.

Approximately once a month, usually on the third or fourth Friday, the Fiscal Agent announces what system securities will be sold that month, usually a note issue and a bond issue, and the selling group begins immediately to solicit interest in the issues. Since the allocations of securities in the selling group are not made until the following Tuesday, dealers reflect all interest to the Fiscal Agent as it is received. During this period, the Fiscal Agent is discussing possible rates and prices with the members of the selling group.

On Wednesday, usually between 2:30 and 3:30 P.M., the Fiscal Agent announces the *coupon rates* and *prices* for the securities, as well as the *concession* to be paid to the selling group. All investors who have indicated an interest in the issue are immediately informed. Generally, indications of interest are not given subject to a specific price level, so most investors are not given the option of canceling at this time. The securities begin trading at 9:30 the following morning, and are usually delivered and paid for the first business day of the following month.

Approximately once a quarter the system announces an additional issue during the first week of the month, usually a note issue. The issuance procedure is approximately the same, with delivery happening at about the middle of the month.

Federal Farm Credit System Securities Trading

System bonds and notes are usually traded by the same traders who deal in other agency securities, and are usually carried on the same screens as the other agencies. In some cases, however, dealers put the system securities on their own page, or part of their own page. Figure 4-1 shows a screen prepared by Merrill Lynch GSI, the government securities subsidiary of Merrill Lynch, Inc. In the upper left-hand corner of the screen are the most recent issues of the FFCB—two notes: a 5.75% issue due 2/2/87 and a 5.80% issue due 5/1/87.

More so than Treasury issues, agency issues are divided into *on-the-run* and *off-the-run* issues. On-the-run issues trade much more actively than do off-the-run issues, so customers very often swap from older issues into the most recent ones around the offering date. There are

Figure 4-1
Telerate screen showing a Federal Farm Credit Bank issues page.

```
TELERATE SYSTEMS
11/10   16:01 EST   [MERRILL LYNCH GSI, NEW YORK]          11/10 15:40 503
        ACTIVE FFCB                       FLOWER BONDS
5.75    02/02/87   100.00    100.01 5.60        11/13/86    4.69     4.44    4.50    +1
5.80    05/01/87   100.00    100.01 5.72   10.125  06/10/92 110.20  111.04   7.64    +2
                                           3 1/2   02/15/90  94.29   96.13   4.70    +7
                                           4 1/4   08/15/92  94.08   95.24   5.11    +9
                                           4       02/15/93  95.07   96.23   4.61    +7
                                           3       02/15/95  95.12   96.28   3.44   +12
                                           3 1/2   11/15/98  95.27   97.11   3.78   +25

                                   FHLMC
                                   8.25  06/01/16   93.04   94.04   8.81    -8
COOPS                              FEDERAL INTERMEDIATE CREDIT BANKS
7.60   12/23/86   100.03    100.05 6.04 -2

THE INFORMATION SET FORTH DOES NOT CONSTITUTE A SOLICITATION BY US OF THE
PURCHASE OR SALE OF ANY SECURITIES OR COMMODITIES
```

75

a large number of FFCB issues, as we can see from Figure 4-2, which is a quote sheet provided by a Primary Dealer. It is set up very much like a Treasury quote sheet. The first column lists the *issue size,* and we can

Figure 4-2
Quote sheet listing Federal Farm Credit Bank issues.

FEDERAL FARM CREDIT BANKS CONSOLIDATED SYSTEMWIDE BONDS*

710	09/02/86	5.60	12/01/86	99 31/32	100 00/32	5.54	2.99	5.54		.4659	5000
1212	06/02/86	6.80	12/01/86	100 00/32	100 02/32	5.69	3.07	5.69		.4570	5000
1002	07/21/80	10.00	12/01/86	100 06/32	100 11/32	4.63	2.50	4.63		.4493	1000
500	10/01/86	5.70	01/05/87	99 30/32	99 31/32	5.86	3.17	5.86		.1948	5000
1006	07/01/86	6.60	01/05/87	100 02/32	100 04/32	5.69	3.07	5.69		.1911	5000
800	01/20/83	9.90	01/20/87	100 23/32	100 29/32	5.23	2.82	5.23		.1500	1000
433	07/23/84	13.20	01/20/87	101 12/32	101 17/32	5.36	2.89	5.36	-1	.1478	1000
514	01/04/82	14 5/8	01/20/87	101 18/32	101 26/32	5.36	2.89	5.36	-1	.1468	1000
904	11/03/86	5.75	02/02/87	100 00/32	100 01/32	5.61	3.03	5.61		.1340	5000
752	08/01/86	6.35	02/02/87	100 03/32	100 04/32	5.72	3.09	5.72		.1318	5000
901	09/02/86	5.70	03/02/87	99 31/32	100 00/32	5.64	3.05	5.64		.0986	5000
716	03/01/84	11.45	03/02/87	101 21/32	101 27/32	5.46	2.95	5.46		.0958	1000
550	09/01/82	12.40	03/02/87	101 31/32	102 04/32	5.51	2.97	5.51		.0954	1000
898	10/01/86	5.80	04/01/87	100 00/32	100 01/32	5.69	3.07	5.69		.0794	5000
513	04/20/82	14 3/8	04/20/87	103 24/32	103 29/32	5.50	2.97	5.50	-2	.0677	1000
643	07/20/82	14.40	04/20/87	103 26/32	103 27/32	5.65	3.05	5.65	-2	.0677	1000
812	11/03/86	5.80	05/01/87	100 00/32	100 01/32	5.73	3.09	5.73		.0664	5000
626	12/02/85	9.125	06/01/87	101 25/32	101 29/32	5.65	3.05	5.65		.0557	1000
734	12/01/82	10.55	06/01/87	102 11/32	102 23/32	5.59	3.02	5.59		.0552	1000
875	10/20/82	10 5/8	07/20/87	103 02/32	103 08/32	5.81	3.14	5.81	-1	.0446	1000
615	03/01/83	10 1/8	09/01/87	103 03/32	103 11/32	5.85	3.16	5.85	-2	.0386	1000
732	01/22/85	10.45	10/20/87	103 30/32	104 06/32	5.86	3.16	5.86		.0331	1000
561	04/22/85	10.55	10/20/87	104 02/32	104 10/32	5.82	3.15	5.82		.0331	1000
715	06/01/83	10.30	12/01/87	104 05/32	104 13/32	5.97	3.22	5.97		.0297	1000
788	12/03/84	10.65	12/01/87	104 18/32	104 26/32	5.92	3.20	5.92		.0296	1000
512	03/03/86	8.20	01/20/88	102 04/32	102 08/32	6.22	3.36	6.22		.0269	1000
751	06/03/85	9.45	01/20/88	103 15/32	103 21/32	6.23	3.37	6.23	-2	.0266	1000
667	03/04/85	10.90	03/01/88	105 10/32	105 22/32	6.31	3.41	6.31	-2	.0241	1000
650	12/01/83	11.35	03/01/88	105 28/32	106 08/32	6.31	3.41	6.31	-2	.0240	1000
512	10/21/85	10.25	04/20/88	105 01/32	105 11/32	6.34	3.42	6.34	-2	.0220	1000
454	04/21/80	12.65	04/20/88	108 08/32	108 20/32	6.34	3.42	6.34	-2	.0216	1000
678	07/20/83	11.50	07/20/88	107 12/32	107 28/32	6.52	3.52	6.52	-2	.0187	1000
604	10/20/80	11.70	07/20/88	107 22/32	108 06/32	6.53	3.52	6.53	-2	.0186	1000
612	09/04/84	12.875	09/01/88	110 06/32	110 18/32	6.60	3.56	6.60	-2	.0173	1000
1075	10/20/83	11.50	10/20/88	108 12/32	108 24/32	6.64	3.59	6.64	-2	.0164	1000
706	01/21/86	8.75	01/23/89	104 02/32	104 06/32	6.67	3.60	6.67	+2	.0150	1000
273	01/23/84	11.65	01/23/89	109 22/32	110 02/32	6.67	3.60	6.67		.0145	1000
638	01/20/81	13.05	01/23/89	112 10/32	112 22/32	6.76	3.65	6.76		.0143	1000
883	04/23/84	12.50	04/23/89	112 06/32	112 18/32	6.85	3.70	6.85	-2	.0130	1000
690	07/21/86	7.35	06/01/89	100 30/32	101 02/32	6.89	3.72	6.89	+4	.0134	1000
273	07/23/84	13.70	07/20/89	115 26/32	116 10/32	6.96	3.76	6.96	-2	.0117	1000
824	09/01/77	7 3/4	09/05/89	101 18/32	102 02/32	6.93	3.74	6.93	+2	.0122	1000
414	10/23/79	10.60	10/23/89	109 04/32	109 20/32	6.95	3.75	6.95	+2	.0112	1000
605	10/22/84	12.45	10/23/89	113 22/32	114 06/32	7.05	3.81	7.05	+2	.0109	1000
482	10/20/81	15.65	10/23/89	122 00/32	122 16/32	7.09	3.83	7.09		.0104	1000
438	01/21/80	10.95	01/22/90	109 28/32	110 12/32	7.26	3.92	7.26	+4	.0104	1000
500	01/22/85	11.15	01/22/90	110 16/32	110 28/32	7.28	3.93	7.28	+4	.0104	1000
444	02/01/83	10.85	02/01/90	109 22/32	110 06/32	7.25	3.92	7.25	+4	.0104	1000
526	04/22/85	11.35	04/20/90	111 26/32	112 06/32	7.29	3.94	7.29	+4	.0097	1000
450	06/01/82	14.10	06/01/90	120 12/32	120 28/32	7.34	3.96	7.34	-2	.0090	1000
533	07/22/85	9.55	07/23/90	106 28/32	107 12/32	7.24	3.91	7.24	-2	.0093	1000
600	07/21/80	10.40	07/23/90	109 14/32	109 30/32	7.29	3.94	7.29	+2	.0092	1000
650	09/01/82	12.50	09/04/90	116 08/32	116 24/32	7.39	3.99	7.39	-2	.0087	1000
740	10/20/82	10.60	10/22/90	110 10/32	110 26/32	7.40	3.99	7.40	-2	.0087	1000
707	04/21/86	7.55	04/22/91	100 16/32	100 24/32	7.35	3.97	7.35	-2	.0083	1000
544	04/20/81	14.10	04/22/91	123 24/32	124 08/32	7.59	4.10	7.59	-2	.0074	1000
662	07/23/79	9.10	07/22/91	105 30/32	106 14/32	7.45	4.02	7.45		.0077	1000
617	07/20/81	14.70	07/22/91	126 28/32	127 12/32	7.66	4.13	7.66		.0070	1000
630	04/20/83	10.60	10/21/91	111 16/32	112 00/32	7.64	4.13	7.64		.0072	1000
487	12/01/81	13.65	12/02/91	124 04/32	124 20/32	7.69	4.15	7.69		.0066	1000
485	01/22/85	11.50	01/20/92	115 20/32	116 04/32	7.68	4.15	7.68	+2	.0068	1000
400	01/20/82	15.20	01/20/92	130 22/32	131 06/32	7.79	4.20	7.79	+2	.0064	1000
824	07/23/84	13.75	07/20/92	125 24/32	126 08/32	7.93	4.28	7.93	+2	.0061	1000
525	01/20/83	10.65	01/20/93	112 24/32	113 08/32	7.90	4.27	7.90	+4	.0060	1000
441	10/20/83	11.80	10/20/93	119 08/32	119 24/32	8.04	4.34	8.04	+6	.0054	1000
435	01/20/84	12.35	03/01/94	122 18/32	123 02/32	8.10	4.38	8.10	+2	.0050	1000
320	04/20/82	14 1/4	04/20/94	133 10/32	133 26/32	8.11	4.38	8.11	+2	.0047	1000
330	09/04/84	13.00	09/01/94	127 10/32	127 26/32	8.12	4.38	8.12	+2	.0047	1000
460	12/03/84	11.45	01/20/94	119 04/32	119 16/32	8.11	4.38	8.11	+2	.0048	1000
377	10/01/82	11.90	10/20/97	125 20/32	126 12/32	8.20	4.43	8.20	-4	.0037	1000

Individual Agency Securities

see that FFCB issues are much smaller than Treasuries. Only a few are larger than $1 billion, while almost every Treasury issue is. The next column shows the *date* on which the note or bond was *issued*. That date is important because it tells the investor or trader how much accrued interest will be attached to the issue when he purchases it, and how long an issue it was when it was offered.

Next come the *coupon* and *maturity* of each issue, followed by the *bid* and *offered* prices, and the *yield to maturity* at the offered price. The next two columns show the *after-tax yield* (assuming a 46% tax rate) and the *full coupon taxable equivalent* yield, a concept made obsolete by the Tax Reform Act of 1986. After the change in price from the previous day comes the *yield value of 1/32d*, which is the inverse of the price volatility of the issue. The last column shows the minimum denomination of the bond or note.

Like Treasury issues, FFCB issues sometimes get out of line, and traders are always looking for opportunities to profit from a correction. It pays, however, to know why the issues are out of line, and how long it might take for the correction to occur. Look, for example, at the two issues due 4/22/91, on either side of the lowest horizontal line. Although they have the same maturity, their yields are far apart, 7.35% vs. 7.59%. What could explain this disparity? The differences in coupon and dollar price mostly. The issue at 7.35% has a 7.55% coupon and a price of 100.16, while the issue at 7.59% has a 14.10% coupon and a price of 123.24. Traditionally, higher prices mean higher yields to maturity for several reasons.

The first is the possibility of *early call*. Many debt securities can be called, or retired, before maturity by the issuer, and a higher-than-market coupon could prompt an issuer to call. FFCB issues are not callable prior to maturity, however, so that can't be the reason for this case. A more likely cause is a reticence on the part of investors to pay a substantial *premium* for an issue. In fact, we can see other examples of YTM differences related to price on this sheet. The two issues maturing 7/23/90 have that relationship, but to a lesser degree. Others, like the two issues of 1/23/89, have the same YTM, and we can even find a reverse relationship, such as the issues maturing 6/1/87. Going back to our originals, maturing 4/22/91, perhaps we should sell some of the 7.55% issue and buy some of the 14.10% issue. If the YTM spread narrows from the current 24 basis points to a more normal 10, we should make about 12/32ds, or $3,750 per million.

Federal Home Loan Bank Bonds

There is no more important key to the success of an economy over a long time span than its ability to *save*. It began with the dawn of an industrial revolution, where agricultural surpluses, when saved, made possible the introduction of basic industrial technology. It leads to the computer age, where massive investments in plant and equipment keep progress rolling. At every stage, the ability to rechannel resources not immediately consumed is the key to the future.

In fact, the story of an efficient economy is the story of reconciliation between the many demands for every saved dollar. One such demand is a need to finance the construction of homes for the general populace. Because the United States has a longstanding bias in favor of individual home ownership, we developed a collection of savings institutions with a mandate to support the single-family home. The American *savings and loan association* is the product of our economic/political evolution, in which the political desire to make funds available for home construction became a national mandate to accumulate savings for the express purpose of financing single-family mortgage loans.

The typical savings and loan association began life, and evolved, as a community service organization. Community leaders, tired of having local homeowners shut out from local bank lending, formed voluntary associations, where the community could save its money in safety and see it invested in loans on local real estate. Many savings and loans started life at weekly meetings, where deposits were taken in and mortgage loans granted. To a very great extent, business was conducted this way for decades, possibly even for a hundred years.

The Great Depression brought a rude end to this method of administrating savings institutions. Community associations were not designed to deal with the violent swings in both interest rates and real estate values brought on by the Depression, and many of them failed. To bring some stability to this sector of the economy, Congress formed the Federal Home Loan Bank Board (FHLBB), the Federal Home Loan Banks (FHLBs), and the Federal Savings and Loan Insurance Corporation (FSLIC). Each of these agencies had a different function.

The *FHLBB* was designed as the *regulatory body* for the thrift industry in the United States, setting national policy and examining individual thrift institutions. The *FSLIC insures deposits* in federally chartered thrifts, and handles the closing and liquidation of failed thrifts.

Individual Agency Securities

The *FHLBs* fulfill for thrifts the classic *central banking function* of maintaining reserves against deposits, acting as a lender to thrifts, and clearing their securities transactions. The government bond market sees the FHLBs in their lender role, as they borrow on their collective credit in order to lend to their members.

The FHLBs themselves, are owned by their member savings associations. There are twelve of them, and they borrow on a collective basis, where they are jointly and severally liable for the debt, which cannot be issued in excess of twelve times their collected net worth. As of 12/31/85, the consolidated balance sheet of the twelve FHLBs looked like this (in millions):

Assets	
Cash and Investments	$ 20,108
Loans to Members	88,835
Other Assets	3,236
Total Assets	$112,179
Liabilities and Capital	
Deposits and Borrowings	$ 25,182
Consolidated Bonds and Notes	74,460
Other Liabilities	611
Capital	10,105
Total Liabilities and Capital	$112,179

For the year ended 12/31/85, the collective income statement of the FHLBs looked like this (in millions):

Revenues	
Interest on Advances	$ 8,678
Interest on Investments	1,484
Other Revenues	519
Total Revenues	$10,681
Expenses	
Interest on Borrowings	$ 7,640
Interest on Deposits	1,490
Other Interest and Costs	242
Operating Expenses	$ 226
Total Expenses	$ 9,598
Net Income	*1,083*

From this we can see that the FHLBs are in substantially better shape than the FFCBs. There is another side to this story, though. The Federal Savings and Loan Insurance Corporation (FSLIC) is in at least as bad shape as the FFCBs. Mid-1986 estimates by the Federal Home Loan Bank Board (FHLBB) indicated that FSLIC would need additional capital of at least $20 billion in order to close and liquidate all the thrifts in the United States that were technically insolvent. In fact, FSLIC had to adopt a program of continuing to run some insolvent thrifts because the Insurance Fund did not have enough reserves to liquidate them.

Several plans have been advanced to take care of FSLIC's capital problems, and the one advanced by the FHLBB could have a substantial impact on the credit quality of the FHLBs. The FHLBB plan would have them use their considerable credit to raise, or assist the FSLIC to raise, the $20 billion in capital. That, in and of itself, would have an impact on the FHLBs' credit quality. In addition, the FHLBB plan assumes that further credit problems with thrifts would be avoided. Should that not be the case, FSLIC could become a financial black hole for the FHLBs. In the meantime, however, the FHLBs continue to issue securities to the public.

Federal Home Loan Bank Issuance Procedures

Like the FFCBs, the FHLBs issue securities monthly, to refund maturity issues and to raise new money. In the FHLB case, however, the schedule for the next year is published by the Fiscal Agent in December. It shows the dates on which the issues will be announced, and the maturing issues for that cycle, but not what issues will be sold or how large they will be. Those decisions are made as the year progresses.

The FHLB schedule is available from any of the thirty-six Primary Dealers, from any of the twelve Federal Home Loan Banks, or from the Fiscal Agent, at the following address:

> Mr. Austin Dowling, Director
> Office of Finance
> Federal Home Loan Banks
> 655 15th Street, NW
> Washington, DC 20005

Generally speaking, the announcements are made in the middle of each month, often the second Tuesday. The issues are usually priced the following day, late in the day, and begin trading at 9:30 the following

Individual Agency Securities

morning. The issues are usually delivered on the 25th of the month, and mature on the 25th of the month (unless that is not a business day, in which case they are delivered and mature on the first business day after the 25th).

The exact makeup of each issuance is determined by the Federal Home Loan Bank Board, on the advice of the Fiscal Agent, who has analyzed the FHLBs' cash flow and has kept in touch with market participants concerning the yield curve and the demand for various issues. Usually, the FHLBs will offer from two to four separate issues, ranging in maturity from two to ten years.

Federal Home Loan Bank Issues Trading

In most Primary Dealers, FHLB issues are traded by the same people who trade other agencies. In many cases, they share the same broker screens as the other agencies. On quote sheets, however, they usually have their own sector. Figure 4-3 shows a quote sheet for all FHLB issues outstanding on November 6, 1986. It has the same structure as the FFCB sheet in Figure 4-2. From left to right, the columns cover: issue size in millions, date issued, coupon rate, date of maturity, bid price, offered price, yield to maturity at the offered price, yield after 46% corporate tax, full coupon taxable equivalent yield (obsolete now), price change from previous day, the change in yield to maturity from 1/32d change in price (expressed in percentage points, so 1 basis point equals 0.0100), and the smallest denomination one could buy.

As usual, the yield to maturity is the common denominator for comparing issues, and it is the method traders use to find issues that are undervalued and overvalued. One comparison they make constantly is between comparable issues of the various agencies. For example, look at Figure 4-2 and find the FFCB 7.35% issue of 6/01/89. It yields 6.89% to maturity. In Figure 4-3, find the FHLB 7.40% issue of 5/25/89, yielding 6.56% to maturity. Although the FHLBs have a higher coupon and a higher price, they have a lower yield, by 33 basis points. Perhaps this is because market participants have some concern about the credit quality of the FFCB, or are these issues just out of line? Let's look at some more issues to see.

The FFCB 7.55% issue of 4/22/91 yields 7.35% to maturity, while the FHLB 7.35% of 4/25/91 yields 7.15% to maturity. The FFCB 8.20% of 1/20/88 yields 6.22%, while the FHLB 8.45% of 1/25/88 yields 6.06% to maturity. In fact, as we look over both quote sheets, it looks

Figure 4-3
Quote sheet listing Federal Home Loan Bank issues.

FEDERAL HOME LOAN BANK BONDS*

655	11/26/84	11.00	11/25/86	100 05/32	100 11/32	3.92	2.12	3.92		.5949	10000
600	11/26/79	11.30	11/25/86	100 06/32	100 11/32	4.20	2.27	4.20	-1	.5942	10000
420	12/26/84	9.375	12/29/86	100 16/32	100 21/32	5.12	2.76	5.12	-1	.2093	10000
.8	06/25/84	13.25	12/29/86	100 30/32	101 04/32	5.16	2.79	5.16	-1	.2060	10000
920	08/26/85	8.65	01/26/87	100 18/32	100 21/32	5.49	2.96	5.49	-1	.1399	10000
905	02/25/85	10.10	02/25/87	101 04/32	101 10/32	5.54	2.99	5.54	-2	.1025	10000
600	05/27/80	10.45	02/25/87	101 08/32	101 14/32	5.47	2.95	5.47	-2	.1023	10000
300	02/27/84	11.05	02/25/87	101 15/32	101 21/32	5.32	2.87	5.32		.1019	10000
900	03/25/85	11.05	03/25/87	101 30/32	102 02/32	5.49	2.96	5.49		.0806	10000
600	08/25/80	11.10	03/25/87	101 31/32	102 06/32	5.21	2.81	5.21		.0804	10000
710	09/26/83	11.25	03/25/87	101 31/32	102 05/32	5.44	2.94	5.44	-1	.0805	10000
300	05/25/77	7.65	05/26/87	100 28/32	101 07/32	5.37	2.90	5.37		.0574	10000
965	05/28/85	9.625	05/26/87	101 30/32	102 10/32	5.31	2.87	5.31		.0567	10000
660	05/25/84	13	05/26/87	103 23/32	104 03/32	5.37	2.90	5.37	-1	.0558	10000
730	06/25/85	8.45	06/25/87	101 19/32	101 25/32	5.53	2.99	5.53		.0499	10000
400	12/27/82	10.30	06/25/87	102 21/32	103 01/32	5.35	2.89	5.35	-1	.0493	10000
550	07/25/83	11.35	07/27/87	103 26/32	104 00/32	5.59	3.02	5.59		.0431	10000
760	07/25/84	13.30	07/27/87	105 05/32	105 11/32	5.61	3.03	5.61	-1	.0426	10000
400	08/25/77	7.60	08/25/87	101 08/32	101 14/32	5.72	3.09	5.72		.0399	10000
640	08/27/84	12.625	08/25/87	105 04/32	105 12/32	5.63	3.04	5.63		.0386	10000
760	09/25/85	9.375	09/25/87	102 29/32	103 03/32	5.72	3.09	5.72		.0358	10000
365	10/25/84	12.05	10/26/87	105 19/32	105 31/32	5.63	3.04	5.63		.0321	10000
470	04/25/84	12.15	10/26/87	105 22/32	106 02/32	5.63	3.04	5.63		.0321	10000
1065	11/25/85	8.70	11/25/87	102 21/32	102 27/32	5.86	3.17	5.86	-4	.0304	10000
300	11/26/82	10.65	11/25/87	104 16/32	104 28/32	5.79	3.13	5.79	-2	.0300	10000
425	11/25/83	11.30	11/25/87	105 06/32	105 18/32	5.76	3.11	5.76	-2	.0298	10000
680	12/26/85	8.05	12/28/87	102 06/32	102 14/32	5.80	3.13	5.80		.0281	10000
435	01/25/86	8.45	01/25/88	102 20/32	102 24/32	6.06	3.27	6.06	-2	.0264	10000
925	01/25/85	10.625	01/25/88	104 28/32	105 08/32	6.07	3.28	6.07	-2	.0260	10000
470	03/25/83	10.20	03/25/88	104 30/32	105 14/32	6.03	3.26	6.03	-2	.0230	10000
420	03/26/84	11.90	03/25/88	107 08/32	107 20/32	6.06	3.27	6.06	-2	.0226	10000
500	04/25/83	10.15	04/25/88	105 08/32	105 20/32	6.08	3.28	6.08	-2	.0217	10000
705	04/25/85	10.375	04/25/88	105 18/32	105 30/32	6.08	3.28	6.08	-2	.0217	10000
525	05/25/83	10.15	05/25/88	105 16/32	105 28/32	6.11	3.30	6.11	-2	.0206	10000
1145	06/26/86	7.25	06/27/88	101 14/32	101 18/32	6.23	3.36	6.23	-2	.0201	10000
820	06/25/85	8.80	06/27/88	103 25/32	103 31/32	6.21	3.35	6.21	-2	.0198	10000
500	06/27/83	10.80	06/27/88	106 20/32	107 04/32	6.15	3.32	6.15	-2	.0194	10000
925	07/25/85	9.15	07/25/88	104 10/32	104 26/32	6.14	3.32	6.14	-2	.0188	10000
745	08/25/86	6.35	08/25/88	100 00/32	100 02/32	6.31	3.41	6.31	-2	.0186	10000
945	08/26/85	9.45	08/25/88	105 02/32	105 10/32	6.27	3.39	6.27	-2	.0180	10000
460	08/25/83	11 5/8	08/25/88	108 12/32	109 04/32	6.18	3.34	6.18	-2	.0175	10000
605	10/27/86	6.35	10/25/88	99 31/32	100 01/32	6.33	3.42	6.33	-2	.0171	10000
655	10/25/85	9.55	10/25/88	105 23/32	105 29/32	6.31	3.41	6.31	-2	.0165	10000
695	10/25/83	11.40	10/25/88	108 28/32	109 08/32	6.32	3.41	6.32	-2	.0162	10000
495	11/25/85	8.90	11/25/88	104 23/32	104 29/32	6.31	3.41	6.31	-2	.0160	10000
400	05/25/82	14.20	11/25/88	114 14/32	114 26/32	6.37	3.44	6.37	-2	.0151	10000
480	12/26/84	10.70	12/27/88	108 04/32	108 16/32	6.38	3.44	6.38	-2	.0150	10000
390	01/24/86	11 3/8	01/25/89	109 20/32	110 04/32	6.39	3.45	6.39	-2	.0144	10000
685	02/25/86	8.30	02/27/89	103 18/32	103 26/32	6.49	3.50	6.49	-2	.0144	10000
425	02/25/85	10.80	02/27/89	108 22/32	109 06/32	6.44	3.48	6.44	-2	.0140	10000
300	02/25/82	15.10	02/27/89	117 22/32	118 06/32	6.47	3.49	6.47	-2	.0133	10000
1250	03/25/86	7.45	03/27/89	101 26/32	101 30/32	6.56	3.54	6.56	-2	.0142	10000
525	04/25/86	6.90	04/25/89	100 20/32	100 28/32	6.51	3.51	6.51	-2	.0138	10000
400	04/26/82	14.25	04/25/89	117 00/32	117 12/32	6.51	3.51	6.51	-2	.0126	10000
1000	05/27/86	7.40	05/25/89	101 26/32	101 30/32	6.56	3.54	6.56	-2	.0133	10000
795	05/28/85	10.20	05/25/89	108 04/32	108 16/32	6.52	3.52	6.52	-2	.0128	10000
1310	07/25/86	7.00	07/25/89	100 28/32	101 00/32	6.59	3.56	6.59	-2	.0127	10000
500	07/26/82	14 1/8	07/25/89	117 30/32	118 14/32	6.59	3.56	6.59	-2	.0114	10000
640	09/25/86	6.75	09/25/89	100 08/32	100 10/32	6.63	3.58	6.63	-2	.0121	10000
335	09/25/84	12.50	09/25/89	114 20/32	115 04/32	6.64	3.59	6.64	-2	.0111	10000
350	03/25/82	14.55	09/25/89	119 30/32	120 14/32	6.64	3.58	6.64	-2	.0107	10000
320	07/25/83	11.55	11/27/89	112 26/32	113 10/32	6.66	3.60	6.66	-2	.0106	10000
410	01/25/85	11.20	01/25/90	112 06/32	112 18/32	6.78	3.66	6.78	-2	.0102	10000
465	03/25/84	11.90	03/26/90	114 18/32	114 30/32	6.87	3.71	6.87	-2	.0096	10000
700	04/25/86	7.05	04/25/90	100 12/32	100 20/32	6.84	3.70	6.84	-2	.0102	10000
1270	06/25/86	7.75	06/25/90	102 12/32	102 16/32	6.96	3.76	6.96	-2	.0097	10000
1080	06/25/85	9.50	06/25/90	107 24/32	108 04/32	6.93	3.74	6.93	-2	.0094	10000
690	07/25/85	9.75	07/25/90	108 22/32	109 06/32	6.90	3.73	6.90	-2	.0092	10000
455	09/25/85	10.30	09/25/90	110 24/32	111 04/32	6.98	3.77	6.98		.0087	10000
300	09/27/82	12.50	09/25/90	118 00/32	118 16/32	6.97	3.77	6.97		.0084	10000
730	10/27/86	7.05	10/25/90	100 04/32	100 06/32	6.99	3.78	6.99		.0091	10000
350	05/25/84	13.70	11/26/90	122 16/32	123 00/32	7.07	3.82	7.07	+2	.0079	10000
390	12/26/85	8.70	12/26/90	105 22/32	105 30/32	7.02	3.79	7.02	-2	.0085	10000
650	12/27/82	10.90	12/26/90	112 30/32	113 14/32	7.09	3.83	7.09	-2	.0082	10000
305	01/27/86	9.10	01/25/91	107 02/32	107 10/32	7.06	3.81	7.06	-2	.0083	10000
300	02/27/84	11 7/8	02/25/91	116 26/32	117 10/32	7.12	3.85	7.12	-2	.0078	10000
1515	03/25/86	7.75	03/25/91	102 00/32	102 08/32	7.14	3.86	7.14	-2	.0083	10000
650	04/25/86	7.35	04/25/91	100 16/32	100 24/32	7.15	3.86	7.15	-2	.0083	10000
950	05/27/86	7.875	05/27/91	102 16/32	102 24/32	7.16	3.86	7.16	-2	.0080	10000
1178	07/25/86	7.50	07/25/91	101 00/32	101 12/32	7.15	3.86	7.15	-2	.0079	10000
1175	08/25/86	7.25	08/26/91	100 00/32	100 08/32	7.13	3.85	7.13	-2	.0078	10000
800	02/25/83	11.10	08/26/91	114 28/32	115 12/32	7.25	3.91	7.25	-2	.0072	10000
761	09/25/86	7.40	09/25/91	100 22/32	100 26/32	7.20	3.89	7.20	-2	.0077	10000
465	09/26/83	11.75	09/25/91	117 24/32	118 08/32	7.24	3.91	7.24	-2	.0070	10000
350	12/26/84	11.40	12/26/91	116 20/32	117 04/32	7.33	3.96	7.33	-2	.0067	10000
845	02/25/86	11.45	02/25/92	117 02/32	117 18/32	7.38	3.99	7.38	+2	.0066	10000
650	10/25/83	11.70	04/27/92	117 30/32	118 14/32	7.53	4.06	7.53	+2	.0064	10000
475	08/25/86	10.35	08/25/92	112 20/32	113 00/32	7.54	4.07	7.54	+2	.0063	10000
550	10/25/82	10.85	10/26/92	115 04/32	115 20/32	7.55	4.08	7.55	+4	.0061	10000
600	11/26/82	11.10	11/25/92	116 12/32	116 28/32	7.57	4.09	7.57	+4	.0060	10000

82

like a spread of 20 basis points is what the market has established. Thus, going back to the first comparison, if we can sell the FHLB 7.40% of 5/25/89 and buy the FFCB 7.35% of 6/01/89 to pick up more than 30 basis points in yield to maturity, we should have done better than the market expects by about 10 basis points. If we can reverse the trade at a spread of -20, we can pocket the 10 basis points, which works out to a little less than a quarter of a point, or $2,388 per million. Not bad money for an essentially risk-free trade. This kind of trading dominates the agency market most days.

Federal National Mortgage Association

The *Federal National Mortgage Association (FNMA)* is unique among the federal agencies, in that it is a *publicly owned corporation*. Originally, when it was chartered in 1938, it was a corporate instrumentality of the United States, like the agencies. But FNMA has gone through several metamorphoses since then.

Its original mandate, which it retains, was to provide support to the *secondary market* for *residential mortgages*. Initially, and to this day, FNMA fulfilled that mandate by purchasing mortgages from approved seller-services, through regular auctions of purchase commitments. Originally, the only mortgages FNMA purchased were insured by the FHA or guaranteed by the VA. As the volume of conventional mortgages grew relative to FHA/VAs, FNMA expanded its program to include conventionals.

In the 1960s FNMA moved from being a government instrumentality to being a publicly held corporation, and its stock is now traded on the *NYSE*. At about the same time, in 1968, FNMA was *split* into two bodies. FNMA retained its original charter and purpose, while a new body, the *Government National Mortgage Association (GNMA)* was formed to guarantee the issuance of mortgage passthrough securities. To accomplish that, GNMA was given the backing of the U.S. Treasury, while FNMA remained a separate entity.

In effect, FNMA became the *world's largest thrift institution*, borrowing money in the public marketplace and using it to purchase mortgages. As such, it suffered the earnings problems inherent to a conservatively run thrift during the high rate periods of the late 1970s and the early 1980s. As we pointed out before, during that period FNMA lost over $275 million, due entirely to the fact that its cost of funds was *variable* and the return on its assets was *fixed*. When the market was at its nadir, FNMA made a decision to sell a large portion of its fixed rate loans and to more closely match the duration of its assets to the duration of its liabilities. As a result, its 12/31/85 balance sheet looked like this (in thousands):

Assets	
Cash and Investments	$ 2,878
Mortgage Portfolio	95,038
Other Assets	1,171
Total Assets	$99,087
Liabilities and Net Worth	
Funded Debt	$93,896
Other Liabilities	3,849
Net Worth	1,342
Total Liabilities and Net Worth	$99,087

For the year ended 12/31/85, FNMA's operations had the following results (in thousands):

Revenues	
Interest Income	$ 9,997
Other Income	345
Total Revenues	$10,342
Expenses	
Interest Expense	$ 9,926
Other Expenses	348
Total Expenses	$10,274
Net Pretax Income	*$68*
Taxes	31
Net After-Tax Income	*$37*

These financials present a picture not unlike a modern thrift institution, where previous interest rate imbalances have weakened the capital structure, and the profitability is still below par. In FNMA's case, as in the case of the thrift industry, the future holds a major key. If rates stay at the levels of the mid-1980s, profitability will improve, and the return on capital could be spectacular. If rates rise sharply, however, FNMA and the thrift industry could be in serious trouble, in spite of having a large proportion of adjustable rate mortgages (ARMs) on the books.

Individual Agency Securities

The reason for this is that, no matter what the contractual ability to adjust mortgage rates, the reality is that the upward range for the interest rate is a function of the homeowner's ability to carry the debt service. If the homeowner can't carry the higher payments, then an ARM may be a lot more fixed than it first appears to be. In the meantime, FNMA continues to raise money in the markets on a regular basis.

Federal National Mortgage Association Issuance Procedures

Like other Fiscal Agents do, FNMA's Fiscal Agent publishes a calendar of expected issues during the month of December for the following year. Like the other agencies, FNMA has issuances once a month. FNMA *announces* the size and maturities of its issues on the first Monday of the month, and *prices* its issues late in the day Tuesday. The issues begin *trading* at 9:30 Wednesday morning, and are delivered on the 10th of the month. They mature on the 10th of the month the required number of years hence, unless the 10th is a holiday, whereupon they mature the next business day.

Generally, FNMA offers *two* issues, one maturing in two to four years, and one maturing in six to eight years. At times, depending upon the agency's cash flow and the bond markets, FNMA may offer as little as one issue or as many as three. Maturities can range from one to ten years. As with the other agencies, the securities are sold by a *group of dealers,* selected by the Fiscal Agent, that allocates securities to the dealers based on their demand and their history of distributing FNMA issues over the years. As with the other agencies, competition to distribute securities and to increase one's selling allotment is fierce.

Federal National Mortgage Association Securities Trading

On many trading desks, and on many brokers' screens, FNMA issues are lumped in with the other agencies. Generally, as with other agencies, the most recent issues are considered *on the run* and occupy a more prominent position in the trading community, as well as on the screen. As with the other agencies, once an issue goes *off the run* it loses both its spot on the screen and a good deal of its liquidity. Traders often say of such issues that they "trade by appointment" meaning that it may take quite some time to move a block at a reasonable price.

On a dealer's quote sheet, FNMAs occupy a section of their own. Figure 4-4 shows one such quote sheet, the one for November 6, 1986.

Figure 4-4
Quote sheet listing Federal National Mortgage Association issues.

6:06 P.M. (EST) QUOTATIONS WEDNESDAY NOVEMBER 5, 1986   YIELDS FOR DELIVERY NOVEMBER 7, 1986
FEDERAL NATIONAL MORTGAGE ASSOCIATION DEBENTURES

Millions Outstdg	Issue Dated	Rate	Maturity	Bid	Asked	Yield to Maturity	After Tax Yield (A)	Corp Taxable Equiv	Change to Prev.Days (32nd)	Yield Value 1/32nd	Minimum Denomination
800	12/10/82	10.95	11/10/86	99 31/32	100 04/32						10000
1.0	06/11/84	13.05	11/10/86	99 31/32	100 05/32						10000
500	12/10/76	7.30	12/10/86	99 26/32	100 13/32	2.77	1.50	2.77	-1	.3307	10000
500	04/11/83	10 1/8	12/10/86	100 11/32	100 16/32	4.46	2.41	4.46		.3272	10000
250	11/22/83	11.05	12/10/86	100 13/32	100 19/32	4.35	2.35	4.35	+1	.3257	10000
700	06/10/83	10.70	01/12/87	100 25/32	100 31/32	5.11	2.76	5.11		.1674	10000
600	12/12/83	11.15	01/12/87	100 28/32	101 02/32	5.03	2.72	5.03		.1670	10000
700	01/18/83	9.90	01/12/87	100 31/32	101 05/32	5.24	2.83	5.24		.1184	10000
1000	02/03/84	11.05	02/10/87	101 08/32	101 13/32	5.39	2.91	5.39		.1179	10000
400	03/10/77	7 3/4	02/10/87	100 19/32	100 25/32	5.36	2.89	5.36		.0913	10000
250	02/28/84	11.25	03/10/87	101 25/32	101 31/32	5.29	2.86	5.29	-1	.0898	10000
700	09/12/83	11.55	03/10/87	101 28/32	102 02/32	5.31	2.87	5.31		.0897	10000
1500	04/10/84	12.25	04/10/87	102 20/32	102 25/32	5.50	2.97	5.50	-2	.0726	10000
500	05/14/82	14.30	04/10/87	103 16/32	103 23/32	5.30	2.86	5.30		.0718	10000
750	05/12/80	11.15	05/11/87	102 18/32	102 24/32	5.61	3.03	5.61	-1	.0612	10000
300	06/10/77	7.65	06/10/87	100 30/32	101 10/32	5.35	2.89	5.35		.0536	10000
1000	11/10/83	11.20	06/10/87	103 00/32	103 12/32	5.31	2.87	5.31		.0525	10000
500	07/10/79	9.10	07/10/87	101 31/32	102 11/32	5.49	2.97	5.49		.0467	10000
500	07/12/82	15.25	07/10/87	106 00/32	106 12/32	5.47	2.95	5.47	-1	.0450	10000
1.0	07/10/84	13.65	07/10/87	105 18/32	105 26/32	5.68	3.07	5.68		.0405	10000
800	08/13/82	14.45	08/10/87	106 09/32	106 17/32	5.50	2.97	5.50		.0402	10000
800	05/10/83	9.85	09/10/87	103 03/32	103 11/32	5.71	3.08	5.71		.0374	10000
200	10/11/77	7 1/2	10/13/87	101 10/32	101 22/32	5.61	3.03	5.61		.0343	10000
400	10/12/82	12 1/8	10/13/87	105 16/32	105 24/32	5.70	3.08	5.70		.0333	10000
1000	10/10/84	12.55	10/13/87	105 30/32	106 06/32	5.64	3.05	5.64		.0332	10000
800	11/12/82	10.85	11/10/87	104 18/32	104 26/32	5.86	3.17	5.86		.0312	10000
1200	11/07/84	11.55	11/10/87	105 09/32	105 17/32	5.82	3.14	5.82		.0311	10000
1000	02/10/83	10.90	12/10/87	105 00/32	105 12/32	5.74	3.10	5.74		.0287	10000
700	01/10/83	10.45	01/11/88	104 28/32	105 08/32	5.76	3.11	5.76		.0267	10000
1000	11/10/84	11.55	01/11/88	106 04/32	106 16/32	5.75	3.10	5.75		.0265	10000
500	04/26/83	10.30	02/10/88	104 22/32	105 02/32	6.05	3.26	6.05	-2	.0252	10000
1000	01/10/85	10.75	02/10/88	105 06/32	105 18/32	6.07	3.28	6.07	-2	.0251	10000
300	02/17/81	14.40	02/10/88	109 16/32	110 00/32	6.01	3.24	6.01	-2	.0243	10000
1000	03/10/83	10.40	03/10/88	105 02/32	105 18/32	6.01	3.25	6.01	-2	.0236	10000
1000	04/11/83	10.45	04/11/88	105 14/32	105 26/32	6.13	3.31	6.13	-2	.0223	10000
1000	05/06/85	10.50	05/10/88	105 28/32	106 08/32	6.10	3.29	6.10	-2	.0211	10000
500	06/10/80	10 1/2	06/10/88	106 06/32	106 18/32	6.10	3.30	6.10	-2	.0200	10000
750	09/10/85	9.40	08/10/88	105 00/32	105 08/32	6.19	3.34	6.19	-2	.0184	10000
300	08/17/81	16 3/8	08/10/88	116 24/32	118 00/32	5.48	2.96	5.48	-2	.0168	10000
500	09/11/78	8.55	09/12/88	103 22/32	104 02/32	6.18	3.34	6.18	-2	.0177	10000
1000	09/10/84	13.20	09/12/88	111 14/32	111 26/32	6.31	3.41	6.31	-2	.0169	10000
600	10/10/85	9.50	10/10/88	105 16/32	105 24/32	6.28	3.39	6.28	-2	.0168	10000
500	05/07/84	12.75	10/10/88	111 02/32	111 14/32	6.34	3.42	6.34	-2	.0163	10000
700	12/10/85	8.95	11/10/88	104 28/32	105 04/32	6.20	3.35	6.20	-2	.0163	10000
500	10/27/82	11.00	11/10/88	108 06/32	108 22/32	6.33	3.42	6.33	-2	.0159	10000
500	11/10/83	11.70	11/10/88	109 22/32	109 30/32	6.35	3.43	6.35	-2	.0158	10000
1000	12/10/84	11.25	12/12/88	109 02/32	109 14/32	6.36	3.44	6.36	-2	.0152	10000
400	12/12/83	11.75	12/12/88	110 02/32	110 14/32	6.35	3.43	6.35	-2	.0151	10000
1000	01/23/85	11.10	01/10/89	109 02/32	109 14/32	6.37	3.44	6.37	-2	.0147	10000
700	02/03/84	11.60	02/10/89	110 06/32	110 22/32	6.43	3.47	6.43	-2	.0141	10000
1000	03/12/84	12.10	03/10/89	111 18/32	111 30/32	6.51	3.52	6.51	-2	.0136	10000
800	03/10/86	7.55	04/10/89	102 02/32	102 06/32	6.56	3.54	6.56	-2	.0139	10000
500	06/11/79	9.30	06/12/89	106 02/32	106 18/32	6.51	3.51	6.51	-2	.0127	10000
750	06/10/85	9.50	06/12/89	106 19/32	106 29/32	6.56	3.54	6.56	-2	.0127	10000
800	06/06/84	8.00	07/10/89	103 08/32	103 12/32	6.59	3.56	6.59	-2	.0126	10000
500	08/05/85	10.05	08/10/89	108 06/32	108 18/32	6.60	3.56	6.60	-2	.0119	10000
.75	08/06/84	13 1/8	08/10/89	115 22/32	116 06/32	6.60	3.56	6.60	-2	.0114	10000
300	10/12/82	12.10	10/10/89	113 24/32	114 08/32	6.65	3.59	6.65	-2	.0110	10000
500	10/10/84	12.75	10/10/89	115 14/32	115 30/32	6.66	3.60	6.66	-2	.0109	10000
1000	11/06/85	9.85	11/10/89	108 07/32	108 17/32	6.67	3.60	6.67	-2	.0111	10000
500	11/07/84	11.80	11/10/89	113 12/32	113 24/32	6.68	3.61	6.68	-2	.0107	10000
400	12/10/82	11.30	12/11/89	112 08/32	112 24/32	6.57	3.60	6.67	-2	.0105	10000
500	01/10/85	11.45	01/10/90	112 24/32	113 04/32	6.78	3.66	6.78	-2	.0103	10000
1000	02/05/85	11.05	02/13/90	111 28/32	112 08/32	6.80	3.67	6.80	-2	.0101	10000
900	02/04/86	8.65	03/12/90	105 06/32	105 14/32	6.80	3.67	6.80	-2	.0103	10000
600	04/10/84	7.35	04/10/90	101 12/32	101 20/32	6.81	3.68	6.81	-2	.0103	10000
700	05/10/83	10.30	05/10/90	109 30/32	110 14/32	6.90	3.73	6.90	-2	.0096	10000
600	05/06/85	11.15	05/10/90	112 20/32	113 00/32	6.91	3.73	6.91	-2	.0094	10000
1500	07/10/85	9.85	07/10/90	108 30/32	109 14/32	6.89	3.72	6.89	-2	.0092	10000
500	09/10/85	10.00	09/10/90	109 22/32	110 02/32	6.96	3.76	6.96	-2	.0089	10000
750	10/10/85	10.15	10/10/90	110 12/32	110 24/32	6.97	3.76	6.97		.0087	10000
1000	11/03/86	7.00	11/12/90	100 00/32	100 02/32	6.98	3.77	6.98	-2	.0091	10000
300	11/12/82	10.90	11/12/90	112 28/32	113 12/32	7.02	3.79	7.02	+2	.0084	10000
200	11/22/83	11.8	12/10/90	116 00/32	116 16/32	7.08	3.82	7.08	-2	.0081	10000
700	01/10/86	8.75	01/10/91	105 28/32	106 04/32	7.03	3.79	7.03	-2	.0085	10000
150	02/28/84	12	03/11/91	117 14/32	117 30/32	7.12	3.85	7.12	-2	.0077	10000
500	05/06/86	7.45	05/10/91	100 28/32	101 04/32	7.15	3.86	7.15	-2	.0082	10000
1000	07/10/86	7.65	07/10/91	101 22/32	101 30/32	7.15	3.86	7.15	-2	.0079	10000
900	09/10/86	7.00	09/10/91	99 16/32	99 24/32	7.06	3.82	7.08		.0077	10000
1000	10/10/86	7.375	10/10/91	100 24/32	100 28/32	7.16	3.87	7.16	-2	.0076	10000
400	10/12/76	7.80	10/10/91	102 12/32	102 28/32	7.10	3.83	7.10		.0075	10000
500	12/10/84	11.75	12/10/91	118 08/32	118 24/32	7.27	3.93	7.27	+2	.0067	10000
200	03/10/72	7.00	03/10/92	98 30/32	99 22/32	7.07	3.83	7.09	+2	.0071	10000
1000	04/10/85	12.00	04/10/92	119 14/32	119 30/32	7.46	4.03	7.46	+6	.0064	10000
200	06/12/72	7.05	06/10/92	99 16/32	100 00/32	7.05	3.81	7.05	+2	.0069	10000
750	06/10/85	10.125	06/10/92	111 08/32	111 24/32	7.51	4.06	7.51	+4	.0065	10000

86

Individual Agency Securities

Figure 4-4
Quote sheet listing Federal National Mortgage Association issues (cont'd).

500	10/10/85	10.60	10/12/92	114 00/32	114 12/32	7.55	4.07	7.55	+2	.0061	10000
500	12/10/85	9.875	12/10/92	110 14/32	111 00/32	7.58	4.10	7.58	+4	.0061	10000
700	01/10/83	10.90	01/11/93	114 28/32	115 12/32	7.72	4.17	7.72	+4	.0060	10000
500	03/10/86	7.90	03/10/93	101 04/32	101 12/32	7.62	4.11	7.62	+6	.0063	10000
500	03/10/83	10.95	03/10/93	115 18/32	116 02/32	7.70	4.16	7.70	+10	.0058	10000
400	04/10/86	7.55	04/12/93	99 28/32	100 04/32	7.52	4.06	7.52	+6	.0062	10000
500	04/11/83	10 7/8	04/12/93	115 16/32	116 00/32	7.67	4.14	7.67	+8	.0058	10000
300	04/26/83	10 3/4	05/10/93	115 00/32	115 16/32	7.68	4.15	7.68	+6	.0057	10000
800	11/03/86	7.75	11/10/93	100 06/32	100 10/32	7.69	4.15	7.69	-2	.0058	10000
500	01/10/85	11.95	01/10/95	123 12/32	123 28/32	7.92	4.28	7.92	+2	.0046	10000
1000	02/05/85	11.50	02/10/95	120 26/32	121 06/32	7.95	4.29	7.95	+2	.0046	10000
700	05/06/85	11.70	05/10/95	122 06/32	122 22/32	7.98	4.31	7.98	+2	.0045	10000
1000	05/22/85	11.15	06/12/95	119 04/32	119 16/32	7.97	4.30	7.97	+2	.0045	10000
500	09/10/85	10.50	09/11/95	115 16/32	116 00/32	7.94	4.29	7.94	+2	.0045	10000
500	11/06/85	10.60	11/10/95	116 10/32	116 22/32	7.97	4.30	7.97	+2	.0045	10000
400	01/10/86	9.20	01/10/96	107 20/32	108 00/32	7.95	4.29	7.95	-2	.0047	10000
500	02/25/86	7	02/10/96	93 10/32	93 26/32	7.95	4.47	8.27	-2	.0051	10000
600	02/04/86	9.35	02/12/96	108 12/32	108 28/32	7.97	4.31	7.97	-2	.0047	10000
500	06/10/86	8.75	06/10/96	104 16/32	105 00/32	7.99	4.32	7.99	-4	.0046	10000
1000	07/10/86	8.00	07/10/96	99 26/32	100 06/32	7.97	4.30	7.97	-4	.0047	10000
1,00	08/05/86	8.15	08/12/96	100 28/32	101 08/32	7.96	4.30	7.96	-4	.0046	10000
200	12/11/72	7.10	12/10/97-82	94 08/32	94 28/32	7.80	4.34	8.03	-2	.0044	10000
250	11/22/83	12.35	12/10/13-93	122 30/32	123 30/32	9.81	5.30	9.81	-2	.0028	10000
250	02/28/84	12.65	03/10/14-94	125 06/32	126 06/32	9.86	5.33	9.86	-2	.0027	10000
250	12/10/85	10.35	12/10/15	117 30/32	118 30/32	8.57	4.63	8.57	-4	.0025	10000
400	03/10/86	8.20	03/10/16	95 20/32	96 08/32	8.55	4.68	8.67		.0030	10000

By now, the structure should be familiar to us. One thing we can see by looking at the yields to maturity—the absence of *liquidity* in some issues can move the prices substantially. In particular, dealers who inadvertently get *short* a FNMA issue can force the price up well beyond its intrinsic value. Look at the 16.375% issue of 8/10/88. At a 5.48% yield to maturity, it is at least 60 basis points *rich* compared to issues surrounding it. Why? Look at the issue size; only $300 million. With such a small issue, a dealer who gets short a block may have terrible trouble finding securities to replace the ones he sold. Opportunities like this present themselves fairly often in the FNMA market, but they can be utilized only by an institution that actually owns the issue. It is sometimes a hit-or-miss proposition, but the profits can be well worth the wait.

MINOR AGENCY SECURITIES

The "big three" agencies may dominate the trading markets, but there are several other agency issuers whose quality is at least as good, even if their presence is significantly less. Because the liquidity afforded these issues by the market is less than that afforded the big three, investors tend to view these securities almost as private placements. Since the yields are higher than more liquid issues, and the quality is just as good, they are often purchased as original offerings and salted away for the duration. That strategy is fine, as long as investment parameters don't change. Should that happen, the investor might pay a substantial penalty for the illiquidity in the form of *discounted bids.*

Student Loan Marketing Association

SLMA is an outgrowth of our nation's preoccupation with higher education. Formed in 1965 (shortly after Russia launched Sputnik) as a part of the *Higher Education Act,* SLMA has a mandate to enhance the availability of loans for college education. Loans can be made directly, either by SLMA or by a lending institution, and guaranteed by SLMA. SLMA itself is a corporation owned by the lending institutions that participate in the SLMA programs, but it is decidedly small potatoes next to the big three.

SLMA Issuance Procedures

Like the big three, SLMA publishes a calendar of projected issues sometime during the month of December for the following year. Most of the securities SLMA issues are *floating rate notes* (FRNs) which mature in six months. The rate, which is reset weekly, is *indexed* to the yield equivalent of the average bid in the six-month Treasury bill auction, and averages between 30 and 35 basis points above the index. Each week's interest is added to the principal, but not compounded, and the whole amount is paid at maturity.

Once a month, usually on the first Friday of the month, SLMA *announces* the size of the FRN to be issued that month, typically 250 to 300 million. The *spread* over the index is set late in the day Monday, and *trading* begins at 9:30 on Tuesday morning. *Settlement* occurs during the second week of the month. SLMA also reserves a place on its calendar several times a year to issue a *fixed-rate, longer term issue,* but those issues are seldom actually offered.

Student Loan Marketing Association Trading

Because SLMA issues are FRN's, changes in market rates of interest do not have the same effect on prices as they do on prices for fixed-rate issues. Each week, SLMA issues adjust to the market rate of interest, so they seldom trade at prices below 99.30, or above 100.02. Even those small changes are due solely to a particular issue's spread over the index. If the current spread is 30 basis points, and a customer

Individual Agency Securities

wants to sell a FRN with a spread of 35 basis points, he will probably get 100.02 for it. Conversely, if his issue is at 30 basis points and the market is at 35, he will probably get 99.30 for it. The only real trading in SLMAs is between owners who need their cash early, as sellers, and investors who need a shorter maturity than six months, as buyers.

OTHER AGENCY ISSUERS

There are some other agencies or instrumentalities of the government that issue securities from time to time, or have in the past. In some cases there are so few issues out that they have relatively little liquidity, as in the case of the U.S. Postal Service—or they are usually regarded as a special class of the corporate bond market, as in the case of the International Bank for Reconstruction and Development (the World Bank) or the Inter-American Development Bank (IADB). In all these cases, security issuance is through an underwriting syndicate of the type used for corporate bonds.

Of course, there is another, very large, class of agency securities. These are the *mortgage-backed securities,* and they are the subject of the next chapter.

CHAPTER FIVE

Mortgage-Backed Securities

As large as we have found the government securities market to be, it is not the largest debt sector of the economy. In 1980, total mortgage debt in the United States outweighed total government debt by about 2-to-1, $1.4 trillion to $0.7 trillion. At that point, mortgages on single-family homes outweighed straight Treasury debt by $955 billion to $738 billion. The explosive growth of Treasury debt has somewhat altered the balance, but mortgage debt, particularly home mortgage debt, is still a very major part of the debt scene. By the second quarter of 1986, total mortgage debt still outweighed total government debt, by $2.4 trillion to $1.7 trillion, but Treasury debt had surpassed home mortgage debt, by $1.7 trillion to $1.5 trillion.

For most of our financial history, lending on single-family homes has been one of the largest financial activities we have had. As our financial system developed and became more formal, lending to finance home purchases moved from an individualistic practice to an institutional one. In fact, the development of financial institutions devoted to lending for the purpose of home ownership was largely responsible for the growth of the home building industry in the United States, and for the strong tradition of single-family home ownership that our country enjoys.

Originally, the vast majority of mortgage lending was done by the dominant lending institutions, commercial banks. Gradually, however, the long-term nature of the loans necessary to finance a home purchase proved to be unsuitable for commercial banks, which had a relatively short-term deposit base. During the nineteenth century there developed institutions with a more stable deposit base, due to the fact that they offered savings accounts, as opposed to checking accounts. Since these deposits were destined to be used very far in the future, they were suitable to be lent for home purchases.

These *thrift institutions* became the mainstay of the mortgage market. They had, however, a very parochial outlook. They were only prepared to lend money in their local area, where they knew the real estate values and could service the loans they made. The rapid migration of the American population southward and westward made this local lending practice obsolete, and brought into being another mortgage specialist, the *mortgage banker*.

The mortgage banker serves as a conduit between the areas where savings are plentiful, like the Northeast and the industrial Midwest, and the areas where population growth is rapid, like the Southeast and the Southwest. First, he originates mortgages in the high growth areas and sells them into the high savings areas. Second, he services mortgages in the high growth areas for lenders in the high savings areas. By fulfilling these two functions, the mortgage banker has contributed immensely to the development of the western and southeastern United States.

Until the middle of the 1960s, the market for single-family home mortgages was made up of traditional mortgage lenders, like thrifts and insurance companies, dealing with mortgage bankers directly. Each mortgage banker developed a list of lenders with whom he did business, and maintained a personal relationship with the mortgage officers in those institutions. Two developments in the 1960s brought that method of doing business to an end.

The first was simply the *growth* of the mortgage business. The explosive population growth of California and Florida, in particular, meant that a more efficient method of raising mortgage money had to be found. Relying upon each mortgage banker's personal contacts was no longer sufficient. The second development was the advent of *interest rate volatility* that accompanied the Vietnam War. The result of this volatility was disintermediation, which cast doubts on the ability of the thrift industry to provide mortgage funds on a continuous basis.

THE PASSTHROUGH SECURITY

In 1968, Congress reacted to these problems by creating the *Government National Mortgage Association (GNMA)* from the Federal National Mortgage Association (FNMA). GNMA, which is a corporate instrumentality of the Department of Housing and Urban Development (HUD), was given a mandate to assist the market for federally insured or guaranteed mortgages, while FNMA retained its mandate to assist the market for conventional mortgages.

The vehicle by which GNMA renders its assistance is the *modified passthrough security*. Unlike a straight mortgage, a GNMA is a security, with standardized terms and a developed and liquid market. It is called a passthrough because the regular monthly payments, as well as any prepayments, are passed through to the security holder, after a servicing fee is deducted. It is modified in that GNMA *guarantees* that the holder will receive the regularly scheduled payments of principal and interest each month.

Thus the passthrough is a hybrid, with some of the features of a bond, and some of the features of a mortgage. The GNMA guarantee, which carries the full faith and credit of the United States, made passthroughs acceptable to all kinds of investors who were not prepared to buy mortgages, but who were willing to accept many of the mortgage characteristics of the passthrough, like unpredictable flows of principal, an unknown final maturity and a new principal amount each month. So widely accepted were GNMA passthroughs among institutional investors, such as pension funds, that the mortgage-backed security (MBS) became the fastest growing sector of the market.

From the first appearance of MBS's on the investment scene in 1970, when the amount outstanding was a humble $5 billion, to the mid-1980s, the growth of these securities has been phenomenal. The $5 billion figure of 1970 grew to $18 billion in 1975, $114 billion in 1980, and almost $370 billion in 1985. (Included in these figures are mortgage-backed securities issued by FNMA and FHLMC, as well as those issued by GNMA.) Perhaps more important than the growth in absolute numbers has been the broadening of the types of investors that mortgage-backed securities have brought to the mortgage market. Because thrift institution deposits became increasingly volatile, they became an unreliable source of funds for long-term mortgages. MBS's brought into the market those institutions that have a regular flow of funds, and a longer term investment horizon, like pension funds and life insurers.

THE CMO AND THE REMIC

As attractive as agency passthroughs were, they still had some serious drawbacks. The fact is that a long-term debt instrument, with uneven and unpredictable repayment flows, does not have a natural investment constituency in the United States. Investors tend to have short-term horizons, like commercial banks or money market funds, or longer term horizons, like pension plans or like insurers. It became obvious that various parts of a mortgage's cash flow appealed to different investors.

In the mid-1980s Wall Street devised two instruments to address those problems. The first on the scene was the *multi-tranche collateralized mortgage obligation (CMO)*. CMOs are issued by single-purpose entities, whose sole function is to hold mortgage assets, usually in the form of agency passthroughs, and issue a strip of securities against that collateral. Each security, or tranche, has a different interest rate, final maturity, and priority for principal payments.

The best way to understand CMOs is to recognize that, although mortgage payments are meticulously divided between principal and interest for the homeowner, they are just a stream of monthly payments for the lender. As an extreme example, one could borrow money under a note that called for very high interest payments, and no principal repayments, and have the lender view the instrument as a much larger zero coupon note, with all of each payment used to reduce principal. The IRS might take exception to your treatment, but more of that later.

CMOs are a much less extreme example of what is essentially a redirection of cash flows. Usually, a CMO is divided into four *tranches*; each with its own interest rate. The first call on monthly cash flow is to make all the interest payments. Any additional cash flow then goes to retire the first tranche. When that tranche is all retired, the extra cash flow goes to the second tranche, and so on, until the CMO is all retired. Often, however, there remains collateral left over, a *residual* which accrues to the original issuer of the CMO. Enterprising issuers have even sold the residual at the same time that they issued the CMO.

Now we have created four securities, with four average lives, more or less predictable, which appeal to four different kinds of investors. If we make one further adjustment, we can even make it more appealing. We can allow the interest on the last tranche to *accrue,* instead of being paid each month. Obviously, the principal amount of that tranche will grow over time, but the unused cash flow will actually be used to retire earlier tranches, so we are even as to principal. But long-term investors prefer interest payments that automatically compound for them, which is what the *accrual tranche,* or *Z tranche,* does.

Thus we have created, out of one investment with less than gripping appeal, four which have natural homes. By thus increasing the overall appeal, we increase the effective price we can get, and this fact has contributed to a phenomenal growth in the issuance of CMOs during the mid-1980s. Every month, Wall Street arbitrageurs bought up millions of dollars in agency passthroughs and converted them to millions of dollars in CMOs. There was, however, one fly in the ointment.

By redirecting and renaming the cash flows, we have had some significant impacts on their *tax treatment.* Interest flows are a tax-deductible expense and taxable income, while principal flows are neither tax-deductible nor taxable. The tax status of the single-purpose issuer was left unclear, making it vulnerable to double taxation on the interest payments.

Seeing a very successful program about to be nipped in the bud, a group of Wall Street firms trekked down to Washington and helped draft part of the Tax Reform Act of 1986. The part they worked on created a new corporate entity, called a *Real Estate Mortgage Investment Conduit (REMIC).* Among its many features, it decrees that anything which qualifies as a REMIC is, for tax purposes, transparent, meaning that the tax treatment of the cash flows depends on how the final recipient treats them. There were some other built-in benefits, like the freedom to account for the transfer of collateral into the REMIC as a sale or a financing, as one wishes, and the automatic exemption of foreign holders from the 30% withholding on interest income.

When it built a fence around this goose that lays the golden egg, Congress was careful about which animals could get into the pen. REMICs can be used only to finance real estate mortgages, and only under controlled conditions. The distribution of the cash flows is regulated by law. In all, though, the REMIC is such an improvement in the area of mortgage finance that it will probably become the dominant method of packaging mortgages for the foreseeable future. For now, though, we need to understand the underlying agency passthrough securities.

GNMA PASSTHROUGHS

As the first mortgage passthrough security, GNMAs were the forerunner of the industry and established the patterns followed, more or less, by all other issuers. The best way to understand GNMA passthroughs is to follow the formation of a single pool.

The first step in forming a GNMA pool is usually the decision by a developer to construct a group of single-family homes on a large parcel of land; in fact, to create a housing development. After obtaining plans from his architect, and arranging construction financing, the developer's next stop is usually at his friendly mortgage banker's office, to obtain a *commitment* for permanent mortgages. The mortgage banker's commitment is subject to the developer's presenting buyers who qualify for mortgages insured by the Federal Housing Administration (FHA) or guaranteed by the Veteran's Administration (VA). The mortgages cannot be for more than the maximum conforming size (currently $168,000) or for more than 90% of the purchase price of the house. The actual rate will be set when the prospective buyers apply for the mortgage. The developer pays the mortgage banker a fee for this commitment. In some cases, the rate can be set at the time of the commitment, for the payment of a higher fee.

Now the developer brings in the bulldozers, and the construction crews, and puts up the big billboard advertising "NEW HOMES FOR SALE—MORTGAGES AVAILABLE!" As the buyers stream in, they are given application forms to fill out, and sent over to the mortgage banker to begin the qualification process. As it becomes clear to the mortgage banker how many loans will close each month, he *presells* an appropriately sized GNMA for delivery two or three months hence.

As the loans close, the mortgage banker takes them to his local bank and borrows the proceeds, using the mortgages as collateral, or *warehouses* the mortgages. When he has accumulated a large enough batch of loans, he applies to GNMA for an individual pool number, and pays GNMA a fee for issuing the security. The loan documents are kept at a custodian bank, the security is issued by GNMA, it is delivered to the buyer of a few months ago against cash, and the cash is used to pay down the warehouse loan.

Each GNMA pool begins life at a specified size, called the *original face amount*, and each pool has a specified interest rate, called the *coupon*, which is .50% below the interest rate on the mortgage. Of those 50 basis points, GNMA keeps 6 as a guarantee fee (although there are signs that the fee may rise to 10 basis points) and the mortgage banker keeps 44 basis points (or 40, if the guarantee fee rises) as his compensation for servicing the pool.

Servicing encompasses collecting the individual mortgage payments on or about the first of the month, remitting the pool payments on the fifteenth of the following month, collecting the escrows and paying the appropriate taxes and insurance, and generally doing the jobs that a mortgage lender does. Each monthly payment is part interest and part principal, so the mortgage banker sends the security holder a form showing how much of the accompanying check covers interest, how much is toward scheduled principal payments, how much represents unscheduled principal (from prepayments, foreclosures, etc.), and the remaining balance on the holder's portion of the pool.

Servicing also involves informing GNMA of the same things with regard to the whole pool, so GNMA can publish a listing of the remaining balance, and the fraction of the original face amount that the balance represents. The fraction, called a *factor*, is multiplied by the original face amount of any holding of that pool to determine the remaining principal at the time of purchase or sale. Each month, GNMA publishes the factors of all its pools in something called a *Factor Book*.

Figure 5-1 is a page from the *GNMA Factor Book*, for December 1986, page 963, to be exact. It contains a great deal of information, and we should learn most of it. The first column contains the *pool number*. Each individual GNMA pool is given a distinct number at the time it is issued, and it is known by that number for the rest of its life. With the pool number, we can go to this book and determine a great deal about the security.

The second column gives the *factor*, or the percentage of the original face amount that remained outstanding as of December 1, 1986. Factors go down each month, both through the reduction of principal due to regular monthly mortgage payments, and through prepayments of mortgages. The third and fourth columns give us information about the *mortgage banker* who originated and services the pool and is called the *issuer*. By using his issuer number, we can look him up in a directory in

Page from a GNMA *Factor Book*.

GNMA MORTGAGE-BACKED SECURITIES — GNMA I PROGRAM

PAGE 963   DEC /86

POOL NO	FACTOR	ISSUER NO	ISSUER	POOL TYPE	ORIGINAL BALANCE	11/86 BALANCE	INTEREST RATE	ISSUE DATE	MATURITY DATE
127698X	.87536002	1463	GMAC MORTGAGE CORPORATION OF PENNSYLVA	SF	5,004,643.77	4,380,865.09	12.500	07/01/85	07/15/15
127699X	.65878972	1463	GMAC MORTGAGE CORPORATION OF PENNSYLVA	SF	5,008,269.48	3,299,396.43	11.500	07/01/85	07/15/15
127702X	.71385702	1463	GMAC MORTGAGE CORPORATION OF PENNSYLVA	SF	3,509,057.66	2,504,965.43	12.000	07/01/85	07/15/15
127703X	.87437797	1463	GMAC MORTGAGE CORPORATION OF PENNSYLVA	SF	4,998,777.35	4,370,820.79	11.500	07/01/85	07/15/15
127704X	.94453015	1463	GMAC MORTGAGE CORPORATION OF PENNSYLVA	SF	5,999,538.31	5,666,744.83	12.000	08/01/85	07/15/15
127705X	.83206029	1463	GMAC MORTGAGE CORPORATION OF PENNSYLVA	SF	3,017,574.04	2,510,803.52	12.000	09/01/85	08/15/15
127706X	.86524161	1463	GMAC MORTGAGE CORPORATION OF PENNSYLVA	SF	4,014,064.49	3,473,135.63	11.500	08/01/85	08/15/15
127707X	.76622532	2743	FIRSTBANK MORTGAGE CO	SF	2,987,265.48	2,294,892.99	11.500	05/01/85	05/15/15
127708X	.73236190	2743	FIRSTBANK MORTGAGE CO	SF	1,004,526.59	735,677.00	11.500	07/01/85	07/15/15
127709X	.64815551	1506	FIDELITY BOND & MORTGAGE COMPANY	SF	1,004,322.89	651,346.31	12.000	02/01/85	02/15/15
127710X	.92326180	1506	FIDELITY BOND & MORTGAGE COMPANY	SF	1,000,480.91	923,705.81	11.500	08/01/85	05/15/15
127711X	.95779656	1506	FIDELITY BOND & MORTGAGE COMPANY	SF	1,017,098.34	974,173.29	11.500	04/01/85	04/15/15
127712X	.93416667	1506	FIDELITY BOND & MORTGAGE COMPANY	SF	1,036,736.73	968,484.90	11.500	09/01/85	09/15/15
127713X	.99407166	1506	FIDELITY BOND & MORTGAGE COMPANY	SF	1,035,682.99	1,029,543.11	11.500	10/01/85	10/15/15
127714X	.88669856	1556	GULF COAST INVESTMENT CORPORATION	BD	1,550,504.49	1,374,830.10	11.000	06/01/85	05/15/15
127716X	.99216063	1556	GULF COAST INVESTMENT CORPORATION	BD	1,010,140.82	1,002,221.95	10.000	06/01/85	05/15/15
127717X	.00000000	1595	THE LOMAS & NETTLETON COMPANY	BD	2,004,400.07	.00	10.000	04/01/85	04/15/15
127720X	.92505472	2637	CTX MORTGAGE COMPANY, INC	SF	1,400,678.00	1,295,703.80	11.500	04/01/85	03/15/15
127721X	.67227981	2219	ALLIANCE MORTGAGE COMPANY	SF	5,495,375.08	3,694,429.70	11.500	04/01/85	05/15/15
127722X	.68711122	2219	ALLIANCE MORTGAGE COMPANY	SF	6,987,864.57	4,791,657.14	12.000	04/01/85	04/15/15
127724X	.62500976	1613	DOMINION BANKSHARES MORTGAGE CORPORAT	SF	2,996,939.20	1,873,116.24	12.000	03/01/85	03/15/15
127725X	.69243086	1613	DOMINION BANKSHARES MORTGAGE CORPORAT	SF	2,994,852.51	2,073,749.07	12.000	03/01/85	03/15/15
127726X	.00000000	1613	DOMINION BANKSHARES MORTGAGE CORPORAT	SF	1,996,611.25	.00	12.000	04/01/85	04/15/15
127727X	.63472602	1613	DOMINION BANKSHARES MORTGAGE CORPORAT	SF	1,995,017.54	1,266,289.54	12.000	04/01/85	04/15/15
127729X	.64547867	1613	DOMINION BANKSHARES MORTGAGE CORPORAT	SF	1,992,849.73	1,286,342.00	12.000	04/01/85	04/15/15
127730X	.62722132	1613	DOMINION BANKSHARES MORTGAGE CORPORAT	SF	1,048,863.03	657,881.80	12.000	04/01/85	02/15/15
127731X	.58129201	1613	DOMINION BANKSHARES MORTGAGE CORPORAT	SF	1,008,592.79	586,286.93	12.500	04/01/85	04/15/15
127732X	.75848709	1613	DOMINION BANKSHARES MORTGAGE CORPORAT	SF	1,023,191.24	776,077.35	11.500	04/01/85	04/15/15
127733X	.45150478	1533	SEAFIRST MORTGAGE CORPORATION	SF	1,255,938.10	567,062.05	12.000	04/01/85	04/15/15
127734X	.80736550	1533	SEAFIRST MORTGAGE CORPORATION	SF	2,022,363.50	1,632,786.51	12.000	04/01/85	03/15/15
127735X	.75346081	1533	SEAFIRST MORTGAGE CORPORATION	SF	1,502,028.36	1,131,719.51	11.500	05/01/85	04/15/15
127736X	.68920619	1533	SEAFIRST MORTGAGE CORPORATION	SF	3,014,989.22	2,077,949.23	12.000	04/01/85	04/15/15
127737X	.92300952	1533	SEAFIRST MORTGAGE CORPORATION	SF	2,445,509.34	2,257,228.41	11.000	05/01/85	04/15/15
127738X	.66474733	1451	MERITOR MORTGAGE CORPORATION EAST	SF	2,016,756.48	1,340,633.48	12.500	04/01/85	04/15/15
127740X	.72886195	1451	MERITOR MORTGAGE CORPORATION EAST	SF	3,007,937.54	2,192,371.22	12.000	05/01/85	04/15/15
127741X	.76638367	1451	MERITOR MORTGAGE CORPORATION EAST	SF	2,007,662.04	1,538,639.40	12.500	05/01/85	05/15/15
127742X	.77933884	1451	MERITOR MORTGAGE CORPORATION EAST	SF	3,506,648.84	2,732,867.65	12.000	04/01/85	04/15/15
127744X	.68688982	1673	THE NEW YORK GUARDIAN MORTGAGEE CORP	SF	2,006,908.88	1,378,545.88	12.000	05/01/85	04/15/15
127745X	.84321811	2692	PLATTE VALLEY FEDERAL SAVINGS AND LOAN	SF	2,997,131.49	2,527,235.54	11.000	08/01/85	08/15/15
127746X	.99448311	1993	THE HAMMOND COMPANY, THE MORTGAGE BANK	SF	1,579,690.17	1,570,975.19	12.500	05/01/85	08/15/15
127750X	.99437277	1993	THE HAMMOND COMPANY, THE MORTGAGE BANK	SF	1,499,694.00	1,491,254.67	11.000	08/01/85	08/15/15
127752X	.61632910	2691	HOME MORTGAGE CO OF EL PASO	SF	1,354,011.40	834,516.63	11.000	04/01/85	04/15/15
127756X	.94387776	1602	BRUMBAUGH & FULTON COMPANY	SF	1,224,124.03	1,155,423.45	11.000	09/01/85	08/15/15

97

Figure 5-1
Page from a GNMA *Factor Book* (cont'd.).

Pool	Factor	Issuer #	Issuer Name	Type	Balance	Rate	Date	Maturity
127757X	.88488116	1673	THE NEW YORK GUARDIAN MORTGAGEE CORP	SF	1,014,456.37	11.000	04/01/85	04/15/15
127758X	.67232794	1673	THE NEW YORK GUARDIAN MORTGAGEE CORP	SF	1,002,447.91	12.000	05/01/85	05/15/15
127759X	.81178708	1673	THE NEW YORK GUARDIAN MORTGAGEE CORP	SF	1,024,797.00	12.000	06/01/85	06/15/15
127760X	.65329995	2180	CHEVY CHASE SAVINGS AND LOAN INC	SF	5,017,648.99	12.000	06/01/85	03/15/15
127761X	.50994848	1723	MERRILL LYNCH MORTGAGE CORPORATION	SF	3,278,029.81	12.000	06/01/85	06/15/15
127762X	.72012224	1723	MERRILL LYNCH MORTGAGE CORPORATION	SF	1,001,851.93	12.000	07/01/85	07/15/15
127763X	.56973186	1723	MERRILL LYNCH MORTGAGE CORPORATION	SF	1,019,723.51	11.500	07/01/85	06/15/15
127764X	.73704885	1723	MERRILL LYNCH MORTGAGE CORPORATION	SF	1,021,187.70	11.500	06/01/85	06/15/15
127765X	.99137714	1723	MERRILL LYNCH MORTGAGE CORPORATION	SF	1,000,587.23	11.500	06/01/85	06/15/15
127766X	.83054361	1723	MERRILL LYNCH MORTGAGE CORPORATION	SF	1,005,362.77	12.500	06/01/85	06/15/15
127767X	.77784966	1723	MERRILL LYNCH MORTGAGE CORPORATION	SF	1,002,457.10	12.500	06/01/85	06/15/15
127768X	.91933992	1723	MERRILL LYNCH MORTGAGE CORPORATION	SF	1,022,248.82	11.500	05/01/85	05/15/15
127769X	.86668328	1723	MERRILL LYNCH MORTGAGE CORPORATION	SF	1,005,332.94	11.000	05/01/85	04/15/15
127770X	.72177434	1723	MERRILL LYNCH MORTGAGE CORPORATION	SF	1,013,419.01	12.500	05/01/85	05/15/15
127771X	.67487628	1723	MERRILL LYNCH MORTGAGE CORPORATION	SF	1,015,588.12	11.500	05/01/85	04/15/15
127775X	.79138328	1723	MERRILL LYNCH MORTGAGE CORPORATION	SF	1,012,915.97	11.500	04/01/85	03/15/15
127776X	.78001407	1723	MERRILL LYNCH MORTGAGE CORPORATION	SF	2,019,867.58	12.000	05/01/85	06/15/15
127777X	.80570612	1723	MERRILL LYNCH MORTGAGE CORPORATION	SF	1,989,808.24	11.500	04/01/85	03/15/15
127778X	.99365530	1723	MERRILL LYNCH MORTGAGE CORPORATION	SF	2,997,656.52	12.000	03/01/85	03/15/15
127779X	.72863096	1723	MERRILL LYNCH MORTGAGE CORPORATION	SF	2,516,165.90	10.000	10/01/85	10/15/15
127782X	.23733819	1723	MERRILL LYNCH MORTGAGE CORPORATION	SF	4,006,931.73	12.000	03/01/85	03/15/15
127786X	.92198416	2770	THE MORTGAGEBANQUE INC	SF	1,030,221.74	12.500	05/01/85	05/15/15
127787X	.76533911	2770	THE MORTGAGEBANQUE INC	SF	1,029,397.73	10.000	06/01/85	05/15/15
127791X	.99149936	2770	THE MORTGAGEBANQUE INC	SF	1,531,141.96	12.000	06/01/85	05/15/15
127799X	.93731138	2770	THE MORTGAGEBANQUE INC	SF	1,039,633.15	11.000	07/01/85	07/15/15
127810X	.58692441	2751	UNITED FEDERAL SAVINGS AND LOAN ASSOCI	SF	1,000,134.22	10.500	05/01/85	04/15/15
127812X	.78417206	2135	FIRST MORTGAGE CORPORATION	SF	1,018,030.46	12.000	03/01/85	03/15/15
127813X	.73677271	2135	FIRST MORTGAGE CORPORATION	SF	2,321,101.62	12.000	03/01/85	03/15/15
127816X	.85240290	2135	FIRST MORTGAGE CORPORATION	SF	1,505,255.56	12.000	04/01/85	04/15/15
127817X	.90272469	1764	CITY FEDERAL SAVINGS BANK	SF	4,365,779.25	12.500	05/01/85	05/15/15
127818X	.71296197	1764	CITY FEDERAL SAVINGS BANK	SF	3,999,871.43	11.500	03/01/85	03/15/15
127819X	.88811915	1764	CITY FEDERAL SAVINGS BANK	SF	8,551,425.44	12.500	03/01/85	03/15/15
127820X	.65907078	2687	YORK ASSOCIATES INC	SF	1,492,138.15	12.500	03/01/85	02/15/15
127821X	.50878237	2712	FIRST FEDERAL OF THE CAROLINAS, FA	SF	1,021,879.43	12.500	04/01/85	03/15/15
127822X	.91654694	2712	FIRST FEDERAL OF THE CAROLINAS, FA	SF	2,007,729.34	12.500	03/01/85	03/15/15
127823X	.54866901	2712	FIRST FEDERAL OF THE CAROLINAS, FA	SF	2,996,630.27	11.000	11/01/85	10/15/15
127824X	.00000000	2712	FIRST FEDERAL OF THE CAROLINAS, FA	PL	3,999,846.18	12.000	03/01/85	03/15/15
127825X	.79845279	2637	CTX MORTGAGE COMPANY, INC	SF	4,360,000.00	12.250	03/01/85	03/15/20
127828X	.70912354	1997	COLONIAL SAVINGS AND LOAN ASSOCIATION	SF	2,427,367.29	11.500	06/01/85	06/15/15
127829X	.75930496	2835	E B MORTGAGE CORPORATION	SF	5,494,428.47	12.000	03/01/85	03/15/15
127830X	.48996682	2621	CITICORP HOMEOWNERS SERVICES, INC	SF	3,896,228.55	12.500	03/01/85	03/15/15
127632X	.78207650	2621	CITICORP HOMEOWNERS SERVICES, INC	SF	1,366,478.13	12.000	03/01/85	03/15/15
127833X	.74760215	2621	CITICORP HOMEOWNERS SERVICES, INC	SF	1,003,211.15	12.500	03/01/85	02/15/15
127834X	.83690373	2621	CITICORP HOMEOWNERS SERVICES, INC	SF	1,435,092.73	12.500	03/01/85	03/15/15
127835X	.83031936	2621	CITICORP HOMEOWNERS SERVICES, INC	SF	1,010,520.97	12.000	04/01/85	04/15/15
127836X	.84025594	2621	CITICORP HOMEOWNERS SERVICES, INC	SF	1,996,885.10	12.000	04/01/85	04/15/15
127837X	.79957795	2621	CITICORP HOMEOWNERS SERVICES, INC	SF	1,001,645.02	11.500	04/01/85	04/15/15
127838X	.95678195	2621	CITICORP HOMEOWNERS SERVICES, INC	SF	1,016,109.07	12.000	04/01/85	04/15/15
127838X	.70114616	2621	CITICORP HOMEOWNERS SERVICES, INC	SF	2,011,146.53	12.000	04/01/85	04/15/00
127839X		2621	CITICORP HOMEOWNERS SERVICES, INC	SF	972,331.83	12.000	04/01/85	04/15/00
		2621	CITICORP HOMEOWNERS SERVICES, INC	SF	1,008,505.58	11.500	04/01/85	04/15/00
					707,109.81			

Mortgage-Backed Securities

the back of the *Factor Book,* and determine his address and telephone number.

Next we see the *pool type.* The vast majority say "SF," for *Single Family.* Although most GNMA pools are single family, there are a few exceptions. Pool number 127824, for example, shows a type called "PL," which stands for Permanent Loan, and indicates that it is a loan on a *multi-family* building. Pool numbers 127714 and 127716 have a type of "BD," showing that they are builder buydown pools, where the builder took out the mortgage before his commitment expired, with the intention of replacing himself with an individual owner as soon as possible.

The next column shows the *original balance,* or the amount outstanding on all the loans in the pool on the day it was issued. This amount is also called the *original face* by GNMA traders. The next column shows the *amount outstanding* at the end of November 1986 when this *Factor Book* was created. Look at pool number 127740, issued by Meritor Mortgage Corporation, East. Its original face amount was $3,007,937.54. Today its factor gives a current balance of $2,192,371.22, the number found in the column labeled "11/86 BALANCE." Each holder of pool number 127740 can determine the current balance of his piece of the pool by multiplying the original face amount of his piece by the factor each month.

The next column shows the *interest rate* on the pool, which is always 1/2 of 1% lower than the rate on the mortgages in the pool. Aside from determining the interest the holder earns on the outstanding balance each month, the interest rate, or coupon, of the pool helps determine how rapidly the pool pays down. We can see how that works by looking at the next column, which shows the *date the pool was issued.* Pools issued at the same time should have about the same prepayment rate, except for coupon differences.

For example, let's look at pool numbers 127786 and 127787. They have the same issuer, The MortgageBanque, Inc., and the same issue date, 6/1/85, but they have very different factors. Pool number 127786, which is a 10% security (and thus has 10.5% mortgages in it), has a factor of 0.92198416, while pool number 127787, which has a coupon of 12% (with mortgages of 12.5% in it), has a factor of 0.76533911. Why has so much more of the 12% security paid down? Because in December 1986, interest rates on mortgages were about 9%, with the result that many more homeowners with 12.5% loans were refinancing than were homeowners with 10.5% mortgages.

This factor difference points up an important trait of mortgages, and thus of mortgage-backed securities. Because the homeowner can prepay his mortgage at any time without penalty, a holder can never predict with certainty how long an individual mortgage will last. In fact, the one prediction one can make is that early prepayment is likely to occur when it is least desired by the holder—when market rates are significantly below the rate on the mortgage. Thus, when your investment yields less than the market rate, you can expect it to last a long time; when it yields more than the market rate, you can expect it to last a much shorter time.

Since all principal payments are passed through to the holders of MBS's, these securities also lead to uncertain lives because of the unpleasant characteristic of being prepaid faster when their rates are above market rates. The combination of this uncertainty, and the non-symmetrical prepayment performance, has restricted the appeal of MBS's among those investors who are used to investing in bonds, where the payment stream is much more predictable. The rapid growth of MBS's in general makes them appear to be universally popular, but there is a much larger universe of potential investors. Recently, the introduction of multi-tranche collateralized mortgage obligations (CMOs) and Real Estate Mortgage Investment Conduits (REMICs) has begun to revolutionize the field of mortgage finance, as we covered earlier.

Major Types of GNMA Mortgage-Backed Securities

GNMA (pronounced Ginnie Mae) was born in 1968 out of the Federal National Mortgage Association, to assist in the creation and marketing of mortgages insured by the Federal Housing Administration and/or guaranteed by the Veteran's Administration. Soon after its creation, GNMA became the main marketing force in the FHA/VA mortgage market.

GNMA originally had two functions: the purchase of FHA/VA loans and the guarantee of GNMA passthrough securities. The purchase program proved to be costly and inefficient, so it withered away, and was eventually dropped. The MBS program, on the other hand, became a roaring success. By the middle 1980s the vast majority of FHA/VA production was going into GNMA passthroughs. So popular was the program that the kinds of GNMAs expanded to encompass all the

Mortgage-Backed Securities

mortgage programs that the FHA/VA allowed. Let's look at each kind of GNMA.

GNMA I 30 Year

This program, which is the original kind of GNMA, is still the largest part of the GNMA market. All the mortgages in the pool have a coupon 1/2 of 1% below the MBS rate. All were created within a year of the pool's issue date, all have 30 years to maturity at the time of issuance, and all are either insured by the FHA or guaranteed by the VA. All the mortgages were issued and are serviced by the same mortgage banker, and principal and interest payments are sent to the holder on the 15th of the month following their receipt. At year end, 1986, there was a total of $200 billion worth of these pools in existence.

GNMA II 30 Year

This program is much newer than the GNMA I program, having begun in 1983, and has fewer pools outstanding. All the mortgages in a GNMA II pool are FHA/VA mortgages, and all had 30-year maturities when they were issued, but the mortgage coupon can be from 1/2 of 1% to 1½% above the MBS coupon. The loans may have been originated and serviced by a variety of mortgage bankers, but principal and interest payments are all made by Chemical Bank, in New York, on the 20th of the month following their receipt.

GNMA I 15 Year (Midgets)

This program is essentially the same as the GNMA I 30-year program, with the exception that the loans in the pool have an original term to maturity of fifteen years. Quicker amortization has the advantage of reducing the interest rate exposure of the lender, allowing him to put a lower interest rate on the loan, but it also results in a higher monthly payment for the homeowner. As a result, 15-year mortgages are less popular than 30-year loans, and there was a total of only $10.5 billion worth of these pools in existence at year end, 1986.

GNMA Graduated-Payment Mortgages (GPMs)

During periods when rates were extraordinarily high, some mortgage lenders devised a scheme of rising payment loans which allowed homeowners to begin paying a lower monthly amount, with the later increases to be offset by hoped-for increases in income. GNMA incorporated these loans into special pools, with many of the characteristics of the GNMA I series. All the loans are 30-year, fixed-rate product. With the drop in rates that took place in the mid-1980s, the need for GPMs was dramatically reduced, and their creation fell off to virtually nothing. As of year end, 1986, there was a total of $10 billion of these pools still in existence.

Other GNMA Programs

Over the years GNMA has been involved in other programs of MBS issuance, but the volumes have been so small that no active market exists in the securities. Two of note are the mobile home pools and the project securities. Mobile home pools are backed by mortgages on mobile homes, with maturities ranging from twelve to twenty years. These loans are often treated as consumer debt, instead of mortgage debt, and carry much higher rates than mortgages. Project pools are backed by mortgages on multi-family housing projects. These loans usually have a term of forty years, with a coupon 1/4 of 1% above the MBS rate. In both these cases, some dealers trade the securities, but not many and not often.

FEDERAL HOME LOAN MORTGAGE CORP (FHLMC)

FHLMC (called Freddie Mac) was formed in July 1970 by the Emergency Home Finance Act of 1970, to perform many of the same functions GNMA performs, but for *conventional* mortgages, as opposed to FHA/VA mortgages. Thus FHLMC acquires loans and guarantees securities, but their securities are called *Participation Certificates (PCs),* and the method of issuance is slightly different. There are, in fact, two methods of issuance. Mortgage bankers can sell new loans to FHLMC, which will create PCs and sell them directly to dealers and/or investors. Thrift institutions can swap older conventional loans with FHLMC, receiving PCs in return, and then sell those PCs to dealers and/or investors.

There are some other differences between GNMA and FHLMC. Where GNMA is owned by the Federal Government, FHLMC is owned by the twelve Federal Home Loan Banks. Unlike GNMAs, PCs do not

Mortgage-Backed Securities

carry the full faith and credit of the U.S. Treasury, and FHLMC guarantees only the *timely payment* of *interest* and the *ultimate payment* of *principal*. PCs exist in book entry form, while GNMAs have only, until 1987, existed in physical form. Let's look at specific PCs.

Types of FHLMC Participation Certificates

30-Year Participation Certificates

As with GNMAs, the basic, original security issued by FHLMC is the most popular. In the case of PCs, the collateral is fixed-rate, conventional mortgages, with original principal amounts not exceeding $168,000, and terms not exceeding thirty years. Mortgage coupons can exceed the PC coupon by from 1/2 of 1% to 2.5%. Although individual mortgage bankers service loans in the pool, principal and interest payments are remitted to PC holders by FHLMC. Because of this two-stage servicing process, the delay between the due date for mortgage payments and the pool payments amounts to *75 days* for PCs, as opposed to *45 days* for GNMAs. At year end, 1986, there was a total of $134 billion of PCs outstanding.

15-Year Participation Certificates (Gnomes)

Gnomes are similar to midgets, in that they are the 15-year version of the 30-year security. Gnomes have the same double servicing structure, the same 75-day payment delay, the same range for mortgage coupons, and the same guarantee structure as the PC does. At year end, 1986, there was a total of $26 billion of Gnomes in existence.

FNMA MORTGAGE-BACKED SECURITIES (FNMA MBS)

In 1980, FNMA got into the MBS business when it introduced the FNMA version of the PC. FNMA MBS's are unique in that they can contain both *conventional* and *FHA/VA* loans, and that FNMA can create them out of its own portfolio of mortgages. The FNMA guarantee covers both interest and principal. Obviously, loans from FNMA's portfolio will have terms considerably shorter then thirty years when the MBS is created. Although the FNMA MBS program is relatively new, there was already a total of $80 billion of the securities outstanding on 12/31/86.

PRIVATE COLLATERALIZED MORTGAGE OBLIGATIONS (CMOs)

The advent of CMOs in the early 1980s accentuated a reversal of the process of homogenization that began with the introduction of the GNMA in 1970. In an effort to create securities with appeal to specific investors, CMO issuers developed a bewildering array of tranches, coupons, and average lives. Such *heterogeneity* may well have the effect of reducing the *liquidity* of each issue, even as it serves to tailor-make securities for individual buyers.

The typical CMO is collateralized by a combination of PCs and FNMA MBS's. It is normally divided into four *tranches*, with estimated average lives in the neighborhood of 2 years, 7 years, 12 years, and 17 years, respectively. Generally, the last tranche is an accrual, or "Z" tranche, where the interest is accrued and not paid. The emphasis here is on "generally," since CMOs have been issued with as few as two tranches, with floating rates on some tranches, and with tranches receiving preferential treatment as to interest and principal payments. With all these oddities, it is no surprise that their trading is much more problematical than that of agency mortgage securities.

AGENCY MBS TRADING

Before anyone begins trading MBS's, he must take two facts to heart. First, MBS *settlements* are utterly unlike those for any other security. Second, the *maturity* and *average life* of an individual security are totally unknown. Let's look at each of these facts.

Mortgage-Backed Securities Settlement

As we have seen, many mortgage-backed securities are sold during the process of creation, as many as four months before they are ready for delivery. This convention of the mortgage market was carried over into GNMAs and the other agency MBS issues, and differentiates MBS trading from all others in the government market.

Additionally, because there is a principal and interest payment every month, which complicates the recordkeeping necessary to pass on the payments, MBS's settle only *one day per month*. Telescoping one month's worth of settlements into one day creates some monumental

Mortgage-Backed Securities

logjams. The first occurs two days before settlement, as traders and customers pass along the *pool information* necessary to calculate the principal and interest necessary to settle the trade. That information consists, in its most basic form, of the pool number and the original face amount of the piece being delivered. From that information, all the rest of the numbers can be calculated.

Because each pool pays down an unknown amount each month, securities which had a principal amount close to $1 million may be closer to $750 thousand a year later. Thus, a seller might have to combine two or more different pools to make an amount approximating the amount sold. Over a period of years, the dealers have evolved terms for *good delivery,* setting out what combinations of securities are acceptable. Good delivery terms vary between securities and from time to time, but every market participant must keep current with them.

Dealing with "Average Life" Uncertainties

The other oddity of MBS's is that, since loans can be prepaid at any time, the concept of "yield to maturity" has no meaning in this market. Each pool will have its own stream of principal payments, and its own *average life,* neither of which can be predicted with certainty. Market participants have developed three methods of dealing with this uncertainty, in varying degrees of sophistication.

The first method depends upon the *FHA's experience* with a huge number of insured loans. Named the *FHA method,* it derives its treatment from the fact that the FHA found that the average single-family loan last about twelve years. As a result the FHA method assumes that the pool will experience 143 regular monthly payments of interest and principal, and then completely pay down in the 144th month. With obvious logic, this method is also called the *twelve-year life* method and is most often used to calculate yields and prices on securities not yet issued.

The second method depends on the recent prepayment history of each pool, and derives from it a *Constant Prepayment Rate* (or *CPR*) which can be converted into an average life, or a duration, for each pool. This method has the obvious advantage of differentiating between pools with rapid prepayments and those with much slower ones. It has the disadvantage of projecting the past into the future without incorporating any judgment about possible speedups or slowdowns.

The third method was developed by the *Public Securities Association,* and is thus called the *PSA method.* The PSA looked at the performance of a large number of single-family mortgages over time, beginning when the mortgages were first closed. They found that the prepayment rate was not constant; instead it moved higher during the first year after closing, and then leveled off for the rest of the mortgage's life. Thus they developed the PSA convention for prepayments: in its first month a pool of mortgages prepays 0.2%, in the second month 0.4%, in the third month 0.6%, and so on to the thirtieth month, where the CPR is 6% per month, where it levels off for the remaining life of the pool.

None of these methods accounts effectively for the possibility of large changes in market rates of interest, so various dealers have begun to develop models to predict the changes in prepayment rates caused by changes in market rates. Needless to say, none of those models had gained wide acceptance by year end, 1986.

THE MORTGAGE-BACKED SECURITIES MARKET

Mortgage-backed securities are traded by a group of dealers whose membership parallels the Primary Dealer Association, but does not duplicate it. In each trading room, MBS's have their own trading desk, and often their own sales force. The sales force is particularly necessary in covering mortgage bankers and thrift institutions, which make up a large part of the MBS market, but not a large part of the government market.

MBS's have their own pages on the brokers' screens, too. Figure 5-2 is one such page, from Telerate. It is interesting because it shows all the agency MBS's on one screen, although it doesn't give complete information about each market. The screen is divided by security and by coupon.

The upper left corner is devoted to GNMAs, and to one coupon in particular. This coupon, called the *current coupon,* is the one currently being produced by mortgage bankers. It is usually the highest coupon whose price is below par, in this case 8%. This is the coupon most actively traded in the market.

We can see that prices are quoted for deliveries in January through April. But notice the prices. As the delivery recedes into the future, the price drops. Is this because the market believes that prices will be lower

Figure 5-2
Telerate screen showing a mortgage-backed securities page.

```
TELERATE SYSTEMS

1/20     11:49 EST       SECONDARY MORTGAGE MARKETS
GNMA 8        11.45   FHLMC PC JAN      11.45    FNMA JAN      11.45
JAN    100.14 -22 +10  10 1/2   105.30-06   UNC   10 1/2   106.10-18  UNC
FEB    100.02 -10      10       105.00-08   +06   10       105.14-22  +06
MAR    99.20  -28      9 1/2    104.06-14   +04   9 1/2    104.20-28  +04
APR    99.06  -14      9        102.16-24   +06   9        102.26-02  +06
GPM    9 1/4%          8 1/2    101.00-08   +08   8 1/2    101.06-14  +08
JAN    104.10 -18 +10  8         99.00-08   +08   8         99.06-14  +08
GNMA JAN               [FED DOING 2 DAY SYSTEM REPOS]
12     108.06 -14 -02  GNMA 15 YR JAN    11.45    FNMA 15 YEAR
11 1/2 107.26 -02 -02  9        104.12-20   +06   9        103.10  -18   +10
11     107.30 -06 -02  8 1/2    102.28-04   +06   8 1/2    101.30  -06   +08
10 1/2 107.26 -02 -04  8        101.10-18   +06   8        100.00  -08   +02
10     107.06 -14 UNC  FHLMC 5 YR (GNOMES)         TREASURY ISSUES
9 1/2  105.16 -24 +04  9        103.06-14   +12   3M BILL       5.34 -30  -02
9      103.16 -26 +06  8 1/2    101.26-02   +12   07.250 11/96 101.20-24  +06
8 1/2  102.00 -08 +08  8         99.26-02   +06   07.500 11/16 102.07-11  +17
7 1/2  98.18  -26      FED FUNDS  BID 6           ASK 6  1/16   LAST 6
```

107

in the future? No, it has only to do with the difference between the yield on these securities and the rate on money borrowed to own them, or the *positive carry.*

Suppose, for instance, that these securities yielded 8%, and the cost of the borrowed money was 5%. If you bought a GNMA at 100 for delivery in January, and sold it at 100 for delivery in April, and financed it at 5%, you would have a risk-free profit of 3% (the positive carry) divided by 4 (for 1/4 of a year), or 24/32ds. In order to compensate for the positive carry, the price of a security must decline by an amount equal to the profit to be gained from the positive carry. This is called *convergence,* and holds true for any forward delivery or futures contract.

In this case, using prices in the middle of the quoted markets, the price decline is 100.18 − 99.10, or 1.08 (in 32ds, remember). That implies a huge positive carry of 5% (1.25 × 4), which means that the GNMA *cost of carry* is 3%. What is more likely is that 8% GNMAs are in short supply, with mortgage bankers closing fewer loans than they had planned on. When this happens, mortgage bankers scramble to buy back securities, creating a temporary shortage in the nearby or *front* months. Astute traders can take advantage of these temporary aberrations.

In the lower left corner are other GNMA coupons, all 30-year securities, for January delivery. Other pages of Telerate, and other brokers' screens may have all these coupons for the same number of deliveries as we see for 8% coupons, but this display is enough for us. Notice the prices for the various coupons. The difference between the 8½% and the 9% coupons, for example, is about 1½ points, but the difference between the 10½% and the 11% coupons is about ⅛ point. Why?

This phenomenon reflects the market's assumption that most people with mortgages carrying rates around 11%, with current rates around 8½%, will refinance their mortgage as soon as possible. Thus, the market assumes that the *average life,* or *duration,* of the high-coupon securities will be very short. Whether that assumption is right or wrong, only time will tell.

The top half of the middle section is devoted to PCs, and the top right is devoted to FNMAs. Let's look at the prices for equivalent coupons in the different securities. The price spread between GNMA 9% coupons and PC 9% coupons is about 1 point, and between GNMA

Mortgage-Backed Securities

9% and FNMA 9% coupons is about ⅝ to ¾ point. In 10% coupons the GNMA-PC spread is about 2 points, and the GNMA-FNMA spread is about 1½ points. In 8% coupons, the spreads are almost identical at about 1¼ points. What is the right spread? Will any of these spreads change soon? Such questions keep MBS traders busy from early in the morning until late in the afternoon.

In the lower middle and right are the 15-year varieties of these securities, and we can do the same spread analysis on them. The 9% spreads are: 1⅛ for GNMA-PC and 1 point for GNMA-FNMA. In the 8% securities, the spreads are 1½ and 1¼, respectively. These spreads can be affected by the smallness of the market, where large trades in a particular coupon can cause large aberrations.

SOME CONCLUDING OBSERVATIONS

Perhaps no security reflects both the power and the problems of our financial system quite like the MBS. The enormous demands of the home mortgage market are not to be denied—they have changed forever both the mortgage market and the bond market. Faced with such immediate demands, Congress and the political system have responded with innovative securities. But the long-term results of these changes are very much up in the air. The advent of the GNMA passthrough brought a welcome homogeneity to the market, but the CMO and the REMIC have set us back on the road to diversity. Where that road leads is anybody's guess.

In the meantime, there is another very important segment of the market to explore. It is short-term by nature, and it is made up of two segments: secured short-term investments and unsecured short-term investments. The Money and Collateral Markets are the next segments of the marketplace for us to look at.

CHAPTER SIX

Money Market Instruments and Financing Transactions

The very large volume of securities traded in the government bond market and the very high degree of liquidity in that market, depends on the circulation of a very large volume of money within the financial system at all times. Economists call this money *transaction balances*, and these are held by a variety of individuals, corporations, and countries. Transaction balances are different from savings, because their express purpose is to facilitate day-to-day transactions, while savings are put away for some future purpose or emergency.

One form of transaction balance is *currency*, the bills and coins that weigh down our pockets or purses. Originally, this was the only kind of transaction balance that existed, but the advent of commercial banks, checks, and electronic money transfer meant a major change in the use of transaction balances. Since money could exist in a purely electronic form, it could be shifted from one account to another instantly, and thus invested overnight. For many years, such intensive cash management was practical only for large corporations or banks, with large amounts to invest. By the last half of the 1970s, though, *money market mutual funds* were developed, which gave individuals an opportunity to participate in the money market, and the development of check-writing privileges for such funds made it practical to invest in the money market. In fact, money market mutual funds had become one of the largest forms of public investing by year end, 1986, holding billions of dollars of the public's money.

Money Market Instruments and Financing Transactions

The growth of these mutual funds represents only part of the growth of transaction balances in the United States. Commercial bank deposits have grown by a very large amount, both in this country and in foreign banks. Thrift institutions have also established transaction accounts, called *money market demand accounts*. Taken together, all these accounts represent an enormous pool of funds to be invested in short-term assets. As far as the government market is concerned, there are two kinds of short-term assets that fit: money market instruments and securities financings.

MONEY MARKET INSTRUMENTS

If the money market is defined to include all suitable short-term investments, then short-term Treasury and agency securities are a part. Indeed they are, but we have already dealt with them, and the market does not really include them in the definition of money market instruments, which would probably read, "short-term investments issued by corporations, not subject to registration under the Securities Act of 1933." Under that definition there are two classes of money market instruments—those issued by banks and those issued by non-bank corporations.

BANK MONEY MARKET INSTRUMENTS

Commercial banks are by far the largest borrowers in the money market. Many of the liabilities on their balance sheets would qualify as money market instruments for someone else. The shortest term liability of all is *Federal Funds*. To understand *Fed Funds*, we must first understand something about the Federal Reserve, and its relationship with its member banks.

Federal Funds

One of the reasons that the Federal Reserve was formed in 1913 was the alarming tendency of the country's banks to lend out all their deposits, keeping no reserves against sudden withdrawals. Thus, the first function of the Fed was to hold required reserves for its member banks. From time to time, some banks have more reserves than they need, and others need more reserves than they have. Thus there developed an active market in reserves at Federal Reserve Banks, called the Federal Funds market, or just the Funds market.

The Funds market is important for several reasons. First, it reflects on the availability of bank reserves. A high Funds rate means that banks are short on reserves, and will be less willing to lend money unless the rate on its loans is high enough to justify borrowing the necessary reserves. Second, Fed Funds are the centerpiece of the money market, as well as of the entire bond market. Everyone in these markets keeps an eye on the Funds rate, simply because everyone else does. Third, and most important, it is the rate the Federal Reserve uses to set monetary policy. The Fed determines whether the banking system has ample reserves, or too few, by watching the movement of the Funds rate, and bases its decision whether or not to intervene in the markets on the level of Funds.

As important as they are, Funds are not widely traded, even within the government market. Only commercial banks can actually trade Funds, and only those banks who are members of the Federal Reserve System. There are brokers who act as go-betweens in Funds trading, but these brokers do not actually settle the trades, since they do not have access to the Fed. Most of the traders in the government market, who watch Funds constantly and base many of their trading decisions on them, have very little idea who trades them, and how they are traded.

In actuality, Funds often trade for longer periods than the overnight Funds whose rate is quoted on many brokers' screens. In fact, Funds can be bought for as long as a month or more, but those who think that they are buying Funds may not actually be doing so. Many customers of commercial banks execute trades in which they think they ''buy'' Funds with their excess money, but they are usually lending their money to their bank at the Funds rate. It is not a big issue, but it points out the arcane nature of the Funds market.

Certificates of Deposit

Funds are not deposits, of course, but rather reserves against deposits. Banks and thrift institutions can raise deposits in the market, without registering their issues with the SEC, by selling *Certificates of Deposit (CDs)*. Although CDs represent a deposit, they do not carry insurance by the Federal Deposit Insurance Corporation (FDIC) or the

Federal Savings and Loan Insurance Corporation (FSLIC). A CD is also different from a regular bank deposit because it is *negotiable*, meaning that it can be transferred to a new owner during its life.

CDs are different from every kind of security we have looked at up to now. For example, they are issued directly by each bank to the buyer to fit his specifications. Every day, banks all over the country post rates at which they will write CDs. Rates are normally quoted for monthly maturities, either early-in-the-month or late-in-the-month. Customers shop around among the banks whose quality is high enough, looking for a bank whose need for money matches the buyer's need to invest funds. The two parties agree on a size, a maturity, and a rate; the bank issues the CD; the customer wires in his money.

Thus every individual CD is a separate security, creating a market that is even more fragmented than the agency or MBS markets. Fragmented markets are very short on liquidity, and this means that many more CDs trade every day in the *primary* market, where they are issued by banks, than in the *secondary* market, where they trade after issuance. The simple fact is that it is almost always easier to fill a buyer's order by finding a bank willing to write a new CD than to find an older CD that matches the buyer's need and is for sale. It shouldn't surprise us, then, that secondary offerings of CDs are usually at a slightly higher yield than the primary offerings by issuing banks.

Bankers' Acceptances

The other major bank money market investment is the *Bankers' Acceptance (BA)*. For most short-term investors, BAs and CDs are treated as interchangeable instruments, but they are really quite different. Where a CD is a *direct* obligation of a bank or thrift, a BA is an *indirect* obligation. Where a CD begins its life when the bank or thrift *borrows* money from a customer, a BA begins its life when a bank *makes a loan* to a customer.

Many bank loans are short-term in nature, to finance inventory or finished goods in transit, or to provide general working capital. The borrower signs a note for the borrowed money, and the note shows the interest rate to be paid and the maturity date when the borrower will pay back the money. Notes like these make up a significant portion of a typical bank's loan portfolio.

Many banks want to sell these notes in order to raise short-term money, but the borrowers are often much less known or accepted in the market than the selling bank is. Thus the bank endorses, or *accepts*, the obligation, putting its own credit on the note. In this way, the bank enhances the value of the asset, and makes it salable in the money markets. In fact, many investors view BAs as superior investments to CDs, because BAs have two obligors, the original borrower and the bank, while CDs have only the bank as an obligor.

BAs are issued and quoted about the same way as CDs are. Banks post rates at which they would sell BAs, with the maturities offered being divided into early-in-the-month and late-in-the-month periods. Investors with short-term money to invest shop around among the banks, or dealers who are in touch with issuing banks, to find BAs issued by an acceptable bank, for the maturity that fits the investor, at the best rate available. The purchase and settlement transactions are essentially the same as a CD transaction. One subtle difference between BAs and CDs from the bank's point of view is that banks can write CDs for any maturity date and in any size that they want because they are creating the instrument, but they can sell only the BAs that they already have in portfolio or are currently creating.

COMMERCIAL PAPER

The other large class of money market instruments is made up of short-term notes issued by corporations, called *commercial paper (CP)*. As long as the maturity of the note is not longer than 270 days from date of issuance, such notes, and the issuing corporation, need not be registered with the SEC, as they would be for a longer-term issue. Since commercial paper need not be registered, companies can sell CP in much the same way that banks sell CDs.

There are, however, a lot more corporations willing to sell CP than there are banks to sell CDs, and the public perceives that commercial companies have a less stable earnings flow than banks do, so CP is rated by both Moody's and Standard & Poors. The rating system is slightly different from the Aaa, Aa, A, etc. of the corporate bond market. CP is rated from A1 to A4, in descending order of quality, by Moody's, and from P1 to P4, in the same descending order, by Standard & Poors. Those issuers rated A1/P1, the highest possible, covet their position in the market.

The market divides CP issuers into two broad classes, *finance companies* and *all others*. Finance companies, particularly the subsidiaries of large industrial manufacturers, hold large portfolios of short-term assets, and issue commercial paper to finance a substantial portion of the portfolios. Among the non-finance company issuers, the nation's largest industrial companies issue CP from time to time, as also do many electric utilities. Generally, A1/P1 CP yields slightly more than CDs issued by the top ten U.S. banks, and the same yield relationship exists between other CP and CDs of the same credit quality.

Although large banks and large corporations issue CDs, BAs, and CP directly to buyers, there is a substantial amount of such paper issued through dealers. Why would an issuer pay a dealer a markup to help him issue his paper, when he has the capability of issuing it directly? Because dealers are in the market every day and have an extensive network of buyers. The key to success in the money market is finding the right buyer for each seller, and vice versa. Dealers, with their sales forces and trading staffs, often provide a valuable service in bringing together buyers and sellers who would never have found each other by themselves.

FINANCING SECURITIES

If the money market is essential for the smooth functioning of banks and other short-term borrowers, the *financing market* is essential for the smooth functioning of the government securities market. Every day, hundreds of billions of dollars' worth of securities are financed, allowing dealers and financial institutions to provide liquidity to the market and affording a safe home for short-term cash portfolios.

Originally, all securities financing was in the form of *secured loans* to holders of the securities, with the securities pledged as collateral. Whether the lender was a bank or a securities dealer, these *broker loans* were the only method of buying securities on margin. In the equity markets, that is still the only way an investor (as opposed to a dealer) can finance a purchase. However, broker loans had two limiting factors in the government market.

First, banks and dealers were not the only ones with short-term cash to invest, but they were the only ones for whom broker loans were practical. Many other short-term investors, like municipalities or mutual funds, were willing to finance government securities but were prohibited from lending money, even if the loan were collateralized. Second, the specter of bankruptcy on the part of the borrower, and the possibility of having the collateral frozen by a bankruptcy referee, made collateralized lending less than perfect as a method of investing short-term cash.

REPURCHASE AND REVERSE REPURCHASE AGREEMENTS

A History of the Repurchase Market

The solution to this dilemma was the introduction of the *repurchase agreement (or repo)*, where the owner of a security sells it to a short-term investor and simultaneously agrees to buy it back at a later date. If title passes to the short-term investor during the financing period, logic tells us that we have solved the two problems with collateralized lending. Since the municipality or mutual fund is buying the security, not lending on it, we have gotten around his prohibition against lending. Since the short-term investor has title to the security during the financing period, he appears to be free to do whatever he wants with the security should the original owner file bankruptcy during the financing period.

Over a period of years, repos became a widely used substitute for broker loans, and began to look a lot like those loans. With the bankruptcy of Lombard, Wall, Inc., a small government dealer, in the early 1980s, the courts were handed the hot potato of dealing with repo collateral, and the judge chose to treat it as if it were collateral for a loan. This startling development threatened to bring the financing market to a standstill, until Congress enacted legislation to clarify the treatment of repo collateral, placing it outside the jurisdiction of the bankruptcy courts.

The checkered history of repos as a financing vehicle was not quite over, though. For many years, the Federal Reserve had observed the convention of calculating the value of a security, for financing purposes, without the *accrued interest*. Drysdale Government Securities, a subsidiary of an old-line municipal bond dealer, discovered that, if they sold securities with substantial accrued interest short, and offered to repo these securities for holders, they could generate substantial working capital from the accrued interest they had received but not paid out.

When coupon payment date came around, of course, the piper had to be paid. The Treasury paid one coupon, but there were two people expecting to receive it, the original owner and the party to whom Drysdale had sold short. Drysdale's solution was to buy back the issue it had shorted, before coupon payment date, and short another issue, perhaps in a larger amount to generate the accrued interest needed. Eventually, this "daisy chain" of short sales and repos came apart, when Drysdale was unable to make a coupon payment in November of 1983. Its entire portfolio of short sales, over $4 billion, was being handled by Chase Manhattan Bank as principal, and the Bank had to absorb a pretax loss of approximately $350 million. Shortly thereafter, the Federal Reserve decreed that all repos must include the accrued interest.

One other crisis shook the repo market in late 1984 and early 1985. In this case, a couple of unregulated dealers had built up a substantial following of unsophisticated thrift institutions and banks, with whom they did repo transactions. In many cases, they convinced the thrifts and banks that it was not worth the extra trouble to actually take delivery of the securities; the dealers would safeguard the securities at a bank instead. For every transaction, the dealer sent out a confirmation, showing that certain securities were being held at a major bank in the thrift's or bank's name. The thrift or bank then sent in the money.

Eventually, these two firms, ESM Government Securities and BBS Government Securities, failed, and the thrifts and banks discovered that the safekeeping bank had no record of holding securities in their name. Some of these institutions suffered losses up to $20 million, simply because they did not want to take delivery, and never verified with the safekeeping bank that their securities were there. In both cases, the managements of the dealer firms have been convicted of or pled guilty to fraud charges, but the thrifts and banks are still out the money. Shortly thereafter, banking and thrift regulators published strong warning that all repo transactions must involve delivery of the securities.

The Financing Market

The first thing to learn about the financing market is that *every transaction has two sides*. If one party is selling and repurchasing securities, the other party is buying and reselling securities. If one party is financing securities that he owns, the opposite party is putting money to work, or borrowing securities he has sold short. If one side is doing a *repurchase agreement (repo)*, the other side is doing a *reverse repurchase agreement (reverse repo or reverse)*.

That seems to be simplicity itself, but market participants often confuse the transaction that is actually occurring. Part of the reason for this confusion is that dealers dominate the market, and transactions tend to be known by the names dealers give them, even if the customer is doing exactly the opposite of what it appears. Perhaps the best example of this phenomenon is found on the regulatory reports required by the Federal Home Loan Bank Board, where there is a category called *Reverse Repos* in the liability section. That same category in an audited balance sheet is called "Securities sold under agreement to repurchase," meaning that it is really a repo, not a reverse. Dealers call these transactions reverses, though, so regulators have come to call them reverses.

With such confusion dominant, it is especially important to understand exactly how a repo/reverse transaction occurs. There are actually two transactions, entered into simultaneously, with different settlement dates. In a typical transaction, a dealer would sell $20 million three-year notes to a money market fund, for same-day settlement, and buy them back for next-day settlement. The price of both transactions is the same, as is the accrued interest added to the principal. When the transaction is closed out, the dealer pays the money market fund interest on the total money raised, at the agreed-upon rate for one day.

Thus we can see that there is a great deal of information to be exchanged in each of these transactions:

Rate. or the interest that the money market fund will charge on the money it has effectively lent to the dealer.

Term. or the period for which the repo/reverse will be in place—it can run from overnight to over a year.

Collateral. or the securities to be purchased and resold; if the securities are in short supply, that can affect the rate.

Delivery. or the method by which securities and money are exchanged.

Pricing. or the relationship between the market price of the security (with accrued interest) and its value in the repo/reverse; the difference between the market price and repo value is called the *haircut*.

Substitution. or the possibility for the dealer to substitute other securities for the ones originally sold.

Types of Repo/Reverse Transactions

There are many kinds of financing transactions, so let's start with the simplest, and most common, the *overnight*. Here, the securities will be repurchased the next business day after they are sold (which can be up to four actual days later in the case of a long weekend). The rate is established at the time the repo/reverse is put on, and there is no right of substitution. Overnight repos are most often used to finance a dealer's position, using very short-term funds.

Term repos are established for a specified period of time at the outset, with the understanding that the funds raised will not be available until the repo/reverse expires. The rate is usually set in the beginning, although it is possible to do a floating rate term repo. The original owner is not assumed to have the right of substitution unless that is agreed to at the outset. Term repos are most often used by financial institutions to raise money for a known period, with the funds being provided by other financial institutions or money market funds.

Open repos are established for an unknown period, by leaving the date of the repurchase blank. Either side can terminate the repo/reverse by notifying the other side before a specified hour each morning, say 10:30 A.M. Most often open repos involve specific securities needed by someone who is short and must make delivery. These *special* repos usually carry rates lower than general collateral, and are left open because the borrower of the security doesn't know how long he will be short. The rate on open repos is set daily, and, since the specific security is needed, there is usually no right of substitution. Open repos are most often used by dealers to obtain securities needed for delivery, with the other side being an investor profiting from the difference between rates, or another dealer financing his long position at advantageous rates.

Repo/reverse *to maturity* is the last type, in which the closing date of the repo/reverse coincides with the maturity of the security. This transaction is a substitute for an outright sale, so the rate must be established initially, and there is no right of substitution. In most cases, there will in fact be no closeout of the repo/reverse, since the maturity and the closeout will coincide. Why would someone want to do a repo to maturity as opposed to a sale? Part of the reason lies in our tax laws. For discount instruments, like Treasury bills, the income from the discount is recognized at maturity, while the interest expense of a repo is recognized over its life. If you own bills that mature next year, and repo them to maturity, you can transfer some of this year's income into next year, while keeping some part of the expense in this year.

THE LANGUAGE OF SECURITIES FINANCING

The government bond market has a language all its own, and nowhere is this more true than in the financing market. One reason for this is that almost all the financing business is done between 8:00 and 10:30 A.M., Eastern Time. Because so many bits of information must be communicated in such a short time, repo traders and customers have developed a shorthand method of communication that almost sounds like code. Let's listen to several trades being negotiated, and explore what is being done.

Financing a Customer's Collateral

Customer: "Where can I put out 100 million three-months for a week, no right of sub?"
Dealer: "6 and an eighth."
Customer: "I can do a steenth, I've seen it away, do you care?"
Dealer: "Okay, done at a steenth."

What actually happened here? First the customer asked the dealer where the customer could repo $100 million of three-month bills for one week, if he didn't have the right to substitute other securities during the week. The dealer responded that he would finance the customer's bills for a week at 6.125%, and the dealer countered, indicating that he would accept a rate of 6 and 1/16th, which he had been offered by another dealer. Given this additional piece of information, the dealer decided to finance the customer's bills at the 6 and 1/16th rate.

Putting a Customer's Money to Work

Customer: "What can you do on 200 million until the 15th, under five years, five pieces."

Dealer: "6%."

Customer: "I need the eighth."

Dealer: "I can do the eighth if I have right of sub."

Customer: "That's fine."

Dealer: "Okay, we'll use 80 million year bills, 50 million old twos, and 70 million threes."

In this case, the customer had $200 million in cash to put to work until the 15th of the month, and needed collateral with maturities of less than five years, and no more than five separate pieces to make up the lot. The dealer, looking at his inventory, decided that he was willing to finance that kind of collateral at 6%. The customer countered that he needed to get 6.125% on his money, and the dealer responded that he would pay that rate if he could substitute collateral. Why would he want to substitute collateral? Because he might sell one of the securities before the 15th, and he didn't want to fail. The customer had no problem with a collateral substitution, so he agreed, and the dealer told him that the collateral would be $80 million of the most recent year bill, $50 million of a two-year note auctioned before the most recent two year, and $70 million of the most recent three-year note.

Finding Securities for a Dealer's Delivery

Dealer: "We are looking for 160 million March 26 bills on open at 4%."

Customer: "I have them, but I will need a replacement."

Dealer: "How about the 9s of March at 6?"

Customer: "Fine."

Here the dealer needed $160 million bills maturing March 26 in order to make a delivery. Because this particular bill is hard to find, the dealer is willing to finance it at 4%, while general collateral is being financed at 6%, but he is not willing to guarantee that rate for a fixed term. The customer has the securities, but he is not willing to finance them without a replacement short-term investment. The dealer needs to finance some Treasury notes, identified as the 9% issue maturing in March, at 6%, giving the customer an interest arbitrage of 2% for as long as the transaction stays open. Not surprisingly, the customer agrees, earning himself $8,767 for each day that the trade stays open.

We can see from this last example that the daily profits and losses in trading money market instruments and financing collateral are not large, but the amounts traded are huge, and those small profits add up, day by day. It shouldn't surprise us, then, that the money market and financing areas often represent one of the largest profit centers a dealer has.

CHAPTER SEVEN

Derivative Instruments

The most important hallmark of the government bond market since the beginning of the 1970s has been *risk*. More than any other aspect of the market, the increase in the risk associated with trading government securities has overshadowed traders and investors. Two developments have been responsible for the tremendous increase in the risk inherent in the market: *higher volume* and *higher volatility*.

Of course, the higher volume of securities that trades every day is largely a result of the large Treasury deficits and the large holdings of securities in the hands of financial institutions. A quick look at Figure 1-1 (in Chapter 1), shows the explosive growth of the Treasury debt outstanding since World War II, and especially since 1970. In many cases, Treasury securities were purchased by investors, both domestic and foreign, who prized their liquidity as well as their safety. Investors who place a premium on liquidity often trade actively, and that has been the case in government securities, with the result that daily trading volume regularly exceeds $100 billion.

Large increases in trading volume serve to increase risk by themselves, but in this case, they were combined with a substantial increase in price volatility. Generally, price volatility in debt securities is a function of *monetary policy*, when the central bankers alter the availability or price of credit. As the strains of the Vietnam War, and the subsequent quadrupling of the price of crude oil, shook the American economy, the Federal Reserve took the lead in trying to control inflation.

High interest rate volatility was an inevitable result, so that between 1965 and 1985 the Treasury had issued securities at yields ranging from 6.125% to over 16%. Such fluctuation in market rates of interest had a profound effect on the prices of issues already outstanding, causing them to fluctuate as much as two points in a day. Coupled with the large positions Primary Dealers were carrying, these price fluctuations threatened the very survival of some dealers. In fact, beginning about 1980, many dealers took steps to increase their capital bases, by selling their firms to large financial institutions or by seeking capital infusions from foreign investors.

While increased capital was an essential ingredient for keeping the liquidity of the market high, an equally important development was *derivative instruments*. A derivative instrument is any instrument whose price is derived from another instrument or instruments. Because the prices of derivative instruments are dependent on the price of another issue, many people feel that they are in some way inferior, but nothing could be further from the truth. In fact, derivative instruments have made a major contribution to the liquidity of the financial markets. The most common derivative instruments are futures, options, and indices.

FINANCIAL FUTURES

The most widely used derivative instrument is the *financial futures contract*. Actually, futures, which came into wide use in 1975, were predated by *financial forwards*, particularly in the GNMA markets.

A *forward contract* is simply a transaction in some instrument for settlement at some agreed-upon date in the future. We have already seen that mortgage bankers have been selling mortgages, and passthrough securities, for delivery many months in the future, as they processed the loans through their pipeline. As long as the mortgage market was small and everyone knew all the players, forward transactions were sufficient. Actually, a large number of passthrough transactions are still done for settlement up to four months in the future.

The widespread popularity of the passthrough brought with it some credit problems, however, making it impossible to include everyone in the forward market. In 1970, approximately two years after the GNMA

Derivative Instruments

passthrough was invented, the Chicago Board of Trade (CBT) introduced a *futures contract* on GNMA passthroughs. After the GNMA futures contract proved that there was a market for exchange-traded derivatives in the debt markets, the CBT introduced the T-bond futures contract in 1970. It proved to be so popular that it remains the highest trading exchange instrument (in terms of underlying dollar volume) to this day.

Futures Versus Forwards

It may appear that the most important difference between futures and forwards is that the former are exchange traded and the latter are not, but that is not the most important difference. It is true that the discipline of the exchange contract, with its homogeneous contract specifications, made many participants more comfortable with futures than they had been with forwards. It is true that the open outcry market gave many institutions some comfort that they were getting the best available prices. It is even true that the availability of exchange prices on virtually all quote machines made investors and traders feel more comfortable with their ability to keep on top of these instruments. But these reasons were not compelling.

What turned the tide for listed derivatives was the presence of the *exchange clearing corporation*. In markets which are exclusively institutional, contraparties can assess each other's creditworthiness, and do business directly on that basis. But we have already seen that financial institutions didn't have enough capital to support the debt markets. When individuals and small businesses are expected to enter the fray, a system needs to be set up to handle a much larger universe of credit decisions.

The clearing corporation does that by stepping between the buyer and seller of listed futures, and becoming the contraparty to every trade. Goldman Sachs may sell some T-bonds futures contracts on the CBT, for a midwestern bank, to Dean Witter, acting for California insurance company, but the bank and the insurance company will deal only with Goldman and Dean Witter, who in turn will deal only with the CBT Clearing Corporation. By enforcing strict credit and margin rules, the clearing corporation makes sure that everyone pays his way every day, which means that the clearing corporation can deal with a wide variety of customers.

Inside a Futures Pit

The second big difference between futures and forwards has to do with how they are traded. Forwards are traded over the counter, in an environment very much like the one prevailing for government bonds. Dealers quote markets to customers, who buy or sell for forward delivery, just like they buy or sell government bonds for immediate delivery.

A futures exchange is an entirely different arrangement. By definition, an exchange is a *physical location* at which all parties who want to buy or sell a specific instrument congregate, in order to be sure of getting the best bid or offer. Since all exchanges are indoors (although the American Stock Exchange began outdoors, and was called the Curb Exchange), there is limited space for buyers and sellers, so a limited number of brokers execute orders for the public.

Originally, the only people who showed up at the NYSE post where a certain instrument was traded were the brokers for the buyers and sellers, but it eventually became apparent that someone was needed to handle limit orders (those specifying a minimum price on sales and a maximum price on buys) and maintain order as prices rose and fell. On stock exchanges this function is handled by a specialist, a broker who remains at one post and specializes in one or more stocks. His job is to watch over the public order book, where limit orders are kept, and to use his own capital to maintain an orderly market, or one where prices change in an orderly way.

Futures exchanges take an entirely different approach to providing liquidity. Instead of a post, futures exchanges have a *pit*, or a sunken area of the floor, in which everyone who wants to trade a certain futures contract stands. Within the pit are two types of exchange members. *Commission brokers* execute orders for customers, and *locals* trade for their own account. Although some trades are done between one commission broker and another, and thus between one customer and another, and commission brokers sometimes trade for their own account, the popular conception is one of commission brokers trading with locals most of the time.

Since an active pit is large, often twenty to thirty feet across, and filled with people, there is no one place for a specialist to stand, so there is no specialist and thus no public order book. Limit orders are held by commission brokers, in their *deck*, and executed if the contract reaches their price and if the commission broker is alert. There is no ticker tape like there is on a stock exchange, since contracts may be trading in several places in the pit at one time. Bids and offers are made by shouting and hand signals, which makes a futures pit look a little like a lunatic asylum.

Inside the asylum, though, business gets done. Hundreds of contracts, representing millions of dollars of securities, are traded by means of shouts and hand signals. After a trade is completed, the commission broker writes it up on a ticket, and hands the ticket to a *runner* standing just outside the pit, who carries it to a nearby phone booth, where a *clerk* reports it to the customer. In many cases, the clerk will have already received a preliminary report of the trade by hand signals from the broker or runner.

The local on the other side of the trade makes a note of it on a pad he uses to keep track of his positions, and continues trading. At the end of the day, he reports all his trades to his *clearing agent*, usually one of the bigger member firms, and settles his accounts with them before the market opens the following day. Since there is no specialist's post, there is no ticker tape reporting each trade. Instead, there are clerks sitting above the pit, called *watchers*, who record price changes as they occur, but not individual trades. Instead of obtaining markets from the specialist, the runners keep an eye on the activity in the pit, and relay the current bid and offer to the clerks by hand signals.

Futures Contract Specifications

The contracts being traded have very specific terms, in order to make them interchangeable. In each case, the contract requires the seller to deliver to the buyer a specific amount of the underlying instrument at a specified time, and the buyer to pay on delivery. The same delivery program is used whether the underlying instrument is eggs, wheat, or bonds, but the specific terms, called *contract specifications*, are a function of the underlying instrument. Contract specs are pretty simple with agricultural commodities, but they become more complicated with government bonds.

The most widely traded futures contract is the *Treasury bond contract* on the Chicago Board of Trade (CBT), which, in early 1987, was trading approximately 300,000 contracts, valued at $100,000 apiece, every day. That $30 billion in volume represents many times the trading volume of Treasury bonds, but the T-bond contract serves as a derivative instrument for every taxable long-term debt instrument in every market in the world.

The T-bond contract calls for delivery of Treasury securities when it expires. In particular, a seller of the T-bond contract can deliver any Treasury bond with at least twenty years to maturity in satisfaction of his futures obligation. That still leaves him a tremendous choice of bonds to deliver; in March 1987 there were 21 bond issues which were deliverable into the T-bond contract. How could one contract accommodate all those deliverable securities?

The CBT solved that problem by making the underlying instrument for the futures contract an imaginary 8% bond with exactly twenty years left to maturity when the contract expires. The contract specifications call for each futures contract to be for $100,000 of that imaginary bond. Other bond issues can also be delivered, in varying amounts depending on their coupons and terms to maturity. The CBT has made up *conversion factors* for every coupon and every maturity imaginable.

Let's look at some conversion factors, selected to conform to some outstanding issues, on 4/1/87.

Coupon	Term	Maturity	Factor
11.25%	27y0m	2/15/2015	1.3574
10.00%	18y3m	5/15/2005	1.1900
9.25%	29y0m	2/15/2016	1.1402
7.50%	29y9m	11/15/2016	0.9434

In the contract specifications, the CBT says that the amount of securities that can be delivered is $100,000 divided by the conversion factors. This means that, for each contract, a seller could deliver $73,670.25 of the 11.25% bond due 2/15/2015; $84,033.61 of the 10% bond of 5/15/2010 (callable 5/15/2005); $87,703.91 of the 9.25% bond of 2/15/2016; and $105,999.58 of the 7.5% bond of 11/15/2016.

Determining Futures Prices

That may be interesting, but it isn't very helpful. What is helpful is that the price of the futures contract multiplied by the conversion factor gives the *delivery price* of each issue. Figure 7-1 shows various prices of the T-bond futures contract for 3/31/87. First, it shows the opening price, then the high, the low, and the price at which the contract closed,

Figure 7-1
Futures prices.

FUTURES PRICES

Tuesday, March 31, 1987
Open Interest Reflects Previous Trading Day.

	Open	High	Low	Settle	Change	Lifetime High	Lifetime Low	Open Interest
Dec	111.75	111.75	107.70	107.70	– 4.30	205.25	107.70	2,028
Mr88	114.00	114.00	110.00	110.00	– 4.00	178.00	110.00	278

Est vol 5,244; vol Mon 1,901; open int 18,336, +205.
COTTON (CTN) – 50,000 lbs.; cents per lb.

May	57.11	57.75	56.75	57.05	– .40	60.15	31.56	9,058
July	55.80	56.50	55.60	55.95	– .35	59.45	32.32	6,633
Oct	55.50	55.85	55.20	55.30	– .60	58.80	33.50	1,882
Dec	55.00	55.61	54.70	54.80	– .61	58.60	34.40	5,263
Mr88	56.50	56.50	56.25	55.70	– .65	58.69	47.50	669

Est vol 3,675; vol Mon 4,993; open int 23,633, +321.
ORANGE JUICE (CTN) – 15,000 lbs.; cents per lb.

May	129.25	129.65	128.65	128.90	– 1.00	138.50	84.50	3,751
July	128.75	129.30	128.40	128.85	– .70	137.40	84.75	2,752
Sept	127.00	127.00	125.50	126.15	– 1.70	135.00	107.50	1,209
Nov	125.40	125.40	124.25	124.35	– 1.65	135.50	108.00	1,089
Ja88	124.00	124.50	124.00	124.05	– 1.85	135.90	115.00	292
Mar	....	....	....	123.40	– 1.85	135.00	121.00	409

Est vol 1,200; vol Mon 3,306; open int 9,561, –289.
SUGAR–WORLD (CSCE) – 112,000 lbs.; cents per lb.

May	6.88	6.91	6.69	6.72	– .18	9.82	6.00	37,084
July	7.05	7.07	6.86	6.87	– .20	9.92	6.17	18,268
Sept	7.15	7.15	6.98	6.98	– .19	8.70	6.24	128
Oct	7.20	7.23	7.05	7.07	– .17	9.60	6.41	24,110
Mr88	7.57	7.60	7.43	7.45	– .17	8.95	7.04	11,233
July	....	....	....	7.80	– .07	8.88	8.51	579

Est vol 13,270; vol Mon 13,632; open int 91,513, –1,404.
SUGAR–DOMESTIC (CSCE) – 112,000 lbs.; cents per lb.

May	21.70	21.70	21.61	21.61	– .10	21.86	20.60	479
July	21.86	21.86	21.85	21.85	– .02	21.94	20.65	2,985
Sept	21.85	21.85	21.85	21.85	– .04	21.94	20.93	1,262
Nov	21.62	21.62	21.60	21.60	– .04	21.67	20.26	1,678
Mar	....	....	....	21.57	+ .01	21.65	21.51	122

Est vol 200; vol Mon 77; open int 6,529, –234.

– METALS & PETROLEUM –

COPPER (CMX) – 25,000 lbs.; cents per lb.

Apr	....	....	....	62.25	– 1.60	63.85	63.55	0
May	63.95	64.15	62.40	62.45	– 1.60	70.00	58.20	41,880
July	63.30	63.60	61.80	62.00	– 1.40	70.00	58.20	25,351
Sept	63.40	63.70	62.00	62.15	– 1.30	70.35	59.40	6,450
Dec	63.60	63.90	63.20	62.35	– 1.25	69.50	60.05	4,254
Mr88	64.25	64.40	63.50	62.85	– 1.30	65.00	60.70	856
May	64.45	64.50	64.45	63.25	– 1.30	65.65	60.90	471
July	....	....	....	63.65	– 1.30	65.80	62.30	129

Est vol 10,000; vol Mon 12,226; open int 79,427, –1,664.
GOLD (CMX) – 100 troy oz.; $ per troy oz.

Apr	421.00	422.50	417.50	418.00	– 3.10	456.00	350.50	16,209
June	426.00	427.20	422.30	422.70	– 3.20	456.00	350.50	68,107
Aug	430.70	430.00	427.00	427.30	– 3.30	460.00	356.00	19,767
Oct	436.00	436.00	431.50	431.70	– 3.40	465.00	361.00	12,727
Dec	440.50	441.50	436.00	436.10	– 3.40	470.00	365.00	17,129
Fb88	441.50	445.80	441.50	440.70	– 3.40	473.00	371.50	9,992
Apr	451.50	451.50	446.00	445.30	– 3.40	479.00	378.00	7,251
June	453.00	453.00	453.00	449.80	– 3.40	484.00	399.00	7,021
Aug	....	....	454.60	– 3.40	483.00	425.00	3,639
Oct	....	....	459.50	– 3.40	465.50	429.00	3,864
Dec	465.50	465.50	464.30	464.30	– 3.40	470.50	430.00	1,527

Est vol 30,000; vol Mon 56,508; open int 167,238, +2,830.
PLATINUM (NYM) – 50 troy oz.; $ per troy oz.

Apr	565.00	565.50	551.00	555.80	– 7.80	689.40	361.00	3,334
July	571.00	571.00	557.50	562.00	– 7.30	695.00	417.00	13,518
Oct	575.00	575.50	562.00	566.10	– 7.30	696.00	464.00	2,673
Jn88	575.00	575.50	568.00	570.40	– 7.50	617.40	474.00	215
Apr	585.00	585.00	580.00	574.80	– 7.60	590.00	498.00	293

Est vol 8,192; vol Mon 9,297; open int 20,045, –1,083.
PALLADIUM (NYM) 100 troy oz.; $ per troy oz.

Apr	....	....	128.90	– .65	122.00	122.00	3
June	130.00	130.00	128.00	128.90	– .65	153.00	112.50	4,189
Sept	129.00	129.50	127.50	128.50	– .65	151.50	114.00	1,551

	Open	High	Low	Settle	Change	Lifetime High	Lifetime Low	Open Interest
Sept	148.00	148.00	148.00	150.00	....	148.00	148.00	100

Actual Tues; vol 2,732; open int 8,791, –188.
GASOLINE, Unleaded (NYM) 42,000 gal.; $ per gal.

Apr	.5240	.5315	.5220	.5267	+ .0047	.5405	.3450	4,244
May	.5370	.5425	.5350	.5380	+ .0027	.5500	.3520	19,228
June	.5435	.5470	.5415	.5417	+ .0008	.5590	.4050	14,556
July	.5415	.5445	.5400	.5401	+ .0008	.5445	.4400	4,591
Aug	.5340	.5360	.5330	.5325	– .0008	.5380	.4920	1,120
Sept	.5255	.5265	.5220	.5245	– .0015	.5290	.4050	762
Oct	.5180	.5180	.5170	.5170	– .0020	.5180	.4725	540
Nov	.5100	.5100	.5090	.5095	– .0020	.5100	.4800	356
Dec	.5025	.5025	.5020	.5025	– .0010	.5025	.4750	579
Ja88	....	....	....	.4945	– .0010	.4858	.4826	179

Est vol 9,374; vol Mon 8,504; open int 46,146, +245.

– WOOD –

LUMBER (CME) – 130,000 bd. ft.; $ per 1,000 bd. ft.

May	192.50	194.50	191.30	192.40	+ .10	203.60	155.50	3,574
July	181.40	182.50	180.00	181.40	+ .60	190.30	155.10	1,682
Sept	174.50	175.70	173.60	175.20	+ 1.00	184.00	159.50	868
Nov	167.50	168.20	166.50	167.60	+ .30	175.00	156.70	339
Jan	166.00	167.50	165.00	167.50	+ 1.50	173.00	156.00	146

Est vol 1,463; vol Mon 1,968; open int 6,709, –140.

– FINANCIAL –

BRITISH POUND (IMM) – 25,000 pounds; $ per pound

June	1.5930	1.6000	1.5900	1.5955	....	1.6105	1.3600	26,135
Sept	1.5840	1.5890	1.5790	1.5845	– .0005	1.6020	1.3420	1,265
Dec	1.5755	1.5770	1.5705	1.5750	– .0005	1.5930	1.3675	268

Est vol 4,746; vol Mon 7,004; open int 37,677, +212.
CANADIAN DOLLAR (IMM) – 100,000 dlrs.; $ per Can $

June	.7611	.7664	.7610	.7656	+ .0020	.7665	.6995	21,133
Sept	.7610	.7653	.7610	.7651	+ .0021	.7659	.6950	4,486
Dec	.7605	.7652	.7600	.7646	+ .0023	.7658	.6900	1,204
Mar	....	....	.7640	+ .0024	.7650	.7052	216

Est vol 7,538; vol Mon 8,873; open int 27,079, –2,231.
JAPANESE YEN (IMM) 12.5 million yen; $ per yen (.00)

| June | .6883 | .6916 | .6855 | .6893 | + .0002 | .6893 | .6121 | 43,524 |
| Sept | .6925 | .6958 | .6900 | .6936 | + .0002 | .6936 | .6160 | 372 |

Est vol 19,002; vol Mon 19,482; open int 43,940, –480.
SWISS FRANC (IMM) – 125,000 francs-$ per franc

| June | .6686 | .6702 | .6659 | .6677 | – .0043 | .6800 | .5870 | 28,200 |
| Sept | .6724 | .6743 | .6702 | .6719 | – .0044 | .6830 | .5960 | 767 |

Est vol 18,729; vol Mon 18,333; open int 28,992, +431.
W. GERMAN MARK (IMM) – 125,000 marks; $ per mark

| June | .5573 | .5594 | .5554 | .5572 | – .0028 | .5692 | .4850 | 41,871 |
| Sept | .5609 | .5625 | .5591 | .5607 | – .0029 | .5725 | .4868 | 1,041 |

Est vol 20,158; vol Mon 27,914; open int 42,973, +1,107.
EURODOLLAR (LIFFE) – $1 million; pts of 100%

June	93.26	93.33	93.25	93.31	+ .03	94.15	90.85	13,884
Sept	93.27	93.33	93.25	93.31	+ .03	94.03	91.65	5,488
Dec	93.21	93.30	93.21	93.28	+ .03	93.88	91.96	2,803
Mr88	93.14	93.18	93.13	93.18	– .03	93.67	92.08	1,408
June	92.97	92.99	92.97	93.01	+ .01	93.39	91.99	766
Sept	92.78	92.78	92.78	92.80	....	93.13	92.37	333
Dec	....	....	....	92.58	– .01	92.90	92.84	107

Est vol 8,459; vol Mon 8,415; open int 24,789, +344.
STERLING (LIFFE) – £500,000; pts of 100%

| June | 90.60 | 90.72 | 90.50 | 90.72 | + .07 | 91.45 | 88.97 | 11,547 |
| Sept | 90.83 | 90.96 | 90.79 | 90.91 | + .07 | 91.31 | 89.02 | 7,130 |

TREASURY BONDS (CBT) – $100,000; pts. 32nds of 100%

June	98-04	98-16	97-13	98-15	+ 23	8.157	– .074	201,367
Sept	97-04	97-15	96-12	97-14	+ 22	8.264	– .073	14,810
Dec	96-05	96-15	95-14	96-14	+ 21	8.370	– .070	4,996
Mr88	95-11	95-16	94-16	95-16	+ 21	8.471	– .071	2,780
June	94-15	94-19	93-20	94-19	+ 20	8.570	– .069	3,362
Sept	93-08	93-24	92-25	93-24	+ 20	8.663	– .070	1,744
Dec	92-22	92-30	92-22	92-30	+ 20	8.754	– .071	529

Est vol 300,000; vol Mon 318,413; open int 229,623, –4,983

or settled, for the day. The change from the previous day's settlement is shown, as well as the yield to maturity for the imaginary bond at that price, and the change in the yield to maturity from the previous day. Finally, the open interest, or number of contracts remaining open as of 3/31/87, is shown. All this information is shown for contracts expiring from June 1987 to December 1988.

Let's concentrate on the June 1987 contract, often called the *front month*. The contract closed at 98-15, or 98.46875 (remember that prices are given in 32ds). That price, multiplied by the conversion factor, gives the delivery price of the above issues. Let's compare delivery prices to actual prices for 3/31/87.

Issue		Factor	Futures Price	Delivery Price	Actual Price
11.25%	2/15/15	1.3574	98-15	133-22	137-27
10.00%	5/15/10-05	1.1900	98-15	117-06	119-10
9.25%	2/15/16	1.1402	98-15	112-16	115-12
7.50%	11/15/16	0.9434	98-15	93-04	96-16

The first thing we see is that the conversion process is fairly consistent across the range of issues, so that delivery prices have about the same relationship to each other as actual prices do. It is not an exact fit however. The 11.25% delivery price is higher than the actual by almost 4 points, while the 10% delivery price is high only by a little less than 2 points. If these were the only issues deliverable, we would say that the 10% issue was the *cheapest to deliver* into the contract, and the contract price would track the price of this issue more closely than any other.

However, the delivery prices are all higher than the actual prices. Why is that? Because we can purchase these bonds to yield about 7.75%, and finance them at about 6.25%. If these delivery price were the same as the actual price, we would buy bonds, sell futures contracts, finance the bonds and wait for delivery date. That trade, known as the *cash and carry trade*, has been around as long as financial futures. Consequently, futures contracts will not trade where delivery prices equal actual prices as long as financing costs are below the yield on bonds. The difference between delivery and actual prices is called the *basis*, and some bond traders sit all day over their computers, waiting for the basis to get out of line.

Comparing Delivery Months

If we look at the rest of the prices in Figure 7-1, we can see that they are not the same for every delivery month. Instead, they fall as the delivery moves into the future. This phenomenon is also a result of the difference between the yield on the securities and the cost of financing, known as the *positive carry*. But, if our calculations are right, the price differences should be an exact reflection of positive carry.

In fact, the difference appears to be much larger than called for. If the positive carry is approximately 1.50%, or 150 basis points per year, then it should be .375%, or 37.5 basis points, per quarter. Thus, the futures price should drop by about 3/8 of a point, or 12/32ds, per quarter, to correct for positive carry. Where the June contract settled at 98-15, the September contract settled at 97-14, over a point lower. That would equate to a positive carry of over 4%, or 400 basis points. Given a yield on the security of 7.75%, the futures market is telling us that the cost of financing is approximately 3.75%. Can this be true?

The explanation lies in the fact that some securities are in tight supply from time to time. If the cheapest-to-deliver bond is in such tight supply that it can be financed at about 3.75%, then the futures market would be right. In late March 1987 that was in fact the case. Many outstanding bond issues had been bought up by Wall Street firms in large numbers, and *stripped* into a string of 0% coupon issues, representing the coupon payments and the final maturity. These stripping operations had reduced the supply of cheapest-to-deliver issues to the point where they were so rare that dealers would finance them at very low rates, in order to have bonds to deliver against short sales.

One reaction to this turn of events would be to sell short a deliverable bond issue which was not in tight supply and buy futures contracts against the short. Being short a bond means paying out the coupon rate, which we have determined to be about 7.75%. Asuming that we can borrow the bonds at approximately 6.25%, we will have a *cost of shorting* of about 150 basis points or about 12/32ds for the quarter. If the basis on the futures contract is about 1 point per quarter, we should be able to make about 20/32ds for the quarter, or about $6,250 per million. The availability of this kind of arbitrage has made the futures markets so liquid that they often provide much of the liquidity needed to support the long bond markets.

OPTIONS ON SECURITIES AND FUTURES

Although futures and *options* are usually mentioned in the same breath, they are anything but the same instrument. The mathematics of futures is relatively simple when compared to the mathematics of options, and there are many more strategies available to options users than there are to futures users. In order to make use of any of these strategies, though, we must first understand the nature of options themselves.

Understanding Options

An option is the right to initiate a transaction, at a specified price, for a specified period of time. The right to purchase something is a *call*, and the right to sell something is a *put*. The specified price is called the *strike price* and the point at which the option becomes worthless is called the *expiration date*. The instrument to be bought or sold is called the *underlying instrument*. The right to initiate the transaction is worth something, and the price that it is worth is called the *premium*.

When a futures contract expires, one party must deliver something, and the other must pay for it. In the case of an option, the owner has the right to buy (or sell) while the seller, or *writer*, of the option has no rights. However, when an option expires the owner no longer has any rights, which is why options are called *wasting assets*. Before the option expires, it has a value, depending on several things.

Option Valuation

An option premium is made up of two parts. One part is the value of being able to initiate the trade immediately, and it is called *intrinsic value*. Intrinsic value can be positive, in which case the option is *in-the-money*; negative, in which case the option is *out-of-the-money*; or exactly zero, in which case the option is *at-the-money*. Thus the most important determinant of option values is the relationship between the strike price and the market price of the underlying instrument, or the instrinsic value.

The second part of an option's value is the value of being able to postpone the decision to buy or sell; this part is called *time value*. Time

Derivative Instruments

value is always positive, which explains why options never have negative premiums. Intrinsic value and time value combine to give us an option's premium. Just as with futures, it is possible to determine the *theoretical value* of an option, or the premium at which a trader would be indifferent between owning the option and owning the corresponding position in the underlying instrument.

In calculating the theoretical value of an option one needs to know the intrinsic value, the term to expiration, the positive (or negative) carry on the underlying instrument, and the *price volatility* of the underlying. You will notice that we do not need to project price direction, because theoretical valuation models assume that we do not know the future path of prices; in fact they assume that there is an equal chance that prices will go down or up in the future.

Deltas or Hedge Ratios

Since options are wasting assets, while the underlying instruments are not, the price performance of options is different from the performance of the underlying. Generally, an option moves a smaller amount than the underlying, which makes sense, since the risk is also less. In fact, the same formula that gives us a theoretical value for an option gives the relationship between the underlying's volatility and the option's.

This relationship is called the *delta*, or *hedge ratio*, and is one of the most important aspects of option strategies. Since many of these strategies involve matching option and underlying positions, understanding how hedge ratios work is the key to using options successfully. Therefore, let's look at some basic rules about option price volatility.

1. *Deltas always fall between 1 and 0.* Options that are deep in the money (have high intrinsic values and high premiums) have high deltas. These options match the underlying in price movement almost exactly. Options that are deep out of the money (have large negative intrinsic values and low premiums) have low deltas. These options barely move when the underlying moves. Options at the money have deltas around 0.5, so they are about half as volatile as the underlying.
2. *Deltas change as the intrinsic value changes.* As the underlying's price moves, the option's volatility moves. For those who use

options to hedge underlyings, this property is especially important. The basic rule is that, as the intrinsic value increases, the delta increases. As the option goes more into the money it moves faster, and, as it goes further out of the money it moves slower. For traders and investors who are trying to maintain a neutral option position, this factor necessitates constant monitoring of the position.

3. *Deltas change as time passes.* Here the rule is a little more complicated. If an option is in the money, its delta *increases* as time passes. If an option is out of the money, its delta *decreases* as time passes. Imagine two calls, one a point out of the money, and one a point in the money. With a year to expiration, their deltas are both about 0.5. As time passes, and the options get closer to expiration, the call in the money becomes more likely to finish in the money, while the call out of the money becomes more likely to finish there. Thus the in-the-money call will track the underlying more closely as time passes, until, right before expiration, its delta is almost 1. Meanwhile, the out-of-the-money call will track the underlying less, as its chances of moving into the money recede.

Options Strategies

Because options are so versatile, they can be combined in many ways, and can result in a myriad of *positions* and *strategies*. Entire books have been devoted to options characteristics and strategies, but we will only take a general look at them here.

Option positions, and the resulting strategies, are divided into four general groups. *Naked positions* are option positions by themselves. *Married positions* are one option position combined with one position in the underlying instrument. *Combinations* are two or more option positions, with no position in the underlying. *Arbitrages* are two option positions and one position in the underlying, which complete a closed circle.

Naked Positions

Long call. This is the risk-limited equivalent of long the underlying. The profit potential is unlimited, while you can lose only the premium, but the long-call holder doesn't fare well if prices stay where they are.

Long put. This is the risk-limited equivalent of short the underlying.

Derivative Instruments

The risk parameters are the same as with the long call, but profits come if the underlying's price falls instead of rises.

Short call. This position has unlimited risk if prices rise, but the premium income accrues to the writer if prices remain the same or fall.

Short put. This position has unlimited risk if prices fall, but the premium income accrues to the writer if prices remain the same or rise.

Married Positions

Covered call. This is long the underlying and short the call. It retains most of the risk involved in falling prices, but generates additional income if prices remain the same. In the case of rising prices, the call writer can expect his securities to be called away. It is the equivalent of a naked put write.

Married put. This is long the underlying and long a put. Here the security holder has bought insurance against significant price decline and paid an option premium for it. His profit potential is unlimited. It is the equivalent of a naked call purchase.

Money market call. This is a cash position and a long call position. The holder can profit from a fall in the price of the underlying, while the call protects him from a sharp rise in prices. If prices remain unchanged, he has wasted his premium. It is the equivalent of a naked put purchase.

Cash secured put write. This is a cash position and a short position in a put. The put premium, added to the earnings on the cash portfolio, are compensation for assuming the risk of falling prices in the underlying. It is the equivalent of a naked call write.

Combinations

Spreads. The purchase of one option and the sale of the same option with a different strike price or expiration. *Bull and bear spreads* use options with the same expiration and different strikes and are designed to show limited profits in one market direction and limited losses in the other. *Calendar spreads* use options with the same strikes but different expirations and are designed to show limited profits from market movement, or from stability, with limited loss potential. The key to spreads is that, if you buy a call (or put), you sell another call (or put).

Straddles and strangles. The purchase or sale of a put and call together. These positions have higher premiums, higher risk, and higher profit potential. When the strike and expiration of the put and call are identical, it is a *straddle*; when they are different, it is a *strangle*. If you sell one of these, you make both premiums when the underlying stays within a range, but you lose on either extreme. If you buy one, you can make money on either end, but it costs you two premiums to do it.

Synthetics. The purchase of a put and sale of a call, which is a *synthetic short position* in the underlying, or the sale of a put and the purchase of a call, which is a *synthetic long position* in the underlying. Based on the two premiums involved, a synthetic position may be more attractive than an actual position.

Arbitrages

An arbitrage is the combination of a synthetic position in options with the opposite position in the underlying. Long a put, short a call, and long the underlying is called a *forward conversion*. Long a call, short a put, and short the underlying is called a *reverse conversion*. Both are equivalent to a cash position, as long as the strike prices and expirations are the same. Option traders use forward and reverse conversions all the time to squeeze small profits out of the market.

OPTIONS MARKETS

Originally, options were strictly an *over-the-counter* market, with lists of stock option bids and offers on the back page of the *Wall Street Journal*. In 1973, all that changed with the formation of the *Chicago Board Options Exchange,* where options were listed and traded on an exchange for the first time. That was so successful that in 1981 the SEC approved listed options on debt securities. Within a year the CFTC had approved options on financial futures. Finally, in the mid-1980s, things came full circle, as options on government and agency securities began trading in volume over the counter.

CBOE Options Market

The first markets, however, were the listed options markets, and the first one approved was the Chicago Board Options Exchange's

Derivative Instruments

(CBOE's) market in options on Treasury securities. The CBOE trades options on Treasury bonds and notes. At about the same time that the CBOE got its approval from the SEC, the American Stock Exchange (AMEX) got approval to trade options on Treasury bills. These markets, although they were the first to get approval, have been the least successful, in terms of trading volume. Part of the reason is that the Treasury markets are almost entirely *institutional*, while both the CBOE and the AMEX are traditionally markets for the *individual investor*.

However, both markets continue to list options on Treasury securities. Figure 7-2 shows the market in options on the Treasury 8.75% bond due 5/15/2017, at about 3:53 P.M. on May 27, 1987, as displayed on Telerate. The first line shows the description of the underlying security, and the ticker symbol for the 8.75% bond (YBN). Below that are the markets for several puts and calls. At this point the bond was trading around 100.

The left column shows the month of expiration for the option and the next column shows the option's strike price. Then there follows a section for calls, beginning with the symbol. On the first line, the symbol for the June 96 call is NFV; N for the 8.75% bond, F for the June call, and V for the 96 strike price. The next column shows the TIME of the last trade, at 2:46 P.M., followed by the BID and ASK prices. Then we have the June 96 puts, symbol NRV; N for the same bond issue, R for the June puts, and V for the 96 strike price. The same information is listed for the June 96 puts—in fact for all the puts and calls.

If the bond is trading at 100, the 96 calls must be 4 points in the money, so the premium of 4–12 to 4–18 is made up of 4 points intrinsic value and about ⅜ point time value. The 96 puts are 4 points out of the money, so the premium of 0–11 to 0–17 is all time value. The 100 puts and calls are at the money, so we can learn something from looking at their premiums. The June 100 options have a little less than a month to go, and both the put and call have premiums around 1.625 points.

Let's look now at the September 100 puts and calls. Since these options have almost four months to run, we might expect their premiums to be four times as large, but they aren't. They are about twice as high, at about 2.875 points for the call and about 3.625 points for the put. We have discovered an important lesson about options: *the premiums of at the money options* increase by the *square root* of the increase in the term to maturity. If the term quadruples, the premium approximately doubles. The further we get into or out of the money, the less this is true.

But the September put and call premiums are not equal, like June's

Figure 7-2
Telerate screen showing the market in options on the Treasury 8.75% bond due 5/15/2017, at about 3:53 P.M. on May 27, 1987.

```
TELERATE SYSTEMS
05/27       15:53 EDT E 30 YR T-BOND $100,000 8.75% 5/15/2017    (YBN)     15013
            CALL TIME  BID   ASK   LAST    PUT  TIME  BID   ASK
 JUN   96   NFV  14:46 4-12  4-18          NRV  14:47 0-11  0-17
 JUN   98   NFX  14:46 2-26  3-00          NRX  14:47 0-25  0-31
 JUN  100   NFA  14:46 1-17  1-23          NRA  14:47 1-16  1-22
 JUN  102   NFC  14:46 0-21  0-27          NRC  14:47 2-20  2-26
 JUN  104   NFE  14:46 0-10  0-16          NRE  14:48 4-05  4-11
 SEP   96   NIV  14:46 5-03  5-13          NUV  14:48 1-26  2-04
 SEP   98   NIX  14:46 3-25  4-03          NUX  14:48 2-19  2-29
 SEP  100   NIA  14:47 2-22  3-00          NUA  14:48 3-16  3-26
 SEP  102   NIC  14:47 1-27  2-05          NUC  09:12 4-15  4-25
 SEP  104   NIE  14:47 1-07  1-15          NUE  14:49 5-27  6-05
```

Derivative Instruments

are. How come? Because short-term interest rates are lower than 8.75%, so we can purchase bonds and finance them at a profit. As long as that is true, we would be more willing to buy bonds and buy puts than sell bonds short and buy calls. In fact, the difference between the premiums should equal the positive carry on the bond, times the fraction of a year left to option expiration. The premium difference of ¾ point for four months equals 2.75% per year, about the positive carry on the bond at that time.

CBT Options Market

At about the same time that the SEC-approved options on bonds began to trade, CFTC-approved options on bond futures began to trade on the Chicago Board of Trade (CBT). Almost from the beginning, this option contract was more successful, largely because the CBT was used to providing a hedging market for institutions and Wall Street traders, who shifted gradually to options for some of their needs. Although futures options were more successful, they had some drawbacks. For example, married strategies were possible in these options only in conjunction with futures, not in conjunction with securities themselves. For another, the basis, or noncorrelation, risk of futures carried over into the futures options.

Nevertheless, CBT futures options became a great success. Figure 7-3 shows the market for futures options at about 11:00 A.M. on May 26, 1987, when the September futures contract was trading at approximately 90.16. The left column shows the strike price and whether the option is a put or call. The first item, C92, is the 92 call on the September futures contract. One oddity about the CBT option is that there is only *one* option expiration per futures expiration. There is no June option on the September futures contract for example. The option expires about a week before the futures contract does.

The CBT display does not show a bid and asked price, like the CBOE does. Instead it shows the trades that have taken place. Under LAST is the most recent trade, in this case at 1 and 41/64ths, followed by the next most recent trade (PREV1) at 1 and 40/64ths, and the trade before that (PREV2) at 1 and 44/64ths. Why are CBT options quoted in 64ths? Because the CBT reasoned that options are about half as volatile as futures, which are quoted in 32ds.

Looking at these prices, we might surmise that futures prices were falling until just prior to 11:08, when they suddenly rose again, since

Figure 7-3
Telerate screen showing the market for futures options at about 11 A.M. on May 26, 1987.

```
05/26   11:08 EDT         TELERATE OPTIONS ON FUTURES SERVICE        952
CBT T-BONDS - SEP 87      SEE PG 2152
        NET   LAST  PREV1  PREV2   LOW   HIGH  OPEN  (RANGE)   PRV CL
C92           141    140    144    130   148   140
P92           349    360    356    349   404   R360  R404
C94           101    100    101     54   103   R60   R102
P94           462    510           462   510   510
C96            38     39     38     30    39   R32   R31
P96
C98            20     19     18     15    20   R15   R17
P98           840                  840   840   840
P100           11     10      9      9    11   R10   R11
P100          1040                1040  1040  1040
C102            5                    5     5     5
P102
C104
P104
PREVIOUS CALLS & PUTS ON PAGE 951
```

call prices were falling and suddenly rose. Let's look at the next row down, the 92 puts (P92). If futures prices were falling, put prices should be rising, and vice versa. That is exactly what happened, with puts going from 3 and 56/64ths to 3 and 60/64ths to 3 and 49/64ths. By looking at the columns labeled LOW and HIGH we can see that futures were near their high for the session, since calls were near their high of 1 and 48/64ths, while puts were at their lows of 3 and 39/64ths.

If the futures contract was near 90.16, 92 puts would be about 1½ points in the money. If that is true, their premium of about 3–50 should be made up of 1–32 intrinsic value and 1–18 time value. But the 92 calls, which are 1½ out of the money, have a premium made up entirely of time value at approximately 1–41. Suppose we bought the September contract at 90.16, bought the 92 put at 3–50 and sold the 92 call at 1–41. Such a position, called a forward conversion, should show a profit of about 23/64ths, or the difference between the time values contained in the option premiums. Aberrations like this are the lifeblood of options traders, who use computers to scan the market and pinpoint opportunities.

SECTION THREE

INSIDE THE GOVERNMENT BOND MARKET

CHAPTER EIGHT

Inside a Primary Dealer: The Trading Desk

Of all the pieces that make up the government bond market, without a doubt the most important ingredient is a group of firms called *Primary Dealers*. Most trades in the market go through at least one Primary Dealer. Primary Dealers submit most of the bids that are awarded securities in Treasury auctions. They underwrite and distribute most of the agency new issue securities. They, and only they, deal directly with the Federal Reserve Bank of New York's Open Market Trading Desk. Finally, they provide most of the liquidity that makes the government bond market the largest, most liquid market in the world.

Despite the fact that these firms are the center of the market, who they are and how they operate is still very much a mystery to the world outside the market itself. In fact, the makeup of the Primary Dealer community is not a constant. In most years, a few primaries are dropped from the list, and a few added. Recently, the list has been expanding as a result of the need for more capital in the government bond market, and subsidiaries of foreign firms have begun to enter the ranks of primaries.

WHAT IS A PRIMARY DEALER?

Although the strict definition of a Primary Dealer is a firm that is a member of the Primary Dealer Association, a division of the Public Securities Association, membership in the select group is actually conferred by the Federal Reserve Bank of New York. The process by which one becomes a Primary Dealer tells us a lot about how the market works.

The first step in becoming a primary is the *commitment* by a securities firm or bank to gear up for the effort. This means commiting capital and manpower to the government bond market. In effect, the infrastructure to support a primary dealership must be built up before the status is granted. Typically, both a trading desk and a sales force are recruited at the same time. Most of the traders and salespeople are hired from firms that are already Primary Dealers, lured away by an opportunity to build a new dealership, as well as a handsome compensation package.

This high-priced talent immediately sets about increasing the firm's *trading volume,* particularly its trading volume with customers, since that has become a prime concern of the Fed. In this effort, the aspiring primary occupies a unique position in the dealer community. First, it must horn in on the territory of the other primaries by doing a substantial amount of business with their customers. At the same time, it is itself a customer, which puts it in a tentative position with those firms that are already primaries.

Some primaries regard the aspiring firms as pariahs and refuse to do business with those who are trying to take food off their table. This makes things especially difficult for the aspiring primary, because the liquidity provided by the primaries is essential to the building effort. Fortunately, other primaries regard the new entrants as bona fide customers, and good ones at that, because they trade heavily and themselves provide no small amount of liquidity.

Thus the aspiring primary finds itself a niche in the market. Perhaps it develops a new cadre of customers, perhaps it brings new expertise to the market, perhaps it simply adds capital, but its trading volume increases, and it begins to report its trading and positions to the Fed. Initially it reports monthly, then weekly, as the Fed decides that it has become a factor in the market. Finally, the Fed decides that it represents enough of the daily trading volume to be recognized as a Primary Dealer. The direct wire is installed, the firm is admitted into the Primary Dealer Association, and the champagne is broken out in the trading room.

DUTIES OF A PRIMARY DEALER

This new honor carries with it some responsibilities. The first is the duty of *making markets* in U.S. Treasury securities, and agency securities. In its narrowest definition, this means making bids and offers in all securities to all qualified customers who request them. However, the market itself is so narrow, and the customer list so restricted, that it is not enough in the eyes of the Fed just to make markets. The Fed measures the effectiveness of making markets in the amount of securities traded with customers. Thus the customer occupies a special place in the government bond market. Every dollar of his business is sought after by Primary Dealers who need to placate the Fed.

The second requirement of a primary is that it *bid on all Treasury securities auctions*. As with the making of markets, just bidding on auctions is not sufficient. A primary who consistently bids so low a price as to buy very little will soon find itself called into the Fed's offices for a "rehabilitative chat." Thus, the ability to submit bids in every auction and win at least some securities is the real requirement. One way to do this is to *establish a short position* before the auction, preferably by selling "when-issued" securities to customers. This strategy can be very profitable, but it can also lead to large losses.

Another, and less risky, strategy is to *collect customer bids* and submit them on the customer's behalf. But why would a customer want a Primary Dealer to submit a bid for him? The main reason is convenience. One of the privileges of Primary Dealer status is the ability to submit bids without having to post the good faith deposit required of the general public. Since the Fed does not pay interest on the good faith deposit and since the deposit could be held for up to two weeks, using the Primary Dealer can be a matter of economics as well as convenience.

At the same time, the Primary Dealer, who normally submits the customer's bid without charge, is often willing to share *market information* with customers who bid through him. Since Treasury auctions are critical times in the market, and often entail large commitments of capital at times of high risk, access to reliable information can be very important, if not lifesaving. One such piece of information is the price at which the dealer expects the auction to *stop*, which is the highest yield that will win any securities. Everyone wants to buy at the stop, and much of the market chatter on the day of the auction is devoted to "stop talk." Getting good information in the stop talk can mean the difference between paying too much for your securities and missing the auction entirely.

Another requirement of a Primary Dealer is the *marketing of* the *new issues* periodically sold by the various *agencies.* The agencies do not auction their securities; they offer them through a sales group, made up mostly of Primary Dealers. The distribution of new issue agency securities is one of the most profitable kinds of business that Primary Dealers can do. The fiscal agents, who occupy the same position as a corporate treasurer, cannot price issue after issue so as to be unattractive to the market, because they must come back so often to borrow. Thus, if a dealer sells his allotment each time, he will, more often than not, make the sales concession with little risk.

Of course, the fiscal agents know this, and they use their ability to allot securities in these offerings to keep a tight rein on the members of the selling group. A dealer who doesn't pull his weight in distributing the agency's issues, who sells too often to other dealers, who doesn't make an active market in issues after the offering period, will find his allotment, and thus his profits, reduced, and he could find himself out of the group altogether.

STRUCTURE OF A PRIMARY DEALER

The essence of most markets is that they look, to the outside observer, disorganized and chaotic. Whether one is looking at an Arabian bazaar, a commodities pit or a Primary Dealer, the impression is one of confusion. Almost always, though, there is a very real form of organization at work below the surface, an organization that is finely tuned to the job at hand.

The primary reason that markets as a whole look disorganized is that the business of buying and selling things is itself a rather helter-skelter proposition. Markets must be able to accommodate all sorts of participants, news events of varying import, and the essentially chaotic process of arriving at equilibrium prices. Although a Primary Dealer's trading room differs from most markets in that it is located entirely within the confines of one corporation, it has all the earmarks of any market.

When one first enters a Primary Dealer's trading room, one could be forgiven for asking, "Where is the market? Where does all the trading happen?" Instead of the physical activity we see in commodity or securities exchanges, we would see a room full of people at desks, albeit small desks, talking on telephones or staring at screens. Occasionally, one of the people will stand up and shout, apparently to no one in particular, something like, "Bid ten million long bonds." From another desk, without looking up, another person will say something like, "Sixteen." After speaking into his telephone for a few seconds, the first person will respond, "Ten you buy at sixteen."

In this way, seemingly without eye contact and in some sort of code, billions of dollars of securities are traded by Primary Dealers. Most of the spoken communication is indeed in code, because a great deal of information must be exchanged in a few words, and it must be accurate because millions of dollars ride on each trade. Considering the speed with which the market moves, and the risk involved, not only must communications be accurate, everyone's role in the trading room must be well understood by all.

WHO DOES WHAT

Most Primary Dealers are divided into three general areas: *trading, sales, and research or economics*. The trading desk is responsible for buying and selling securities and derivative instruments for the firm's account. The sales force is responsible for contacting customers and buying and selling securities with those customers. The economics department is responsible for tracking economic developments and for keeping a sharp eye on the Fed. Its research output is made available both to the trading desk and, through the sales force, to customers.

Although many market participants cling to the old idea that profits and losses are made by the trading desk, while the sales force generates customer inquiry and the economists play the role of "Fed watchers," the truth is something quite different. The fact is that the commodity Primary Dealers trade isn't securities, and it isn't money—it is *information. The Primary Dealers who consistently make money do so because they are good traders of information, while those firms that struggle to make money usually do so because they don't know how to trade information well.*

This trading of information is made harder by the fact that all business in this market is done as principal, not as agent. Thus the Primary Dealer makes his money by buying and selling directly with others in the market, and his profits come out of the hides of, among others, his customers. Principal trading has the tendency to make adversaries out of trading partners; the Primary Dealer and his customer face this tendency every day. Good primaries deal with it by clearly defining people's roles, and seeing to it that people within the trading room interact, both with each other and with the customer.

The Trading Desk

At the center of the trading room, psychologically as well as physically, is the *trading desk*. It is in fact a group of desks, occupied by people who buy and sell securities, futures, options, or money for the firm's account. These people are *traders,* and their job is the oldest one in the government bond market. For many years the mission of a Primary Dealer was regarded as simply the buying and selling of securities. As long as that was true, the trader was the preeminent person in the dealership. Times have changed somewhat, but the trader still holds a lot of the cards. Traders are divided along the lines of the securities they trade.

Treasury Bill Traders

Since bills trade the highest volume of all government securities, the *Treasury bill desk* is often thought of as the linchpin of the entire trading desk. In recent years, the bill desk has slipped a little in importance, partly because the Treasury has shifted its issuing emphasis away from bills somewhat. Still, a good bill desk can make a Primary Dealer a force to be reckoned with.

Bill traders have two parts to their job. The first is the *day-to-day trading* of existing bills, and the second is *bidding* on the weekly auctions of 13-week and 26-week bills, as well as the monthly auction of 52-week bills. No other security is issued as often as bills, so no other traders have as much responsibility to bid on and distribute securities.

Most bill desks employ at least two traders, and possibly as many as four. With two traders, the "list" is divided either along maturity lines, or along liquidity lines. In the maturity case, the most common point of division is the bill that was most recently the current six-month bill. In this case, one trader bids on the three-month bill and the other bids on the six-month bill, as well as the monthly auction of year bills.

Another method of dividing the list is to give one trader the most active issues, usually the current and when-issued three-month, six-month and one-year issues, while the other trader takes the "off-the-run" issues. Although the first trader has the much smaller list to trade, he may trade more volume, because the "on the runs" trade so much more actively. In this case, one trader bids all the auctions, while the other deals with a large list of securities on a daily basis.

The more traders assigned to bills, the more the list is broken down. With three traders, one might take all issues out to, and including, the when-issued three month. The second would trade from there to the when-issued six month, and the third trader would cover the remainder out to the year bill. With four traders, the additional person might be assigned the arbitrages involving the futures contract or options.

However many traders are on the bill desk, one thing is sure: *they all work together as a team.* The bill market may be large in trading volume, but it is small in terms of participants. As a result, the customers are well known to the traders, and everyone in the market has to know where the bodies are buried. In this market most of all, good information is the key to success, so traders, and salesmen, share everything they know or hear. This close teamwork breeds something of a fortress mentality, making the bill desk appear elitist. However, the reality is that the volume of securities traded, the competition in the market, and the razor-thin profit margins make close cooperation a necessity.

Treasury Coupon Traders

If the bill desk is close knit, the coupon desk is just the opposite. At this desk sit the people who trade *Treasury notes and bonds,* which are called coupon securities because years ago they actually had coupons attached. Twice a year, on the semi-anniversary of each issue's original sale, as well as its maturity, the securities pay interest. Today the interest is credited to the bank account of the holder of record, but in the past the holder had to clip a coupon and take it in to the bank to get his interest payment. There haven't been any coupons on Treasury issues for many years, but the old names die hard.

As much as bills are homogeneous, coupon securities are heterogeneous. As much as bill customers are few and well known, coupon customers are many and varied. As much as the bill desk works as a tight unit, the coupon desk is disparate. In fact, it is really several desks, split up according to the maturity of the issues.

Short Coupon Traders

Short coupons are generally thought of as those maturing in *less than two years*. This demarcation is natural because the two-year note is the only coupon issue auctioned monthly, and customers tend to think in terms of the two year as a break point. Actually, some dealers break the list down even more, having one trader specialize in issues maturing in a year or less, and another trading issues from one to two years.

Of all the coupons, the short end is most like the bill market. In fact, issues shorter than a year trade almost exclusively against the closest maturing bill. Generally, a coupon security will yield more than a bill with the same maturity, by a spread of about 20 basis points. Why? There are two reasons. The first is that bill issues are usually larger and more liquid than note issues. The second, and more important, is purely mathematical.

Bills do not carry accrued interest, and their yield is calculated that way. Coupon securities, however, do carry accrued interest, although their yield calculation does not take that into account. Why does that make a difference? Because the coupon buyer does not earn interest on the accrued interest he has paid the seller. How big a difference does this make? If the average coupon is 7%, and the average accrued interest is 91 days, this means that the coupon security buyer is paying out an average of 1.75 points on which he earns no interest for the remaining 91 days. For $1 million of securities, that amounts to an extra outlay of $17,500 for 91 days. Interest on that money at 7% would amount to about $300, which is equal to about 1/32d. Many markets in one-year and under securities have a spread of less than 1/32d.

Needless to say, short coupon traders keep a very sharp pencil because the spreads in the market, and thus the profit opportunities, are very thin. On the other hand, the volume that trades in short coupons can be enormous. It is not unusual to see trades of $500 million of short coupons, and that kind of block size highlights one of the real dangers of trading short coupons: *short squeezes*.

Unlike bill issues, which all have about the same size, coupon issues can have widely different amounts outstanding, or floats. Sprinkled in among the recent two-year note issues we can find older five-year notes, ten-year notes, and even long bonds. Next to an issue with a float of $6 billion or more we might find an issue of less than $1 billion. Since a trader is as likely to be short as long any particular issue, short coupon traders must be constantly on guard against getting short a large amount of some issue with a very small float. That mistake is a trader's nightmare.

The solution to that nightmare is to find a *holder* of the issue, and buy the securities back. Fortunately, the short coupon market shares with the bill market a small universe of customers, primarily bank portfolios, corporate cash managers, and money market mutual funds. Because the risk of a short squeeze is so large in short coupons, traders make sure they know as much as possible about where blocks of small issues are held.

At the long end of this segment of the market, the action is dominated by the *monthly auction* of two-year notes. The trader, in addition to preparing the bids on each auction, and trading the issue after the auction, does a lot of business in the period between the announcement of the issue (when trading can begin) and the auction date. Years ago, most of the distribution of Treasury new issues was accomplished by dealers either after the auction or by submitting customer bids. In recent years, much more of the distribution has been accomplished by trading in *when-issued securities,* before the auction itself. Since the two-year note is auctioned more often than any other coupon, the two-year trader spends much of his time trading between the most recently issued two-year and the when-issued one.

Intermediate Coupon Traders

The intermediate sector of the Treasury list generally runs from the two-year note to the ten-year note. This sector has more issues in it than any other (except agencies), and a wider variety of customers. At one time or another, every government securities customer makes a foray into the intermediate sector. From a money market fund getting bullish by adding some three-year notes, to a pension fund pulling in its horns by shortening up to the ten-year note, the intermediate traders see more customers than anyone.

Because there are so many issues, and so many customers, Primary Dealers tend to divide the intermediate coupon list more than either the short end or the long end. For example, one trader might take the issues from the two year to the three year, another the three year to the five year, another the five to the seven, and the last the seven to the ten. With fewer traders, the split might be two to four, four to seven, and seven to ten. In some smaller shops, two traders might split the list at the five year.

However the intermediate list is split, one thing is sure: *this sector is the great meeting ground of the government bond market.* If you imagine the Arabian bazaars that are sometimes depicted in the movies—with a thousand booths and chaos everywhere—that is a good approximation of the intermediate sector.

As a result, the intermediate coupon desk does not have the close-knit quality that one usually finds on a bill desk. Here each trader tends to work much more in a world of his own. That is not to say they don't communicate with each other, because they do. But their communication is much more like that of air traffic controllers, sharing terse updates on what is happening on their screens. Only later, after the trading day is over, will the intermediate traders relax and share war stories.

And they may have some real stories to tell. The intermediate customer base is much less defined than any other market, so these traders have a much less friendly world to deal in. Instead of well-known customers, with well-defined parameters and objectives, these traders deal with shadowy shapes in the twilight. Customers can move easily from three-year notes to five-year notes, as their market projections change, and as they see opportunities develop. That is the most natural thing in the world to them, but they may well be moving from one trader to another at the same time. Each trader has his own trading style, and customers can be rather perplexed when they get an unexpected response to a familiar request.

What all this means is that, in the intermediate sector, the salesman's role becomes doubly important. A little later, we will discuss the sales force in detail, but here we need to know that one of their crucial jobs is to *run interference* between the customer and the trader. Some traders like to maximize the communication between themselves and the customers while others regard customers as a necessary evil. Some traders are paranoid, others will talk to anyone. Some traders have big egos, and like to take big positions, others are much more comfortable close to the shore. It is the salesman who is responsible for making all these traders appear to the customer as a well-oiled machine.

As with all the other traders, the intermediate jockeys must also *prepare bids* for the various auctions in their area. In two cases, the three year and the ten year, the bids are part of the *quarterly refunding*. These auctions, along with the long bond, represent a quarterly event of almost religious significance. From the announcement of the issues to be sold, through the when-issued period, to the preparation and submission of bids, these four events (in early February, May, August, and November) attract the attention of everyone in the market. Like religious feasts, they have assumed an importance out of proportion to their actual role, but market participants seem to like it that way.

Long Coupon Traders

At the far end of the spectrum, and often of the desk itself, sits the long bond trader, or traders. For many years, from the early 1950s to the late 1960s, this was truly the forgotten sector, because during those years the Treasury couldn't issue long bonds at all. Only when Congress granted limited relief from the 4¼% interest ceiling on bond issues was the Treasury able to get back in the bond market.

Once it did get back in, it encountered a bunch of new investors. Actually, these investors weren't really new, they had simply been left behind when rates went above the 4¼% ceiling. Primarily made up of life insurers and pension funds, this class mostly *manages retirement savings*. Since their time horizon is relatively long, and since their cash flow is relatively predictable, they have an appetite for long-term, fixed-rate investments.

When the Treasury exited the long bond market, these investors shifted to corporate bonds, and they made their home in that market for many years. When the Treasury reappeared in the early 1970s, long bond traders had to learn about a whole group of customers all over again. Trading practices had been established in the corporate market that were quite different from those in governments, and it took a little while for both sides to get used to the change.

For instance, corporate trades settle on the fifth business day after trade date, and payment is made in clearinghouse funds. Governments settle the next business day, and in Federal Funds. In many cases, pension funds and life companies began buying governments by swapping out of corporates and were surprised to find the government being presented for payment long before the corporates were due to be delivered out. Many long bond trades are still done against corporate bonds, so the long bond trader must keep himself constantly aware of the condition of the corporate market. For commercial bank dealers, the close relationship of long governments to corporates raises an additional problem, because the Glass-Steagall Act has prohibited banks from trading corporates for many years. As a result, many bank dealers are not as strong in long bonds as they are in the shorter end of the list.

One area where these banks can participate is the *futures market*, and the Chicago Board of Trade (CBT) bond futures contract has had a major impact on the liquidity of the long government market. So important has the futures market become that many dealers assign a trader to do nothing but follow the relationship between the cash bond and the contract. Aided by computers, and with a direct line to the CBT floor, these *basis traders* try to make tiny profits by arbitraging between any of the bonds on the list and the CBT contract. Sometimes the cash bond seems to be moved by the contract, and sometimes it appears to be the opposite, but one thing is certain: there are times, when prices are highly volatile, that most of the liquidity in the long bond market is provided by the locals in the CBT bond pit.

The Agency Traders

There is no CBT contract for the agency traders, and their market has significantly *less liquidity* as a result. When you couple a mind-boggling array of issues with some very real credit concerns about some of the issuers, you get a market that looks more like the corporate bond market than anything else in governments.

As a result, the agency trader's job is more like a corporate bond trader's than like anyone else's. Similar to a corporate bond trader, he must deal with credit risk, which plays a major role in how his securities trade. There was a time, not so many years ago, when agency issues were as homogeneous as Treasury securities. Each issuer occupied its rightful place in the quality spectrum, and the spreads between issuers were both narrow and static. In the modern world, all that has changed.

Since the late 1970s, and especially in the mid-1980s, the credit quality of the various agencies has followed a bumpy path. First, FNMA suffered losses, due to the interest rate spike of the late 1970s and early

1980s. As a result, its debt issues fell out of favor, and began to trade at spreads of almost 100 basis points to Treasury issues. Things got so bad that the options exchanges delisted options on FNMA's common stock because its price had fallen so far.

FNMA's fortunes have improved immensely since then, largely because its management attacked its maturity mismatch problem with a vengeance. In the meantime, the Farm Credit Agencies have suffered a worse fate. In their case, the earnings problems were a result of a general credit deterioration in their loan portfolio, as opposed to a rate mismatch. Credit problems are potentially more damaging than rate problems because they attack the principal value of an asset instead of its earnings value. As a result, the market downgraded the Farm Credit System more than it did FNMA, to the extent of a spread of almost 150 basis point over Treasuries.

In the end, however, market participants concluded that Congress could not afford to abandon either the farming sector or the housing sector, returning some semblance of stability to the agency market. For the agency trader, that stability was welcome, because he very definitely has two jobs to do.

First, he must *trade* a bewildering array of agency debt issues. Not only do they range from maturities of a few days to more than twenty years, but they also range in coupon from very high to very low. Perhaps worse than that, the issues range in size from a few hundred million to over a billion. With several issuers to keep track of, a variety of coupons and maturities for each issuer, and the added bogey of issue size, the agency trader spends a lot of his time avoiding the land mines in his market.

Second, he must *underwrite and distribute* each new issue of agency securities. Here, he acts more like a corporate syndicate department than a government securities trader. As a distributer instead of a trader, he is focused on passing customer interest, and the rates at which it exists, to the fiscal agent, instead of using that information to buy and sell for his own account. As an underwriter, he is more dependent upon the fiscal agent's price ideas than on his own trading prowess. As a marketing entity, he is more concerned with what the customer thinks than with what he thinks.

All this means that the agency trader, more than any Treasury trader, is dependent upon his *customer information flow*. Good agency traders develop good rapport either with their sales force or with their own customer base, but it is virtually impossible to be successful trading agencies with only the brokers. In this respect, agency traders stand out as different from Treasury traders.

Mortgage-Backed Securities Traders

In the Mortgage Backed Securities (MBS) market, the difference is even more striking. In some cases, the dealer will have a separate department that deals only with MBS. Some of the securities are actually corporate bonds, in that they are registered under the Securities Act of 1933. Many of the customers, mortgage bankers in particular, never come into contact with the government bond market in any form other than MBS.

In fact, the MBS trader is really a hybrid between a government bond trader and a corporate bond trader. Some aspects of the way he does business are very much government bond ways. For example, he has *screens,* very much like government bond screens, for those MBS's issued by GNMA, FHLMC, or FNMA. All his trades settle in *Federal Funds,* as do governments. And many of his securities are *wire transferrable,* as are governments.

On the other hand, the MBS trader is very much in a world of his own. Many of his securities are issued directly by mortgage bankers, very much the way bank CDs and commercial paper are. In those cases, there is no public information about how many securities are being issued, and at what prices. Thus, he must keep an open pipeline of information to mortgage bankers, and other mortgage lenders, to determine the supply position of the market.

The demand side of the market has become even more complex in the middle eighties. The reason is the advent of the *CMO,* which turns a fixed-rate, 30-year, level-debt-service mortgage into a series of securities, with different assumed average lives and interest rates. The most common collateral for CMOs has been agency MBS's, so the demand for CMOs has created a corresponding demand for agency MBS's. As Wall Street arbitrageurs find new and interesting ways to structure CMOs, their attention shifts from one kind of MBS to another, making first one kind rich and then another.

There is another aspect of CMO creation which wreaks even more havoc with the MBS market. CMOs tend to be created in issues averaging around $300 to $400 million, and the whole issue closes at once.

This means that, at a certain point in time, there can be a terrific demand for a specific MBS security, in order to collateralize a CMO. Since most CMO indentures require that the collateral be physically present—not just purchased—these CMO closings often give rise to a huge short squeeze. Thus, the MBS trader who is not aware of an impending CMO issue can find himself short securities under very difficult circumstances.

The Matched Book Traders

The last, and often least understood, trading desk is the one that deals in the *short-term financing* of government securities. In many dealers, these traders are thought of as operations people, and in others they are not even housed in the trading room, yet they represent a tremendous resource, as well as a profit opportunity.

Every time a securities trader "goes home" long or short a security, a *matched book trader* must facilitate that position. Not only must he finance the securities (in the case of a long position), or borrow them (in the case of a short position), he must also work with his clearance department to ensure that all deliveries are accomplished. In terms of realizing the profits that the traders put on their books, no one is more important.

And how important is the matched book trader? Look at it this way: Most coupon traders are happy if they can make 1/32d on every trade. That's $312.50 per million. Bill traders are happy with 1 basis point, or $50 per million on the six-month bill. At the same time, a fail to deliver costs the dealer the entire coupon for the day. If the average security has a coupon of 7%, one day's fail costs $191.78, over 60% of the average coupon trader's profit, and 400% of the bill trader's profit. Two day's fail turns almost any profit into a loss.

No less important is the cost of borrowing securities, because short positions can last much longer than fails do. If securities have been sold short in large amounts, the rate at which they can be financed (or borrowed) drops, as they become *special* in the financing market. It is not unusual to see securities financed at rates 2% below general collateral. That 2% equates to $55 a day, which means that the price of the shorted security must fall by more than 1/32d a week for the position to break even.

Unlike most other trading desks, the matched book desk knows a great deal about its market needs, but it faces intense time pressures. Every morning, every dealer knows what securities it will have to finance for that day, and which ones it will have to borrow. At the same time customers, made up of cash investors (mostly cash managers and money market funds), and securities holders, mostly pension funds and insurance companies, know what their cash needs and securities' availability will be for the day. Thus the repo desk's day starts early, usually about 8:00 A.M. New York time. For the next two hours, these traders are very busy matching up cash investors with securities financers, and matching securities holders with securities borrowers.

In most cases, a fully staffed matched book desk will have three traders. One does the *overnight book,* which is made up mostly of general collateral. Another manages the *term book,* where repos are done for specified terms, usually at the request of money market funds. Finally there is the *specials trader,* who manages the book of securities needed to cover short positions. Even more than the bill desk, these traders must work together, because securities move from trader to trader on a moment's notice. The term trader might need collateral from the overnight book to fill an unexpected request, and the specials trader might be sending collateral back to the overnight desk at the same time as someone on the coupon desk covers a short position.

From 10:00 A.M. until after lunch, most matched book desks have a slack period, but things pick up again as the interdealer wire gets close to closing for the day. Any deliveries not made by that time will result in fails, so the matched book desk works closely with the "cage" to move collateral around, in order to make deliveries out where they have failed to come in. For an astute matched book desk, making these deliveries and earning the extra day's interest on the money generated, represents a major portion of their daily profits, and can make them one of the most profitable trading desks in the room.

CHAPTER NINE

Inside a Primary Dealer: The Sales Force and the Economics Department

If the trading desk is the nerve center of the Primary Dealer, and many people in the government bond market believe so, then the dealer's eyes and ears are the *sales force* and the *economics department*. Just as the greatest brain in the world is useless without its eyes and ears, the best trading desk in the market has a hard time making money consistently without the help of a good sales force and economics department.

For many years, however, both these groups labored in the shadow of the trading desk. Both salesmen and economists were considered something of a third wheel, tagging along behind the real moneymakers who traded securities. At some dealers, that feeling still pervades the dealership. In those shops, good traders earn more than good salesmen or economists, management jobs are reserved for the traders, and the dealer's market strategy is dictated by the traders.

That approach is decidedly an old-fashioned one. The facts of the modern market are that a dealer needs to utilize all the talents of all its people to succeed. Each department plays an important role, and nothing is gained by downplaying the importance of one department or another.

THE SALES FORCE

If the trader's job is clearly defined, the salesman's job is fluid. If traders know exactly how they will be judged and who keeps the score, a salesman often feels that he is serving two masters. More than any other department, the sales force bridges the gap between the dealer and its customers.

As we have seen already, customers tend to deal in certain kinds of securities more than others. For example, money market mutual funds invest mostly in securities with a year or less to maturity, and do a great deal of term repo. Savings and loan associations concentrate on Treasury issues with about five years to maturity (and agencies with three years to maturity) for their liquidity portfolios and mortgage-backed securities for their real estate portfolio. Commercial bank portfolios tend to concentrate on securities of from one to three years, while their trust departments are more likely to trade securities from ten years out.

Specialization in the Sales Force

Since each sector of the market has its own lore and technology, no salesperson can expect to be an expert in all the sectors at once. In the same way, each class of customer has its own objectives and regulations, and no salesperson can be expected to be equally knowledgeable about them all. As a result, salespeople tend to specialize as much as traders do.

One group of salespeople concentrates on the *short end* of the market. These people cover the growing category of money market mutual funds, which the public looks at as a substitute for a checking account. They also cover corporate cash portfolios, which usually have a very short time horizon, and most of the foreign holders of exchange reserves. Finally, they talk to municipal tax offices, which invest tax receipts for short periods before they are spent.

Because of the short-term nature of their customers' interests, the salespeople become experts in bills, very short notes, and repos, as well as the money market instruments that fall in the same maturity sector. They keep close track of the yield spreads between bills and notes with the same maturities, and they are experts on the cost of financing all kinds of short-term instruments.

The short sector of the market operates on very thin spreads, so

The Sales Force and the Economics Department

these salespeople keep a sharp eye on every price in their market sector. At the same time, some of the customers in this sector are enormous, large enough to control a single issue by themselves. Since being on the wrong side of a trade in one of those issues can be disastrous, these salespeople are forever trying to learn which customer is doing what with which security, and rumors about auction coups (where a customer or dealer attempts to stop an auction short of everyone's expectations) are a daily fact of life.

A little further out on the maturity spectrum are the salespeople who talk mostly to bank portfolios, corporate cash portfolios, and savings and loan liquidity accounts. Although these customers often trade in bills and very short notes, they do most of their business in the maturity range of from one to five years.

Because the *intermediate sector* of the market has such a wide variety of players, the salespeople have a much larger job to do in keeping track of their customers and their customers' needs. As customers move from maturity sector to maturity sector, they may move from an area in which the salesman has substantial expertise to one where he is very much at a loss. A salesperson who knows the two-year market in detail may feel much less sure about the five-year note. Since salespeople communicate their strengths and weaknesses subconsciously, customers may avoid talking to a certain salesperson about the area of the market where he is weakest.

As a result, salespeople in the intermediate area of the market tend to rely on each other's expertise about various sectors of the market. They also rely on the traders, but the age-old tradition that salespeople and traders work opposite sides of the street makes most salespeople more comfortable exposing their shortcomings to a fellow salesperson than to a trader. Whomever they choose, the salespeople in the intermediate market get outside help more often than any others.

Those salespeople who deal mostly with pension funds and insurance companies, and thus deal mostly in *longer maturities*, need a lot less help on government securities, but they have other needs. Many of their customers look upon government bonds as substitutes for other investments, such as corporate bonds, or even common stocks. These customers, instead of moving around the government market, move in and out of it. When governments are rich versus corporates, or when the stock market is on a tear, these customers may disappear from the government market for months at a time.

Other long bond customers use the CBT futures contract, or options, as a *hedge* for their positions. As we might expect, large institutions that are active in futures or options can afford sophisticated analytical tools, including computers. A trader who doesn't have comparable tools will find himself at a disadvantage in these markets and may treat these customers with even more suspicion than others. The salesperson who covers accounts like these has a special job of running interference between the customer and the trader.

The Job of the Sales Force

Whether his customers have the latest tools and technology, or are the smallest, most unsophisticated institutions, the salesperson essentially has two jobs: *to maximize both the quantity and quality of the information flow in the trading room, and to maximize the quantity and quality of business done with customers.* Although everyone agrees with the second half of that statement, many salespeople will not agree with the first half; they will say that their job is solely to maximize the amount of customer business the dealership does. In fact, many managements will say that salespeople are there just to do customer business, because any customer business is better than street business.

However, as long as business is done as principal, instead of as agent, with whom the dealer does it does not have any qualitative implication per se. Customer business does not, in and of itself, generate profits. Some customers are so tough to deal with that certain dealers write them off completely and tell salespeople not to cover them at all. Yet those same customers are quite profitable for another dealership.

Why? The answer lies in understanding the real commodity traded in the government bond market. It isn't securities, and it isn't money—it is *information*. Dealers may make markets in bonds and do trades in bills or notes, but the securities don't determine whether the dealer makes or loses money. In a principal market the prices paid for securities, and the prices at which they are sold, are the only determinants of profits or losses. Being long or short, and the prices at which the positions were established, makes all the difference.

That being the case, the key to profitability is the quality of the information the dealership is working with. In particular, information about what is happening in the marketplace. Who is long, and who is short? Who owns securities at higher prices and is just waiting for a rally

The Sales Force and the Economics Department

to sell into? Who needs to buy and is just waiting for another downtick to jump in? Who is short and needs to borrow to make delivery?

That kind of information comes from outside the dealership. Some of it comes from other dealers, or the brokers who act as their go-betweens. Most of it, however, comes from customers. It is customers who see blocks of securities offered by one dealer, and relay that information to another dealer. It is customers who have blocks of securities of their own to sell, or are looking for blocks to buy. It is customers who hear from other dealers where they expect new issues to be auctioned. And it is the salespeople who talk to the customers about all these things.

Thus, although the government market is thought of as being a vast pool of securities, or a vast pool of money, it is best understood as a *vast pool of information*. The information is passed from participant to participant in exchange for other information, and in exchange for trades accomplished. When a customer asks a dealer to bid on a block of bonds, he is communicating the information that he has that block for sale. And, when the dealer makes a bid, he is communicating the level at which he is willing to do business. But there is a great deal more information that can be exchanged.

Is this block all the securities the customer has for sale? Does he have a price in mind at which he will sell them? What prices will other dealers pay him for this block? Is the dealer long or short this security? Would he pay a higher price than his bid for the block if it were offered to him? Has another block of this same security traded recently? At a higher price, or a lower one?

It would be extraordinary if either the dealer or customer volunteered much of this information unless it was expected to bring some information in return. In fact, the information exchange is a little like the mating dance of wild birds, with advances coming in small steps, taken by both parties. In this dance, the salesperson plays a crucial role. He is constantly talking to both the customer and the trader, taking the temperature of both sides, offering and soliciting information in small steps until a transaction is arrived at. Let's listen to one such three-way conversation between a customer, a salesperson, and a trader.

Customer (to salesperson): "What can you pay for $10 million of the ten-year note?"

Salesperson (to trader): "Bid $10 million ten years, please."

Trader: "Sixteen."

Salesperson (to customer): "We can pay 99.16."

Customer: "No thanks—I'll pass."

Salesperson: "Well, what price do you need?"

Customer: Someone else will pay me seventeen. I need to get eighteen."

Salesperson (to trader): "He's seeing seventeen away. He will sell at eighteen. Do you care?"

Trader: "I see them offered at eighteen plus, but I'm short, so I can pay him seventeen plus. That's my best."

Salesperson (to customer): "We see them offered at eighteen plus. Our best is seventeen plus."

Customer: "Okay, ten I sell you at seventeen plus."

Salesman (to trader): "Ten you buy at seventeen plus." *(to customer)* "We are buying $10 million of the ten-year note at 99.17+. Thank you for the trade."

From a situation that started out with minimal information (a request for a bid and a response) this conversation evolved into a substantial information exchange and a trade. Both the customer and the dealer knew that they would not give up much information without getting something in return, and the salesperson kept the information exchange moving in the right direction until a trade occurred. You might have noticed that the salesperson did not relay to the customer the trader's information that he was short the issue. Why not? The salesperson might have known that this particular customer would only use that information to try to extract a higher bid from the trader, and might have tried to buy more securities in order to squeeze the dealer. The salesperson rightly concluded that, when information doesn't help the trader, or help get a trade done, it is better not passed along.

THE ECONOMICS DEPARTMENT

If the job of the salesperson is a little nebulous, the job of the economist is steeped in *tradition*. As long as traders have bought and sold securities, as long as the Treasury has issued them, as long as interest rates have risen and fallen, a dealer has needed someone to make sense of it all. That someone is the *money market economist* and his department.

Most companies, particularly those that do business in many

markets or many countries, have an *economics department*, whose job it is to survey the panoply of forces outside the control of management, and to recommend how management should deal with these forces. Whether the companies manufacture computers, write insurance, or fly people from place to place, they all use economists like the lookouts in the crow's-nest of a sailing ship, to warn them of approaching danger and to help guide the ship home.

In the old days, economics was a little like manning a sailing ship without advanced navigational devices. Under those conditions, vigilance was at a premium, but all too often the ship ran aground. Today of course, ships are equipped with radar, SONAR, LORAN, and lots of other acronyms that make the trip a lot safer. Every once in awhile, though, all that modern technology breaks down, and another ship goes to the bottom.

For the money market economist, the tools available for guidance are also better than they used to be. Now government computers spew out reams of information on every aspect of the economy. Economic and analytical services take all that data and rework it more ways than most of us could imagine. When all these people are done, the money market economist goes to work, adding his expertise to the process. It is no wonder that the economist's predictions are better today than they have been. Nonetheless, every once in awhile something crucial is overlooked, and all the dealership's best laid plans blow up. When that happens, everyone plays a part, but the economist often bears more than his share of the blame.

The Money Market Economist's Job

The money market economist and his department really have three jobs. The first is to *advise the traders and the management* about the changes occurring in the economy, both national and international. The economist doesn't set trading policy, but his input is very important, and he sits in on all the policy meetings. In particular, he has an important place at the ritual morning meeting where the strategy for the day is mapped out. The second job is to assist in *marketing the dealership's expertise to its customer base*. In this function he publishes a weekly or monthly market letter, looking at things economic from his unique perspective. Large, active customers receive a pile of these market letters in every Monday's mail. They keep the ones they really value, glance at a few others, and throw the rest away. But there is a third, unique job the money market economist does.

In many dealerships, the economics department is referred to as *"the Fed watchers."* This title bears witness to one of their most important functions, keeping tabs on the Federal Reserve. In a later section, we will take a closer look at the Fed, but for now it is important to know that, through executing monetary policy, the Fed has a major impact on the business of a dealer. Things are made more complicated by the fact that the Fed operates in a cocoon of secrecy, never revealing or commenting on its actions or motives. Thus, although the economist has many other jobs, divining what is happening behind the walls at 33 Liberty Street is one of his most crucial.

Reading The Fed's Tea Leaves

The Federal Reserve impacts a dealer's P&L because it is the implementer of the nation's monetary policy, which controls the availability and cost of credit. As every student of Economics 101 knows, the Fed has three avenues for controlling monetary policy: *reserve ratios,* the *discount rate,* and *open market operations.*

Reserve ratios determine the portion of each deposit dollar that banks must keep at their district Federal Reserve Bank, as a precaution against runs and illiquidity. Once, all banks had the same reserve ratio, and it applied to all deposits. Today the Fed employs a sliding scale of reserves, higher for money center banks, and lower for country banks. Periodically, especially during periods of very tight money, the Fed imposes special reserve requirements against certain kinds of deposits. Changes in reserve ratios happen infrequently, and are regarded as the most heavy-handed of the Fed's tools.

The *discount rate* is the interest rate that the Fed charges its member banks when it lends to them against certain kinds of collateral. Originally, the Fed lent only against very short-term paper, and determined the interest rate by discounting the paper from par. Hence the place where the Fed lends this money is called the discount window, and the rate is the discount rate. Today, the Fed lends against collateral the same way dealers do, and generally for very short periods of time. The discount rate, which used to be a market rate, is now much more ceremonial and tends to follow market rates instead of leading them. Thus dealers interpret discount rate changes as ratifying rate changes that have already occurred in the market.

Open market operations are the transactions the Fed performs, as often as daily, in the government bond market and are by far the most important indicator the market follows. Because these transactions impact the available reserves in the banking system and because they impact the cost of credit, everyone who participates in the market knows the four kinds of open market operations, and what they signify.

1. The *purchase* of securities for the System Account adds reserves to the system permanently, and is considered the most expansionary open market action the Fed can take.
2. Entering into *repo* transactions for the System Account, where the Fed buys securities from dealers and agrees to sell them back to the dealers at a later date, adds reserves to the system on a temporary basis, and is considered mildly expansionary.
3. Entering into *reverse repos,* or *matched sales,* for the System Account, where the Fed sells securities to dealers and agrees to buy them back later, drains reserves from the system temporarily and is considered mildly restrictive.
4. The *sale* of securities for the System Account drains reserves from the system permanently and is considered the most restrictive open market action the Fed can take.

Just to make things a little more complicated, the Fed can undertake any of these actions for the *account of a customer,* usually a foreign central bank, instead of for the System Account. Conventional wisdom says the customer actions have no impact on the reserves in the system and thus no monetary policy implications, but some economists read something into every Fed action, including customer actions.

Determining the significance and hidden meanings of Fed actions begins with understanding the flow of reserves into and out of the banking system. The primary flow comes from the Treasury. When the Treasury pays out money, it adds reserves to the system whether the payments are for Social Security, interest on the debt, or military contracts. When the Treasury collects taxes, it drains reserves from the system, whether those taxes are payroll withholding, corporate profits, or individual income tax filings.

If the Treasury's inflows and outflows were matched, the system would be in balance, but they aren't. For instance, the Treasury makes large Social Security payments around the first of each month. On the other hand, it receives corporate income tax payments on or about the fifteenth of March, June, September, and December. Thus the Fed must either *add* or *drain reserves* within the system every week to keep reserve availability from fluctuating and interest rates from jumping around.

One of the money market economist's most important jobs is to determine whether each week is an *add week* or a *drain week*, and how much needs to be added or drained. Every economist has his proprietary method of doing this, which he hopes will give him a better handle on exactly how large the add need or drain need is. Most economists start with the Treasury's projected dispersals and collections, factor in the flow of funds overseas, and finish with some projections for bank loan and deposit creation for the week. This gives them a handle on the projected oversupply or shortfall in the reserves necessary to support the level of bank deposits.

The next step involves a lot more guesswork. How the Fed responds to a projected reserve shortfall or oversupply is a function of where interest rates are and where the Fed wants them. The interest rate the Fed focuses on is the rate for excess reserve deposits lent overnight, or the *Federal Funds rate*. Not only does the Fed keep an eye on this rate, so does everyone else in the market. Because it is so important, the *Funds rate* has become a symbol for the level of rates throughout the whole market.

Although the Funds rate is a market rate, determined by the supply of and demand for Fed Funds, it is very much a child of the Federal Reserve. One of the hallowed beliefs in the market is, "You can't fight the Fed." If they want the Funds rate up, it will go up, and vice versa. Since the Fed is so secretive about the decisions behind monetary policy, as well as about their actions, watching the Funds rate, and how the Fed reacts to it, is the primary method of determining monetary policy and the changes that have occurred.

Once the economist has determined whether the Fed needs to add or drain reserves, he then looks at the Funds rate, to see if it is at the high or low end of what he thinks is the Fed's target band, or if it is in the middle. From these two factors, and a few that only the economist knows, he makes a projection of the day's "Fed activity," which is expected to happen between 11:30 and 11:45 A.M. Let's look at some sample projections, to get a flavor for the economist's job.

"Today the Fed has a $1 billion add job to do, and, with the Funds Rate at $6\frac{7}{8}\%$, near the high of the current range of $6\frac{1}{2}$ to 7, we expect a bill pass."

Here the economist sees a need for reserves to be added, and sees Funds a little higher than the Fed might like, so he is calling for a permanent addition of reserves through a purchase of bills for the System Account, or a *bill pass*.

"This whole week the Fed has had a large drain job to do, but Funds are above the range at 7-1/16, so we are looking for matched sales at most, or perhaps a customer sale." This time the Fed has to drain reserves from the system, an action which would raise rates by itself. With rates already too high, the economist expects the Fed to make the drain temporary by doing matched sales for the system. In fact, rates may be so high that the Fed may simply sell securities for the account of a customer and do nothing for the System Account.

"So far this week the Fed has completed its add need, but Funds still remain high, so we are looking for a customer buy or a multi-day repo, but we may see a coupon pass if the Fed is unhappy with Funds." In this case the economist has determined that the Fed has taken all the action it needs to in order to balance the reserve position. In spite of that, the Funds Rate is too high, so the economist expects the Fed to take further action to nudge the Funds Rate down. Perhaps they will buy securities for the account of a customer, perhaps they will finance dealer positions for a period of several days, or perhaps they will buy notes and bonds for the System Account (called a *coupon pass*).

There are some other things the economics department must pay attention to of course. The market, like the rest of the business world, pays attention to the economic news and numbers, like unemployment, GNP, industrial production, the consumer price index, and the balance of payments. In each case the market has built into it some expectation for each number; how the market reacts to an announced number, as well as how it reacts to the daily Fed activity, makes up the pattern of trading, the subject of the next chapter.

CHAPTER TEN

Trading Government Securities

The crux of the government securities business is *trading*, the buying and selling of securities and their financing, for the firm's own account. For all the salespeople and the economists, for all the calls to customers, for all the swaps and arbitrages shown by dealer to investors, the money is made or lost by the purchase and sale (not necessarily in that order) of securities by the dealer.

On its face, nothing could be simpler. You buy securities for less and you sell them for more. The market's motto could well be that old saw, "Buy cheap, sell dear." A short portrayal of a very complex business, but one that really captures its essence. Every person in the market—every salesperson, every economist, and every trader—is focused on the same objective, to make money for the firm by buying cheap and selling dear.

Of course, there are a million ingredients in the potpourri that makes up the market, and these are remixed every day. Every morning, the salespeople and the traders gather to plan their strategy for the day; their meetings are filled with tidbits of information. Who is long, and who is short? Which issues are in short supply, and which are all around? What do customers think about the market, what do they expect the Fed to do? And what will they do if the Fed does what they expect?

THE KEY TO SUCCESS

If you listen to those morning meetings, and if you listen to what goes on in a trading room, it becomes apparent that the commodity being traded here is not government securities, and it isn't even money—*it is information*. The common thread in all the conversations in a trading room is the gathering of information, its interpretation, and its assimilation in a trading program.

Of course, if information has value, it is not given away. What customers know about what dealers are doing, and what dealers know about what customers are doing, are pieces of information with real monetary value. What may sound like pleasant conversations between people in a trading room or between dealers and customers, are really a complex series of information exchanges.

Sometimes the monetary value of the information is made painfully obvious. One salesman is famous for having said to a customer, who called to ask a question, "This isn't the Dow Jones News Wire. If you want information, do a trade!" It is a measure of this salesman's reputation and charisma that the customer did do a trade, and duly got his answer. Far more often, the value of information is shown by the intricate dance of exchange it engenders. The salesman offers a nugget, and asks a question. If he gets an answer, he volunteers a little more. And so it goes. In these dances we can see the trading styles of Primary Dealers.

TRADING STYLES OF PRIMARY DEALERS

Generally, dealers' trading styles fall into two approaches: *order flow trading* and *position trading*. It would be convenient to find that these two styles are mutually exclusive, and that a dealer does either one or the other, but that isn't how it works. No dealer can be effective trading entirely order flow or entirely position because the market is too large and too diverse. But each dealer emphasizes and combines these two aspects a little differently.

Order Flow Trading

Order flow trading involves maintaining a wide network of customer contacts all over the world, and using those contacts to maximize the amount of customer business the firm does. This approach is based on the philosophy that customer business is the best kind of business, and that customers have the best information in the market. It also assumes that customers have enough loyalty to the dealers who give them good service that they will come back again and again to do business.

The hardest part of order flow trading is managing the customer relationship. Customers, no less than dealers, have their own interests first in their minds, so it is easy for any relationship, no matter how good, to deteriorate into an adversarial contest. Customers have business to do, and they need the dealers to do it, but there is no need on their part for any *particular* dealer to do well. Thus the dealer must begin the process of icebreaking by offering the customer something of value, usually information. In return for that information the dealer expects the customer to volunteer information of his own or perhaps to do business at the dealer's quoted levels.

If both sides of the exchange are happy with the progress of the relationship, more steps are taken. The dealer offers more detailed insights into its market predictions and perhaps more research products. Customers reveal more about the securities they own and what trades they are thinking about making. Dealers may offer to run specialized analyses on the customer's portfolio, which requires that the customer send in a copy of his holding list. The dealer may want to borrow some of those securities to facilitate short sales, which reveals to the customer the dealer's trading positions.

As cozy as this relationship sounds, it is somewhat self-limiting. No matter how similar the dealer's and customer's interests may seem, they really do have different goals. Eventually, these different goals limit the amount of information exchanged, as it becomes dangerous for either the dealer or the customer to tell the other more about how they are doing business. Whoever calls a halt to this mating dance is usually portrayed by the other as opportunistic or ungrateful, but it is really due to the facts of business life.

Position Trading

Position trading, on the other hand, takes as a given that everyone in the market is an adversary of everyone else and builds a trading philosophy on that fact. It is natural to assume that such a trading philosophy embodies a great deal more risk, and it does embody some more, but the facts are that the market is made up of a large number of forces in balance. A participant who can play those forces well need not have any other allies to succeed.

For the position trader, as for everyone else, the essence of trading is information. For the position trader, however, information doesn't come from allies or customers—it comes from the market itself. Just as a good quarterback can read the opponent's defense, and just as poker players read each other's eyes, the position trader reads the market. He gets the same flow of economic information as everyone else, and he sees the same requests for bids and offers as every other dealer, but he relies on his ability to anticipate the market's reaction and read its pulse.

For example, on days when economic news is announced, the position trader will be assiduous in anticipating the market's reaction. Does everyone think that the unemployment rate will be unchanged? What will the market do if it is actually up .2%? If the trader expects a rally in that case, and his call on the unemployment number is right, but there is no rally, does that mean that everyone was expecting a good number and has bought already? In that case, should he now sell? How long does he wait after the number is announced before he makes up his mind?

For the position trader, the world is an ever-changing place. Every minute, every second, brings another squiggle in prices, another bit of input. No tidbit of information is unimportant, and everything is blended into the kaleidoscope that makes up the market. For him, the market is a living, breathing being, like a dragon that lies in wait. Only by being cleverer, and never resting, can the position trader slay the dragon and win the fair lady. In this struggle, customer relationships are nothing more than encumbrances. There must be no entanglements to cloud his icy glare at the market.

In the end dealers, and customers for that matter, combine these two trading styles. No one in the market is purely dependent on relationships for information, and no one disregards them totally. Everyone develops a few relationships, even if there are only one or two. And everyone knows that the market is a jungle, so every piece of information is suspect. Among all the dealers and all the customers that one could talk to, there is a tremendous range of approaches. What happens, in the end, is that customers and dealers with the same approach end up talking to each other. Some become good friends, and some become worthy adversaries.

MARKET PHILOSOPHIES—
FUNDAMENTAL AND TECHNICAL

After one's style of handling information, one's trading philosophy is next in importance. Here we are concerned solely with what determines the future course of prices. In this case there are also two approaches, much more widely known in the securities industry. Those who depend on the economic facts that underlie the market, without looking at the performance of the market itself, are said to be *trading on the fundamentals*. Those who believe that all the economic facts are already in the market and look only to price performance in the market as a guide, are said to be *trading on the technicals*. For years the ideological battle between the fundamentalists and the technicians has raged on Wall Street, and the fact that neither side has won is good evidence that there is merit in both approaches.

Trading on the fundamentals is trading on the economic announcements that surface every week. It is also trading on the views of the market participants. What will next week's trade figures be? What do those figures bode for the value of the dollars in the exchange markets? If the dollar slides in the exchange markets, what will the Fed do, and what will the other central banks do? Based on what they do, what will foreign holders of dollars, and dollar securities, do with their holdings? And what will all the buyers of governments do when the Treasury next sells securities?

For the technician, all these questions are chaff in the wind. For him, the answers to these questions are already in the market, if only he can read them. He wants to know what has happened to prices in the recent past. Have they been making new highs, or have they shown signs of running out of steam? What are the trends of the past several weeks? Does the market show signs of reversing those trends, and when will we know that the reversal has really occurred? Does the market tell us that real investors are accumulating securities or liquidating them? The answers to these questions, and a thousand others, are hidden in the market, waiting to be discovered.

Given these philosophies, it shouldn't surprise us that dealers who tend to trade order flow are more inclined toward fundamentals, and those who trade positions are more inclined toward technicals. Of course, even that is an oversimplification. There are plenty of technicians who command a loyal customer following, just like there are fundamentalists who trust only their own information. As with styles, there are no examples of total commitments to a single philosophy. Everyone, even the most devout technician, waits nervously for the major economic announcements. And even the most ardent fundamentalist knows the basic trading rule: "Never stand in the market's way!" The trading fraternity is littered with the economic corpses of those who knew better than the market and stood their ground.

METHODS OF TRADING—NAKED VS. SPREAD

If the final objective of trading is the making of money, the final ingredient is the method of trading, or the way in which the trader establishes positions. Here, as with style and philosophy, the world seems divided into two camps: those who take *naked* positions in the hopes of reaping large rewards, and those who take offsetting positions, looking to take advantage of *spreads*. As with style and philosophy, the choice here is often a function of personality—whether one falls into Keynes's class of plunger or hedger.

Naked Trading

Naked traders are not those who disrobe before they sit down at their desks, but those who either buy or sell, without taking any offsetting positions to reduce the risk. They reason that the real profits come from calling the market right, not from trying to get between the market's wall and its wallpaper. They subscribe to the belief that, "All the angels that can dance on the head of a pin can't help the trader whose sense of market direction is wrong."

Their road is straight, but rough. When they are right, and on a roll, they can make unbelievable amounts of money, enough to put the spread trader to shame. By the nature of their method, they must be concerned with the macro picture, because that is what determines the macro moves in the market. They must also have enough capital and financing sources to hold the size positions necessary to take advantage of market moves. And, finally, they must have nerves of steel.

The steel nerves come into play because naked trading involves tremendous amounts of risk. The positions which can generate those astronomical profits can also generate numbing losses. The trader's creed would probably be, "Cut your losses, and let your profits run." That is easier said than done, though. Markets never move in a straight line, so every position can be both a winner and a loser in a short space of time. Naked traders have hair triggers, because they are always exposed to large losses, and this leaves them vulnerable to the classic whipsaw, where the trader abandons a position just before it begins to work for him.

Naked traders are likely to trade more viscerally than intellectually, depending on "feel" rather than logic. Like streak shooters in basketball, they can run hot and cold. When they are hot, the market feels like a living being, which reveals all its secrets to them, and to them alone. When they are cold, all the signals are confusing, they always seem to be going the wrong way, and everyone is out to get them. When they are on a streak, these traders are glorious to behold, but when they are in a slump, no one is more miserable.

Spread Trading

As much as naked trading is for the plunger, *spread trading* is for the hedger. As much as the naked trader works on feel and runs hot and cold, the spread trader works on logic and aims for consistency. Where the naked trader takes big risks to make big profits, the spread trader makes his money in nickels and dimes, hoping they add up every day.

It might sound, from that description, like spread trading is a riskless, mechanical, wimpy game for the faint of heart, but that is really not the case. Good spread trading takes courage, too, and sharp wits; it just requires less of a death wish. Spread traders get as many ups and downs as naked traders, they just get them in smaller doses. One thing is for sure: spread trading is a science. It requires that the trader control his positions, monitor his risk/reward ratios, and, above all, keep his ego out of the equation.

And the equation is the essence of spread trading. A spread trader starts from the premise that there is always an equilibrium relationship between any two issues on the list. What contributes to that equilibrium may be anyone's guess, and what makes two issues move off the equilibrium may be a mystery, but this is the arena of the *arbitrage*.

THE NATURE OF ARBITRAGE

Arbitrage was originally defined as trading that embodied no risk and profited from tiny aberrations. Buying a security in one market and selling it at another price in another was the original arbitrage. As markets have grown and matured, the opportunity to take riskless profits has evaporated, leaving a much chancier business. But the idea of arbitrage is still the same; to abjure the bigger, riskier pie in the sky in favor of the johnnycakes closer at hand. The forms of arbitrage, however, are many and varied.

In order to "put on" an arbitrage, the trader starts from no position, either long or short, and assumes a long position and a short position, or a combination of long and short positions, which gives him a "risk neutral" stance. In assuming these positions, the trader must first know what the historical spread has been between the issues and have an idea of why the current spread is out of equilibrium. It is not enough to assume that, because two issues are trading at a spread quite different from their historical average, they will automatically return to that average spread. Many arbitrageurs have made just that assumption, only to be caught in a fundamental, long-term, shift in spreads. That is the time when spread trading loses its charm and becomes the hardest work of all.

There is a good deal more to controlling risk than setting long and short positions. No two securities, or derivative instruments, move the same amount in price for the same movement in yield. In determining the position sizes, the arbitrageur must calculate the price volatility of each instrument and establish positions that are the inverse of those volatilities. And it isn't enough to say that a four-year note should be twice as volatile as a two-year note. The trader must do the math every time.

Just to complicate the decision, the trader must also determine the availability of the security he is selling short. The rules of the government market require timely delivery of any security sold, so if many dealers do the same arbitrage, the security sold short could be in very tight supply. If that is true, the cost of borrowing that security can amount to as much as 8% per year, or about 3/4 of 1/32d per day. At that cost, the trader's patience with a spread trade can wear thin very quickly.

Kinds of Arbitrage

Probably the most common kind of arbitrage is *yield curve trading*. This arbitrage attempts to take advantage of projected changes in the yield curve by buying one security and selling another with a different maturity. One such trade involves just two issues, say the two-year and three-year notes. If the trader thinks that the two year is cheap, he will buy that and sell the three year, in amounts that are the inverse of their volatility. Thus he might sell $50 million three years and buy $70 million two years. He reasons that, no matter which way the market goes, the different amounts of securities will result in roughly the same dollar profits and losses, except for the hoped-for correction in spread.

Another popular yield curve trade is the *butterfly*. Here the trader takes one position in the middle of the curve, and opposite positions on either end. The middle position would be roughly twice as large as either of the wings. For example, our trader might buy the two-year and four-year notes and sell twice as many of the three-year notes. This trade focuses the attention on the exact security that is out of line, since that will be the one in the middle. By going both ways for the arbitrage, the trader minimizes the chance that he will pick the wrong issue as the offset, and increases his chances of winning. He also increases the complications in the trade as well.

Another arbitrage involves securities and futures, and is called the *basis trade*. This strategy, which used to be called the "cash and carry" trade (because its first use was to allow people to buy securities and carry them), involves the assumption of one position in the security and the opposite position in the futures contract. Its original form was usually the purchase of the security and the sale of the contract, but it is now done both ways.

There is an equilibrium relationship between the security and the contract, of course, based on the net positive carry available to those who buy the security and finance it. If I can buy bonds with a current yield of 10% and finance them at 7%, I have a net positive carry of 3%, or 3/4 of 1% per calendar quarter. If I can sell the 90-day futures contract for a price less than 3/4 point below today's price, I can buy the bonds, finance them, sell the futures contract, and lock up a profit. Voilà! Easy money.

Except, of course, if the financing rate changes during the next three months. Then I might do a lot better or a lot worse. But, all things considered, the basis trade is one of the easier arbitrages. And that is why everyone wants to do it. Every significant dealer, not just every Primary Dealer, has someone who "watches the basis." With all those eyes on it, it seldom gets very far out of line, and many basis traders spend a lot of time staring at the screens and very little time doing trades.

Another game, with more risk but a lot more action, *is auction arbitrage*. This is based on the assumption that, prior to an auction, most dealers sell short the issues nearest to the when-issued security. Then they bid in the auction, and use their short positions to swap customers out of the existing issues into the new one. This process is the way in which dealers hedge themselves against having to bid for large amounts of new securities in uncertain markets.

If everyone sets up for the auctions this way, then the existing issues will be relatively cheap when compared to the when-issued securities. Furthermore, since all the dealers are short the existing issues, they will finance those securities at very attractive rates. Thus, the orthodox wisdom says that you should buy the existing issues, short the when-issued ones, and wait for the dealers to reverse themselves. In the meantime, you can finance your securities at attractive rates, and not have to borrow the when-issued security.

It sounds too good to be true, and doing this blindly is inviting disaster. Sometimes the dealers sell more when-issued securities than existing ones, so the spread never materializes. Sometimes everyone wants to trade out of older issues into newer ones, so the spread never seems to come back into line. And sometimes all hell breaks loose. A few years ago, the Japanese developed a pattern of "rolling out," or selling existing issues in order to swap into new ones. Finally, every large dealer caught onto the pattern, and they all set up for it during the same auction. Every dealer went short the existing issues, and they all bid in the auction.

Only the Japanese didn't roll this time. They just stepped up and bought the new issue with their accumulated cash. The dealers were caught short massive amounts of securities, sometimes more than had originally been issued. At the same time, they were frozen out of the auction, so they were just short. Since the market was rising sharply, as a result of the aggressive bidding of the Japanese, the dealers suffered massive losses. It took them many months to make back what one auction arbitrage had cost them. Perhaps this emphasizes the most important lesson about trading government securities: the market is like a big jungle cat—it might doze off now and then so you can sneak into its lair, but it is never so fast asleep that you can pull its tail.

CHAPTER ELEVEN

The Language of the Market

The government bond business is a highly technical business and, as such, has developed its own vocabulary. Like any technical vocabulary, it sounds very foreign to the uninitiated, but makes perfect sense to those who use it every day. But the government securities business is different from some other technical businesses in two important ways.

First, the business is often done in high pressure and chaotic conditions. At those times, speed of communications becomes paramount, so the language often reverts to shorthand or abbreviated code. Second, a great deal of money often rides on the information exchanged, so the language, including its shorthand, must be accurate and expressive even under stressful conditions. Over many years, the government bond market has evolved just such a language.

Like any language that has taken years to evolve, this one is laden with nuances. Not only do certain words have a specific denotation, they carry one or more connotations. Some of the connotations are based on unwritten rules of business procedure in the market—rules that were understood by everyone when the market itself was much smaller, but are often misunderstood now that the market has become gigantic.

Thus a simple glossary is less useful here than a guided tour of the language, complete with the time-honored traditions of doing business. In this tour, we will not divide words alphabetically, but by function, and the definitions will be more explanatory than those in a glossary. So, let's get started. The terminology is divided into four basic groups: trading terminology, auction terminology, financing terminology, and settlement terminology.

TRADING TERMINOLOGY

Bid: The willingness to *buy* a security at a specified price. The amount must also be specified, either by the bidder or by the customer asking for the bid. Both customers and dealers can make bids. A bid is good for as long as the other party stays on the telephone.

Offer: The willingness to *sell* a security at a specified price. Here, too, the amount must be specified. Both customers and dealers can make offers, and the offer is good for as long as the other party stays on the telephone.

Market: A bid and an offer for the *same* security given *simultaneously*. Usually only dealers make markets, as they are required to do so by the Federal Reserve. If the dealer does not specify an exact size to the market, it is assumed to be for a "round lot" in the security. Customers asking for markets are transmitting less information to the dealer than those asking for bids or offers.

The market has two other connotations. One refers to the government bond market *as a whole,* as in the question, "What is the market doing?" The other refers to an *exchange market,* which is given as information and is not binding on the dealer, as a government securities market is.

Indication: Prices at which one would *probably* do business, but *not* a *binding* number. Indications are asked for and provided, by either a customer or a dealer, when a trade is not imminent. Dealers are usually more willing to provide a series of indications to a customer than a series of markets. Indications are often identified with the phrases, "just a number," "nothing to do," or "ballpark," signaling the indication giver that a bid or offer is not being asked for.

Quote: A bid *indication* and an offering *indication* given at the *same time*. Sometimes, when a customer asks, "How is the ten-year note?" the dealer will respond, " Do you want a quote or a market?" That is not a frivolous question, since the dealer is trying to determine the depth of the customer's interest in the issue. Likewise, when a dealer responds to a request for a quote by giving

The Language of the Market

a market, he is telling the customer that he is active in the issue, and wants to pursue the conversation.

Run: A *series* of market (or quotes) on a predetermined series of issues. Since the issues and their order are *known* ahead of time, the trader will normally give only the *fractional* part of the price. Thus, a bill run quoted "8–6, 23–21, zip–98," would be a quote of 8.08–8.06 for the three-month bill, 8.23–8.28 for the six-month bill, and 9.00–8.98 for the year bill. Runs are given out less now than they were before the advent of brokers' screens, although they are still used in new issues, and some agency issues.

Order: A bid or offer *left* with a dealer by a customer. Once an order is left, the dealer can execute the trade *without* having to recheck the bid or offer with the customer. Orders are normally left for a *specified period* of time, for a few minutes for actively traded issues up to many days for illiquid issues. It is possible for a customer to cancel an order prior to expiration, but only under certain conditions.

Firm: Able to be executed *without* being rechecked. Bids, offers, markets, and orders are firm. Both customers and dealers can leave a bid or offer firm, but it is done more often by customers.

Subject: Unable to be executed *without* being rechecked. Indications and quotes are subject. Orders whose time period lapses go from firm to subject, and must be rechecked before being executed. If a customer hangs up the phone after receiving a bid, offer, or market, that which was firm becomes subject.

Counter: A *response* to a bid, offer, market, or order, giving a *different* price at which the trade can be done. Some customers always counter a dealer's price, so dealers may shade their prices to those accounts, in anticipation of a counter. A counter turns what was a *firm* price into a *subject* one, just as if the customer had hung up the telephone.

Pull: To *cancel* a bid, offer, or order before the time limit expires. Dealers pull bids and offers in the brokers' markets all the time, but orders can be pulled only after calling the dealer and giving him a....

Fill-Or-Kill: Notification that a bid, offer, or order must be executed *immediately* or *canceled*. A customer will normally give a dealer a fill-or-kill when another dealer is willing to do the customer's business at the customer's price. Instead of leaving the first dealer high and dry, the customer must give him a chance to complete the order, in case he has done a part of it.

All-Or-None: A bid, offer, market, or order that must be executed in its *entirety* or not at all. All-or-none orders are usually confined to large transactions, where the dealer is concerned that he may not be able to do the whole trade at once, or where the customer does not want to receive partial reports. All-or-none orders must be so specified at the outset and may be pulled, after giving a fill-or-kill. In this case, the dealer would have to execute the entire order or give it all back, even if he had done only part of it. In the broker's market, all-or-none orders stand behind any orders at the same price which are not all-or-none.

Swap: A trade involving the *purchase* of one security and the *sale* of another which is currently owned. Swaps are generally presented and discussed in terms of *spread,* not absolute prices. When the issues are compared in terms of yield, the swapper is said to *pick up* or *give up* yield. When the comparison is in terms of price, the swapper is said to *take out* or *pay up* money. Although swaps are presented as one trade, dealers or customers may in fact do only one side of the swap, if the price is right. When a dealer does a swap by buying one issue and selling the other *short* it is called an....

Arbitrage: A swap in which a dealer or trader starts with *no position,* buys one issue, and sells the other short. The arbitrageur will normally *weight* the positions according to the volatility of the issues, so that he expects to make money no matter which way the market moves. Arbitrages are *put on* to take advantage of what the arbitrageur thinks is a temporary aberration in the spreads.

Roll: A swap (or arbitrage) from the most *recently issued* security into security *about to be auctioned* (from the *regular-way* security into the *"when-issued"* security). Since bills are the most frequently issued securities, the most common rolls are bill rolls. Since the buyer doesn't pay for the when-issued security and doesn't earn interest on it either, the spread in this swap is usually a function of the difference between the yield on the security and the cost of carry.

Reverse Roll: A swap (or arbitrage) from the *when-issued* security to the *regular-way* security. Any time one party does a roll, the opposite side does a reverse roll. Not only are rolls and reverse rolls done in bills, they are done in a variety of note issues, particularly the two-year note, and some agency issues. Rolls and reverse rolls are among the most popular trades around auction time.

Pass: An *open market operation* by the Federal Reserve Bank of New York in which the Fed's trading desk calls all the Primary Dealers and requests bids or offerings from them all. When the operation involves bills, it is called a *bill pass,* and when the Fed buys or sells notes or bonds, it is called a *coupon pass.* The Fed can do a pass for the System as well as for the account of a customer. From time to time, the Fed will execute trades without doing a pass, but those trades never have any monetary policy implications.

AUCTION TERMINOLOGY

Competitive: Bids which *specify* the price or yield at which the bidder is willing to buy securities and the *amount* the bidder is willing to buy at that price.

Non-competitive: Bids which *do not* specify the price or yield at which the bidder is willing to buy securities, only the amount he is willing to buy. The total of these bids is *subtracted* from the total securities to be awarded before any securities are awarded. Because non-competitive bids are thought to be submitted by real investors, the size of the non-competitive bids is taken as a measure of retail interest in the auction.

High: The high price bid in the auction. When bids are specified in yield, the high bid actually has the lowest number. The Federal Reserve, which actually conducts Treasury auctions, *begins* awarding securities at the high.

Stop: The low bid that is awarded securities. This is the price or yield at which the Fed *runs out* of securities, so bidders at the stop almost never get all they have bid for. Professionals in the market are always *shooting for the stop,* and pre-auction discussions about the low bid are known as *stop talk.* In terms of assessing the success of an auction, the stop is the most important single number.

Average: The *weighted* average of the bids that were awarded securities, arrived at by multiplying each bid level by the amount awarded, adding up those numbers, and dividing the result by the total amount sold. The press usually makes a great deal of the average, as opposed to the stop, but market professionals regard the average as much less important than the stop. All non-competitive bids are awarded at the average price or yield.

Tail: The *difference* between the average and the stop. The tail is important to professionals in measuring the *unanimity* of market opinion on the *value* of the auctioned securities. Normally, the size of the tail is *directly* related to the *maturity* of the auctioned security, so a 2 basis point tail on a two-year note auction would not be nearly as bullish as a 2 basis point tail on a thirty-year bond auction.

Cover: The *ratio* of the total amount *bid for* to the total amount *to be auctioned.* A cover of more than two is usually thought to represent good interest in the issue, while a cover of less than 1.25 usually indicates a close call for the Treasury.

New York District: The *volume* bid for, and awarded, in the New York Federal Reserve District. The professionals have felt for years that the New York District bids represent dealer bids, and those in other Federal Reserve Districts represent customer bids. Thus, the larger the proportion awarded in New York, the weaker the auction is thought to be. This reasoning has been less valid in recent years, because many customers have taken to submitting their bids through Primary Dealers.

FINANCING TERMINOLOGY

Repurchase Agreement (Repo): A two-part transaction where a party *sells* securities and agrees to buy them back (or *repurchase* them) at a later date. Repos are a method of *financing securities* owned which is more popular than a collateralized loan, because repo collateral becomes the property of the financer during the repo, thus insulating it from bankruptcy proceedings.

Reverse Repurchase Agreement (Reverse Repo): The *purchase* and subsequent *resale* of securities. *Reverses* are a method of *investing money* for the short term with great safety, as well as a method of *borrowing* securities sold short. The opposite of every repo is a reverse, a fact that leads to a great deal of confusion in the market. For example, savings and loan associations have an item on the liability side of their balance sheet called "Reverse Repos" although it is clearly a financing, and thus a repo. At the same time, when the Federal Reserve finances dealer positions (and

The Language of the Market

therefore does reverses for itself), the street professionals universally say that "the Fed is doing repos." In fact, the Fed never uses the term reverse repos, preferring to call them "Matched Sales."

Rate: The interest rate charged on the money raised through a repo, calculated on a *money market basis,* as opposed to a bond basis or bill basis.

Term: The *period* that the repo/reverse will be in place. There are four terms normally used.

Overnight: Since the opening transaction for all repo/reverses settles the same day as the trade is made, the closing transaction for an overnight is the *next business day*. It is important to remember that the closing transaction for an overnight on Friday is Monday. In cases like Memorial Day and Labor Day, overnights actually last *three* days.

Fixed Term: A period *longer* than overnight, but less than the term to maturity of the issue. Money market funds and other short-term investors often use fixed term reverses as an *alternative* to the purchase of short bills or short CDs. In the case of a dealer putting inventory out on fixed-term repo, he will often give a rate concession if he has the *right of substitution,* so he can replace the securities being used as collateral in case he sells them during the term.

Open: A period *undetermined* at the outset of the transaction. The transaction will be closed whenever either side exercises its *option* to do so. The rate on open repo/reverses is *reset* every day. The most common use of opens is to *borrow* securities sold short, since the trader doesn't know how long it will be until he covers.

To Maturity: A period *exactly matching* the term to maturity of the security. Obviously, a repo to maturity is equivalent to a *sale*, except that some institutions book profits or losses on sales, but not on repos. Also, the tax recognition of interest income and expense can be different for securities sold as opposed to repoed to maturity. Several regulators have changed the treatment of repos to maturity in the last few years, making them less profitable.

Special: A reverse repo involving a *particular* security needed to make delivery in the case of a *short sale*. Securities *on special* can be financed at rates lower than the rates for general collateral, because they are in short supply. Some customers take advantage of specials through *collateral swaps,* where they sell as repos collateral that is in heavy demand and replace it with *general collateral,* and earn an incremental yield spread.

Haircut: The *difference* between the market value of the collateral and the funds advanced through the repo. The haircut acts as a *margin deposit* to protect the financer of the securities against adverse price movement. Haircuts run from a few basis points for bills to more than a point for long bonds and mortgage backs. The size of the haircut can also be affected by the creditworthiness of the party providing the securities for repo.

Repricing: The *closing* of a repo/reverse and *reopening* of the same transaction, with the *same securities.* A repricing acts as a *mark to the market,* adjusting the financing value of the securities to reflect current market prices, and bringing the accrued interest for both the securities and the financing up to date. Repricings are most often done with open repos, and some longer fixed-term repos. Overnights are automatically repriced every day, and repos to maturity are never repriced, because the financer isn't looking to the original owner to take the securities back.

Safekeeping Repo: A financing transaction in which the financer *doesn't* take delivery of the securities at his clearing bank, leaving the securities on deposit in a *safekeeping* account at the contraparty's bank. Because safekeeping repos require fewer deliveries, they often carry high interest rates. Although this kind of transaction was popular in years past, it is much less so now, because some financers were not careful enough in checking to make sure the securities were actually on deposit. A couple of dealers who were running sizable safekeeping repo books went out of business, and their customers discovered that there were no securities on deposit at all, leaving them as *unsecured lenders* to a dealer in bankruptcy.

Dollar Roll: A repo/reverse transaction in *mortage-backed securities.* Since MBS's have *twelve* coupon payments a year (instead of two), and because each pool of MBS is *different* from all others, the normal repo/reverse doesn't work well. Instead, *specific* MBS's are purchased for delivery immediately, and an *unspecified* pool (with the same coupon) is sold back for a later date. In this case, the interest rate on the repo is established by selling back at a *different price* than the original one. For example, a dollar roll in 8% MBS opened at 100 would be closed out a month later at 99.75 if the financing cost were 5%. The difference between the yield on

The Language of the Market

the security (8%) and the cost of financing (5%), or 3%, is reflected as 1/4 of a point lower price (3% divided by 12).

SETTLEMENT TERMINOLOGY

Regular Way: Trades that settle on the *next business day* after trade date. *All* trades in the government bond market that are not otherwise specified at the outset settle regular way. Some market participants mistakenly say that regular-way trades settle the next day, but that is clearly not true for trades made on Fridays or days before holidays.

Cash: Trades that settle the *same day* that the trade is made. All *financing* trades settle cash. Because many dealers put their inventory out on repo early in the day, the availability of securities for cash settlement may be very suspect after about noon. As a result, cash trades become hard to do late in the day, and no trader will confirm cash trades without checking availability first.

Skip Day: Trades that settle the next business day *after* regular-way trades. Customers sometimes request skip day settlements when their securities settle at a bank in another city, and they need an extra day to get settlement instructions to the bank.

Corporate: Trades that settle *five business days* after trade date. Customers request corporate settlement when they are *swapping* between corporates and governments, and they need simultaneous settlement to avoid borrowing in order to take delivery of the governments.

MBS: Trades in mortgage-backed securities that settle one day each month. Because the factor information, which is essential for settlement of MBS's, is not available until about the fifth of the month and participants need several days to transmit settlement information around, it isn't practical to settle MBS trades the same way as others. Since so many trades must be settled on the same day, market participants maximize use of the....

Pair-Off: The settlement of *two* trades, a purchase and a sale, with the same contraparty by *netting out* the settlement amounts instead of effecting two deliveries. Pair-offs are used in securities other than mortgage backs, but their use is heavily concentrated in MBS.

Fed Funds: Funds on deposit at *Federal Reserve Banks*. Fed Funds are good the *same* day. All government trades, unless otherwise specified, settle in Fed Funds, as opposed to....

Clearinghouse Funds: Funds on deposit at a *clearinghouse bank.* Clearinghouse funds are good the *next business day.* All corporate and municipal bond trades settle in clearinghouse funds.

Wireable: Securities which exist as *entries* on the Federal Reserve's *computer,* rather than as physical pieces of paper. Settlements in wireable securities are accomplished by transferring securities in one direction and money in the opposite direction. All government and agency securities are wireable, with the exception of some MBS, and those will become wireable within a few years.

Fail: An *inability* to deliver securities. Fails are one of the largest causes of *losses* in the government bond market, because interest accrues only to the specified settlement date, and not for the extra day. Thus a fail requires the seller to finance the security for an extra day without receiving an extra day's interest.

Bounce: A *refusal* to accept delivery of securities. Having securities bounced is the *most common cause* of fails. There are only two valid reasons to bounce a delivery: *money differences* and *time.* Money differences refer to a discrepancy between the amount of money expected by the seller and the amount of money the buyer expects to pay, most often due to a disagreement about the amount of accrued interest due.

Dealer Time: The point at which the *dealer-to-dealer* wire at the Fed closes down for the day. Dealers can deliver to each other until this wire shuts down, currently 3:00 P.M. Sometimes, when the computer or a terminal is down at one of the member banks, the closing of the Fed wire is delayed.

Customer Time: Traditionally, the point *after which* customers can no longer deliver to dealers, and the point *until which* dealers may deliver to customers. Although it isn't written down anywhere, dealers expect to deliver to customers for fifteen minutes after the Fed wire closes, and expect to stop receiving fifteen minutes before the Fed wire closes. Some customers who do a lot of trading request and often get treated as dealers, as far as deliveries go.

Turn Around: Getting securities in *from* a *seller* and delivering them *to* a *buyer* before the Fed wire shuts down. The fifteen-minute differences between dealer and customer times is designed to allow dealers to turn around securities and avoid fails. Customers who are active traders request dealer time in order to be able to turn around securities.

Partial: A delivery of *some* of a sale but *not all at once.* When dealers make a large sale and cover it back in small pieces, they face the possibility that some of the securities may fail, causing the dealer to fail on the whole delivery unless he can make a partial delivery. Since buyers usually expect the entire delivery, the seller usually must call ahead to arrange a partial delivery.

CHAPTER TWELVE

A Day in the Life of a Dealer

Many years ago the government bond market looked very different than it does today. The number of dealers was smaller, the kinds of securities were fewer, and it operated on a rigid schedule. By tradition, if not by fiat, the market originally opened promptly at 10:00 A.M. and closed promptly at 3:30 P.M. Over time, as the pressures on the market increased, it changed in many ways, and one of the ways was its hours of operation.

Back in the good old days, all the customers who mattered were in the United States, and they all operated on Eastern Time. Even if they were located in California, customers rose before the sun in order to be at their desks in time for the New York opening. When the market closed in New York, those Californians still had most of the afternoon left to surf or sit in their hot tubs.

Today, government bond customers cover the globe, from Europe through the Middle East to Japan. In response to the globalization of the market, dealers have opened branch offices in Europe (usually in London) and in Japan (usually in Tokyo). These offices, which originally contained only salespeople, are sometimes staffed by traders as well. Thus the market has moved from a localized, 9-to-5 business to a worldwide market that trades 24 hours a day.

Since someone has to be in charge during trading hours, and those hours never stop, dealers have evolved two methods of 24-hour trading.

A Day in the Life of a Dealer

Some dealers man their New York trading desks around the clock, with three shifts of traders and management to handle business as the active trading moves around the world. Other dealers "pass the book" around the world, with traders and management in London, Tokyo, and New York. With this approach, when a trading day ends in one market, the positions and trading strategy are passed to the next office.

THE QUIET HOURS

A typical trading day is best observed by visiting a typical dealer. In our case, it will be an imaginary dealer, Stone, Forrest, & Rivers, known to the bond trade as SFR. This dealership began life when three top performers at one of the old-line dealerships left to form their own firm in the late sixties. As the market grew, SFR prospered until it became apparent that it needed more capital to compete. Recently, SFR was acquired by a German bank, filling up the capital coffers and making rich men out of its founders.

As one might expect with European ownership, SFR follows the "pass the book" method of trading. Our visit will be to the New York office, located in one of the new office buildings on Water Street near the South Street Seaport. SFR's new trading room, with the latest in electronic equipment, was one of the advantages of its acquisition by its German parent. Today is the first Tuesday in August, and, although we might expect many people to be enjoying their summer vacations, today will be busy. This is the second day of Refunding Week, and the Treasury is scheduled to auction three-year notes today. As we enter the trading room, it is...

7:30 A.M. Eastern Time

At this hour, there are very few people around and not much activity, so this is a good time to see how the trading room is laid out. In order to counteract the normal tension of trading, SFR has chosen a relatively innocuous color scheme. The walls and floor are beige, with blond wooden desks. These colors, under the cool fluorescent lights, contrast with the eerie green of the computer screens that adorn every desk.

In a trading room, physical proximity takes precedence over the luxury of personal space, so these desks are much smaller than the typical office desk, and are arranged in quadrants, four desks facing a center computer post. Each desk is dominated by a series of small monitors, arranged in two horizontal rows, which show brokers markets, and a telephone console. The traders have consoles with nearly a hundred buttons on them, each button representing a direct line to a broker or another dealer. Salespeople's phones have fewer direct lines, although each salesperson has some, and a speed dialer to facilitate calls to out-of-town customers. Aside from these differences, there is nothing to distinguish a trader's desk from a salesperson's.

Scattered around the room are microphones, on desks, and in the ceiling are speakers. These are part of an intercom system, known as the *"open mike,"* which connects the main trading room with SFR's branch network. Since these microphones are on all the time, the people in the branches can hear everything that goes on in the trading room, reducing the isolation they feel. Also spread around the room are large TV monitors, hung from the ceiling, which show other markets and late-breaking news items.

Around the perimeter of the trading floor are offices and conference rooms, with glass doors and windows looking out on the floor. Some of the offices are "second homes" for people in charge of parts of the trading operation: the head trader, the sales manager, and the head of operations. Also housed here are the economist and his staff, the computer experts, and certain key members of the operations group. In a corner office, larger than the rest, sits the department manager, when he is not out on the floor. His office has a full complement of screens, and a microphone and speaker.

The manager is in there now, with the head trader, talking on the speaker phone to SFR's London office. It is 1:30 P.M. in London, and the London branch manager is updating New York on the day's trading activity, as well as the extent of European interest in today's all-important three-year note auction. As we enter, the branch manager is just finishing his report.

"So we haven't seen much interest in the issue richer than a 50," he is saying. "Every time the WI traded there we did good business with Swiss banks and British building societies. The Street being what it is, the auction will probably stop at a 49."

What he means is that customers haven't been willing to buy the three-year note at a yield less than 7.50%. Every time the when-issued

A Day in the Life of a Dealer

three year did trade at 7.50%, certain kinds of customers bought it, but the dealers, seeing interest at that level, will probably try to get customers to pay more by stopping the auction short of 7.50%, perhaps at 7.49%.

"Okay, John," replies the manager, "we are nursing a good-sized short in the WI, at slightly lower prices, so we won't be very aggressive sellers here. If the dealers knock it down into the auction, we will bid to buy, but we are too bearish to step up to these levels."

The manager means that the trading desk has sold the when-issued three-year note short, expecting prices to fall going into the auction. They have risen instead, presenting management with a decision. Do they throw in the towel on this short and cover it, taking the loss, or do they hold onto the position, hoping to buy back later at lower prices?

The manager reveals that they do not want to sell any more securities here, and won't bid aggressively in the auction at current levels. However, sometimes the dealers drive prices down just before an auction, hoping to scare customers away and give themselves a chance to buy cheap securities. If that happens today, the manager plans to use the opportunity to buy back his short position and move on to another strategy.

As this conversation proceeds in the manager's office, people are trickling in on the trading floor, most carrying breakfast and coffee in paper bags. They sit at their desks and immediately check their screens to see what has been happening to the market overnight. After exchanging a few cryptic comments about the market, they settle down to do some paperwork.

Records are the lifeblood of the government securities business. Not only records of trades made, but records of past prices and spreads between issues, both in terms of price and yield. For salespeople, there are records of what customers own, what they sold or bought, what swaps they did between what issues for what spreads, and what they said they would do in the future. Early in the morning is a good time to update all these records.

It is also a good time to compare notes on the market. The traders are talking to their counterparts in London, to their counterparts at other dealerships, to the brokers, and to the salespeople. Salespeople compare notes with each other, with salespeople at other firms, and with those customers who are early birds.

Although New York is not trading actively yet, one desk is already busy. Since today's settlements and financings are a result of yesterday's trades, the *matched book desk* is already busy financing yesterday's purchases and finding collateral for yesterday's short sales. The secret to success for this desk is developing a network of customers who own or finance collateral, so there will be a parade of salespeople to and from this trading desk until about 10:00 A.M. There is no time here to discuss yesterday's baseball game or next week's vacation. These traders are too busy negotiating, trading, and writing tickets.

8:15 A.M. Eastern Time

People have been coming into the trading room for the past 45 minutes, and the noise level has been gradually rising. Suddenly, the noise drops as the intercom crackles to life and the morning meeting begins. This daily ritual starts with the economist's pronouncements, followed by any trader who wants to share his market insights, any salesman with a specific need, and ends with any housekeeping matters that managers may have. The economist leads off.

"Yesterday we expected the Fed to accomplish its add through a small system repo, but they surprised us by doing a bill pass. Either the add need was bigger than we thought, or they are unhappy with funds at 7%. We rechecked our cash flow projections for the Treasury, and we still see only a small add need, which we think they completed yesterday. Thus, we think the bill pass was a rate protest, and we would expect another one today if funds stay in the 7% range."

"On the economic front, everyone is looking for tomorrow's balance-of-trade figures to show another drop in net imports. We think the drop will be a lot smaller than projected, largely because oil stockpiles are being built up. We will stick with our projection of $11 billion, down slightly from last month's $12 billion."

As the economist covers several other matters, salespeople take detailed notes on what he is saying, to be used later in conversations with customers. Traders write less, incorporating his comments into their own market outlooks. As soon as he is finished, the three-year note trader begins talking about today's auction.

"The trading in the WI has been spotty, with some buying at 7.50% and cheaper, but interest has picked up in the last few days. The bill pass seems to have convinced some people that the Fed may be leaning toward ease, which has made the shorts nervous, us among

A Day in the Life of a Dealer

them. I still think the auction will stop at 50 or 49, but I am less sure of that than yesterday. I want feedback today on what your customers are hearing. If it looks like someone is going to coup this auction, I want to bring that short in right away."

A few salespeople add comments they have heard from customers, both about customers' interest in the three year and what customers have heard from other dealers. Then the bill traders discuss yesterday's auction of three- and six-month bills.

"The three month came right as advertised at 6.54%, but the six month was a little stronger than the talk at 6.83%. Apparently, two money funds stepped into the auction and stopped the six month cold. We heard that they had been buying the WI sixes aggressively, and it seems they are trying to create a short squeeze. Luckily, we stepped up in the auction and bought three hundred, so we are positioned for a rally. If sixes go special when they are delivered, we will know that we were right. In the meantime, we will be sellers at 6.80% or richer."

Following the bill traders, the agency trader comments on the upcoming sale by FNMA, the long bond trader points out that the CBT bond contract has been trading cheap to the cash market as traders short futures to get ready for Thursday's bond auction, and the mortgage-backed securities trader alerts everyone to a shortage of FHLMC PCs due to the recent closing of a $500 million collateralized mortgage obligation.

Two salespeople outline programs their customers have. One is moving from five-year notes into ten-year notes, as he becomes more bullish, and another is reducing coupons on his MBS portfolio, by swapping out of 13% issues and into 8% issues. Then the sales manager reminds everyone that commission runs, which show the amount of business done, by account and product, are due, and that the firm's tickets to the U.S. Open tennis tournament are available, for those who reserved them, from his secretary. Finally, the manager sums up the meeting, and sets the tone for the day.

"We have been bearish for the last several days because we think that the economy is stronger than others do, but yesterday's Fed activity was a surprise. I think that the Fed is a little confused about the Treasury's cash position, but I am willing to be convinced that they really are trying to ease. Today's activity will tell the tale. Meanwhile, we will be better buyers than sellers. Have a good day."

With that, the intercom goes silent, and the general noise level picks up again. It is now 8:30 A.M.

Chapter Twelve

TRADING BEGINS

9:00 A.M. Eastern Time

There is no official opening bell for the government bond market, but this hour is as close as the market gets to an official opening. This is the point at which SFR's London traders pass the book to the New York office. It is also the point at which the Chicago Board of Trade bond contract opens for trading. Finally, it is the hour at which many customers expect to begin trading.

In the trading room, one can feel the intensity pick up a little, as the real trading day begins. All across the country, customers and other dealers are doing their first real trades of the New York trading day, and the first few moments often set the tone for the whole day. The brokers' screens, many of which have been largely blank, fill up with numbers and begin flashing as trades begin to take place. Traders get busy with street and customer business; none more so than the three-year note trader.

"Bank of Montreal would like a bid on $20 million WIs."
"Forty-nine bid."
"Twenty you buy at 49."
"FCA is looking for $50 million WIs at 48. Can you help?"
"Sorry, 47+ is my best."
"Nothing done, thank you."
"Harvard can offer $40 million WIs at 48+."
"Forty I buy at 48+. Show FCA his $50 million at 48."
"He bought 25 there already; he can do 25 more."
"Twenty-five I sell him at 48."

Other traders are working on their own positions, and doing their own trades.

"Sales force, I can offer $100 million six months at 6.80%. There is a 6.81 bid in the street."
"Where can Scudder sell us $10 million long bonds?"
"I will pay them 16."
"They need 17. Can we pay it?"
"Not now, but I will take an order."

A Day in the Life of a Dealer

"Okay, you have $10 million long bonds for ten minutes at 17."

"You can sell $70 million six months to Exxon at 6.80, if you are still there."

"Fine, seventy I sell at 6.80%."

As the tide of inquiry and trades ebbs and flows, the management is keeping a sharp eye on the trend of business, as well as the direction of the market. Are customers asking for more bids or more offerings? Are they getting stronger prices from other dealers, or weaker ones? Are they haggling about the dealer's bids but taking his offerings, or vice versa? Are securities trading "BID HIT" on the screens, or are they trading "TAKEN"? All these things tell the market's story, if only the management can decipher it.

10:00 A.M. Eastern Time

By now, the opening rush of business has slowed down. Those customers who needed to establish their positions for the day have made their trades. The matched book desk has almost completed its work, with only some small positions left to be financed. Now the market's attention turns to Fed funds, for everyone has decided that the funds level will dictate the Fed's activity for the day.

Even if the level of activity has ebbed, important things are happening. At about this point, the manager makes a crucial decision in his office, and buzzes the three-year note trader on his private line.

"Where is the WI now?"

"47+ −6+, last taken at 47."

"I think this short is just too dangerous. Futures are right up against a resistance level, and if they break out they could go another half point. Funds are still $6^{15}/_{16}$ to 7, which means the Fed will probably be in again. Oil is trading down and bills are trading up. What are you seeing from retail?"

"Some of the players are starting to nibble, and a few that swore they wouldn't go through 7.50 are trying to buy from me on the bid side. I think you are right about the short. In fact, I have been covering small amounts all morning."

"What are we short now?"

"Two hundred, down from three hundred."

"Okay, let's buy the rest and go long 200. If you have to pay more than 46, call me first."

"Right."

Immediately the intercom comes to life, and the three-year note trader has everyone's attention.

"Sales force, we are buyers of the WI three year. The market is 7.47+ to 7.46+. We will pay 7.47 for size. If you see any at 46+, don't hang up!"

Now the good salesperson proves his worth. To simply call a customer and repeat what the trader said would be to tip the dealer's hand to someone who might use the information against the house. The first order of business is to determine if the customer owns any WIs, and whether he might be in a selling mood.

"Mike, it's Terry at SFR. Are you long any WI three years?"

"Yes. I bought 50 yesterday at 51. Why?"

"We are looking for some. The market is 47+ − 46+. Would you sell any at 47?"

"It's that strong, huh? Well, I guess I could let them go at 46+."

"Let me see if we can pay that. Hold on... We can't pay it right now, but I may be able to get you 46+ if I have an order."

"Okay, you've got them for ten minutes at 46+."

Meanwhile, the trader is getting information from the government brokers about the street market.

"Offering out at 46+, 46 is best now."

"WI trades up at 46+, buyer wanted more."

At this point, the trader makes his move.

"Terry, buy those WIs at 46+. Sales force, I am paying 46+ for WIs; I have bought them there."

After buying $150 million at 46+, the trader is shown a block of $100 at 46 by a broker, *"eyes only."* This means that the broker has instructions to show the offering only to the big buyer, and not to the rest of the dealers. The trader immediately buys the offering, and then gives the broker a small offering at 46 to show to the street.

"Sales force, I am bidding 46 for 100 WIs. They are offered there on the screen."

Seeing the 7.46 offering, several customers are happy to sell there, and the trader completes his $200 million long position at that price. As soon as he completes his purchases, he pulls his offering at 7.46, and replaces it with a bid at the same price.

A Day in the Life of a Dealer

FIRST MOMENT OF TRUTH

11:30 A.M. Eastern Time

The day's first moment of truth has arrived. It is *Fed time*, the point in every day when the Federal Reserve Bank of New York executes its open market transactions. Having recently changed from bearish to bullish, SFR has a major investment in this particular operation by the Fed.

Since the Fed never comments on any of its actions and never articulates monetary policy (beyond the chairman's public appearances before Congress), open market operations become doubly important. Not only do they have the obvious effect of adding or draining bank reserves, they also provide a window into the Fed's thinking and policies. That window may have frosted glass panes, and we may only be able to make out general shapes and not details, but it is the only window we have.

The reason market participants pay so much attention to Fed time is that open market operations can have two very distinct causes. In one case a temporary imbalance in bank reserves, which is not reflected in the funds rate, may require the Fed to add or drain, even though it is happy with where the rates are. This kind of action is known as *technical*.

Conversely, even though the Fed is not concerned with reserve imbalances, it may be unhappy with where funds are trading and may enter the market to add or drain in order to show its displeasure with current rates. This kind of action is called a *rate protest*. Since the Fed never tells the market what reason prompted a particular action, much of the market's time is spent determining what the reason is. There are a couple of guidelines the market uses in trying to figure out the Fed's motivations.

The first guideline is *recent history*. The Fed seldom makes abrupt changes in monetary policy through open market operations alone; it uses reserve requirements and the discount rate for that. Thus, if they did matched sales with funds at 7% yesterday and bought coupon securities today with funds at the same rate, the market would conclude that there were some powerful technical forces at work, not that the Fed had done a 180-degree turn in one day. The second guideline is that *overnight* repo or matched sales are thought of as *rate protests*, while *multi-day* operations are thought to be *technical* in nature. Beyond that, a lot of guesswork is involved.

The difference between technical and rate protest will be particularly important today, because Fed funds have edged off since 10:00 A.M. They are now 6⅞ to $6^{15}/_{16}$, a little below the magic level of 7% which prompted the Fed to intervene yesterday. Whatever they do today will tell the market a lot about the direction of rates over the next few days.

Thus, by 11:35, everyone is seated, ready for action. All the traders have one eye on the firm's direct line to the Fed's trading desk, and the salespeople focus their attention on the senior trader, who has the responsibility for answering the Fed line. A few phone conversations are going on, but even these don't have the participants' full attention.

At 11:38, the light on the Fed line blinks, and the senior trader answers it at once. All eyes in the room are on him as he listens intently for a few seconds, puts down the phone and grabs the nearest microphone.

"Two day repo for the System! Two day repo for the System!" reverberates across the intercom. Immediately, since the Fed has called all the Primary Dealers at approximately the same time, the market reacts.

The first reaction is disappointment. People who bought securities because they thought the Fed was easing hurry to lighten their positions. Their urgency is heightened by the fact that they will have to bid on $10 billion of three-year notes in less than an hour and a half. What bids there are get hit immediately, and the market starts to fade.

The manager is now on the trading floor, standing behind the three-year note trader. His face is impassive, but his emotions are high. Is this a classic whipsaw, where a dealer gets short in a rising market, covers and watches the market fall in his face? Has the Fed totally botched it, leaving him long a bundle of securities with no help on the horizon? Or is there some better, more logical explanation? Most important, what is he to do about the auction?

At a time like this, there are plenty of people with explanations, but precious few with real insight. The economist calls, to defend his earlier projections.

"We said that the Fed's actions would be a function of the funds rate, and they are. We have seen the funds rate drop slightly, removing the Fed's need to protest. This was a technical action, based on some imbalance we haven't seen yet. Don't give up, we are right."

The traders, with a more immediate horizon, can only react to what they see before them. In particular, the three-year note trader.

"Look, boss, they're hitting 48 bids all over. Everybody's a seller, now. Let's bag it, blow out the position here, and take another look at auction time."

But the manager must look at all aspects of the market. Dealers buy and sell in an instant, but customers are much more deliberate. Between customers and the funds rate, he will be able to see what is really happening. So he listens to the flow of customer inquiry.

"Offer $50 million WIs to Dominion Bank."

"Forty-eight."

"He needs 50."

"No thanks."

"Alliance Capital can offer you $25 million WIs at 47."

"They have traded at 48 already; I won't pay more than 50."

"He's going to stay at 47."

"The World Bank has been buying WIs at 49. Do you want to sell any there?"

The manager puts his hand on the trader's shoulder and shakes his head. The World Bank is one of those accounts that can accumulate huge positions, and the fact that they are buying is the most bullish thing the manager has seen. He is also encouraged that customers, unlike dealers, are not rushing to hit bids, and some are bottom fishing.

The trader takes the hint. "At 47, $100 million at 47," he says.

"Nothing done."

As if on cue, Fed funds tick down again, making them $6^{13}/_{16}$ to $6\frac{7}{8}$. Prices stabilize and begin to edge up again. The manager rubs his eyes and heads back to his office.

12:45 P.M. Eastern Time

After the excitement of Fed time, things have quieted down considerably. Metal carts with lunch trays have arrived and been distributed by the kitchen staff. The market itself doesn't take a lunch break, so the participants seldom go out to eat. They eat at their desks instead, talking on the phone and watching the screens all the while. The manager, eating in his office, has made a few personal calls, never taking his eye off the market.

Now, we have arrived at the day's second moment of truth, the auction itself. Since the Treasury has been using this method of issuing securities for about fifteen years, market participants may feel that this is the only method the Treasury has ever used. Nothing could be further from the truth. In the 1960s, when it did not have such a voracious appetite for money, the Treasury refinanced outstanding issues through rights offerings. Owners of maturing securities turned them in and received new ones in exchange, so the only way to obtain new securities was to buy the maturing ones.

As markets have moved, and the Treasury's cash position has changed, other methods have been tried. Dutch auctions have been used, where all securities are awarded to successful bidders at the lowest successful bid. The Treasury has also tried subscription offerings, where it set the terms beforehand and allowed people to subscribe for what they wanted. Over time, though, the competitive auction evolved as the issuing method of choice.

In a competitive auction, each bidder specifies the amount of securities he is bidding for and the price he is willing to pay. In the case of a *new issue*, the bidder specifies the *yield to maturity*, out to two decimal places, and the Treasury specifies the coupon and dollar price after all the bids are in. In the case of a *reopened issue*, the bidder specifies the *dollar price*, out to three decimal places.

Now is the time for SFR to prepare its bids for the three-year note. The trader has a pile of tender forms on his desk, already filled out with everything but the amount and the yield. The sales manager holds a brief meeting on the trading floor, with all the salespeople in attendance.

"As you already know, we have changed our posture in the last couple of hours. We think that the Fed was reacting to a temporary oversupply of reserves by not doing another bill pass. Funds, which are now below 6⅞, are telling us that. The WI is trading 7.47 to 7.46. We think the stop will be 7.46. If customers have to buy, we recommend that they bid 7.45. It looks to us like there are some size buyers in the issue."

A few salespeople add comments about what their customers are thinking or seeing, and they all go back to their desks to begin rounding up bids. Dealers traditionally submit customer bids without commission or spread, as a courtesy, so SFR will have a goodly number of bids to

A Day in the Life of a Dealer

prepare. For the next ten minutes, salespeople come over to the trader, or call out to him, with customer bids to be entered.

At the same time, the manager is working with the trader to prepare the firm's own bid. Dealers have an inside track here, because they can see what customers are bidding before they prepare their own bid. An unscrupulous dealer, seeing large customer interest, could *front run*, or submit a large bid of his own just above the customer level, hoping to freeze the customers out and sell them securities at a higher price after the auction.

SFR values its customers too much to attempt that, but there is no denying that customer input affects SFR's own bids. As customer bids come in, it becomes apparent to the manager and the trader that interest is higher than they had originally thought. Some customers are taking the chance of buying at a 7.48 or 7.47, but many more are stepping up to 7.46 and even to 7.45.

There are customers whose auction information is invariably poor, so that they always pay too much or miss the securities entirely. Other customers always seem to get good auction information and are always around the low price, or stop. After many years in the market, the manager knows who has good information and who doesn't, and this time the smart money is bidding to buy. Even those customers who are scaling their bids are putting the higher volume on the lower yields.

It is now 12:55 P.M., and time to put in the firm's own bid. There is a hurried conference around the trading desk, and the decision is made to bid for $200 million at 7.45, $200 million at 7.46, and $200 million at 7.47.

While some dealers telephone their bids to clerks standing in the Federal Reserve Bank of New York, SFR follows the old-fashioned practice of having the tenders hand carried from their offices to the Fed. They believe that the risk of mistakes due to faulty communication on the telephone outweighs the risk of having the runner miss the deadline. So one of the secretaries has summoned an elevator and immobilized it. As soon as the last tender is filled out, a young clerk, known for his athletic ability, dashes to the elevator with the tenders. Upon reaching the ground floor, he sets off on a dead run for the Fed, two blocks distant, and arrives, slightly winded, with a minute to spare. He hands in the tenders, and receives back a time-stamped receipt, signifying that his tenders were submitted in time.

Back at SFR, the market continues to trade, almost as if nothing much has happened. But appearances are deceiving. In an attempt to buy securities cheaply in the auction or to convince others to pay a high price, market participants sometimes make bids or offers in large size right before the bids are submitted. After 1:00 P.M., nothing can affect those bids, so the market is much more concerned with what everyone bids and where the auction will stop. Now, those dealers who bid cheaply may be concerned about missing the auction entirely, particularly if they hear others discussing more aggressive bids than theirs. Those who become convinced that they paid too much may be in a hurry to dump the securities they are afraid they bought. The fact is, though, that no one knows how the auction went until the results are announced, sometime after 4 P.M.

Once the auction is over, some of the other securities come back into focus, and the flow of business is more evenly spread across the room. The six-month bill trader is still a seller, but at 6.78% now. The long bond trader is in the midst of putting on a sizable arbitrage against the CBT bond contract. The MBS traders are still looking for securities to fill out a CMO. And the agency trader is busy taking orders for FNMA's new issue. It is business as usual again.

2:45 P.M. Eastern Time

For almost two hours, the market has been humming along. With the three-year note auction behind it, and several more hours until the results are announced, the market has begun to turn its attention to the ten-year note, which will be auctioned tomorrow. Ten-year note buyers are often different from three-year note buyers, so the marketing job must be done all over again.

Fed funds seem to have stabilized at 6¾%, and the market has taken some encouragement from the ¼ point drop. Customers have become more aggressive in buying securities. The WI three year is now trading at 7.45%, with plenty of bidders at that level. In fact, the manager is even starting to believe that he may have missed the auction entirely.

Two areas of the trading floor have become especially busy as 3:00 P.M. approaches. One is the long bond trader, who is completing his futures arbitrage. The CBT closes at 3:00, so he will be frozen out until tomorrow morning if he doesn't finish in the next five minutes. He sits, staring at the brokers' screens, speaking to a clerk on the floor of the CBT on one phone and a bond broker on another.

"What's bid?"
"Seventeen."
"At 18."
"Seventeens trade."

Since the trader is trying to sell futures and buy long bonds, the fact that futures are not trading up is making his job more difficult. He has a bid for bonds in the brokers market, based on the futures price. As futures move, he must adjust his bond bid to keep the arbitrage in line. It is a little like juggling while walking on a tightrope, and requires him to carry on two conversations at once.

"At 17... 21 best on the bond."
"Bid along with you at 21, offered at 22."
"Seventeens trade, you sold 30."
"Take 3 million at 22."
"You buy 3 bonds at 22, seller would do more."
"What's bid?"
"Seventeen for 50."
"Sell 50 at 17... take 5 more at 22."

In this last exchange, the trader is taking something of a risk, since he can't be sure both trades will be executed as he ordered. Someone else could sell futures at 17 before his order gets to the floor, or someone else could take the 22 offering on the bond. These risks are manageable, though, and in this case the trader completes his arbitrage before the market closes.

The other busy area is the matched book desk—3:00 P.M. is the normal cutoff time for deliveries of securities between dealers, which means that any securities not delivered by that time must be carried overnight by the delivering party. Since the dealer would have paid for the securities, he would have to finance them overnight. However the official settlement date would still be the previous day, so he would not get an extra day's accrued interest to offset the financing cost.

If financing costs are 8%, then *failing to deliver* $10 million in securities costs the dealer $2,192. That equates to 70% of 1/32d, the normal profit margin for many trades. Thus delivery problems could wipe out most, if not all, of the gross profit margins a dealer earns. For that reason, the matched book desk is busy at this hour, in constant contact with the clearance department about which securities are coming in and which are being delivered out.

One of the most perplexing problems this desk faces is the need to put blocks of securities together to make deliveries to customers and other dealers. If SFR had sold a customer $100 million in bills—which it had bought in blocks of $10 million, $20 million, $25 million, $40 million, and $5 million—and the last $5 million failed to come in, the whole delivery of $100 million could be rejected. Thus, dealers make certain that, in large trades with customers, they can deliver *partials*, as long as they call the customer to let him know what is coming.

4:00 P.M. Eastern Time

The day is beginning to wind down, but there are still a couple of important things to be attended to. The first happens right at 4:00, when the news flashes across the Dow Jones ticker, "TREASURY TO AUCTION $13 BILLION OF BILLS." That isn't really news to anyone in the bill market, or perhaps to anyone at SFR. This is the ritual bill announcement, which is made every Tuesday at 4:00, detailing the amount of the bill auction to be held next Monday.

If it isn't really news, why does anyone care? Because the Federal Reserve mandated several years ago that there could be no when-issued trading in a security until its sale had been officially announced by the Treasury. Since there is a bill auction every week, the market could trade when-issued bills for many weeks in advance, if it were not for this rule. However, since there is such a rule, this is the first moment that bill traders can get their teeth into next week's bills.

Trading begins immediately, of course, but it sounds a little different from the other kinds of trading we have been hearing.

"How can we do the three-month forward roll for Northern Trust?"

"Plus two."

"He would do $100 million at plus 2½."

"Okay, $100 million done at 2½. Use 47 and 49½."

"IBM will show you the six-month reverse roll at give 1."

"Everyone wants to do give 1. I have done give 1½ with customers already. Does he want to do give 1½?"

"Sorry, he's going to stay at give 1."

These people are talking about bill rolls, both forward and reverse. A roll is a kind of swap, between the when-issued bill and the most recently issued one. These bills obviously mature a week apart, with the when-issued bill maturing later. A forward roll is the sale of the regular-way bill and the purchase of the when-issued one. A reverse roll is the

A Day in the Life of a Dealer

sale of the when-issued and purchase of the regular way. Like all swaps, rolls are presented with price spreads instead of absolute prices, which are determined only after the trade is done.

Northern Trust wanted to sell regular-way bills, and buy when-issued ones, maturing a week later than the sale candidate. Since Northern will not be earning any interest for that week and won't be using any money to pay for bills, the spread for the roll is a function of two things. The first is the yield curve, or the amount by which yields change as maturities change. The second is the positive carry, or the net profit to be gained by holding bills, financing them, and earning the interest differential. Northern has determined that the combination of those two factors makes the swap worth 2½ basis points. SFR does the trade at that spread, and determines that they will be buying the regular-way bills at 6.47% and selling the WI at 6.495%.

IBM, on the other hand, wants to sell the WI and buy the regular way. Why would someone want to sell a bill that hasn't been issued yet and buy one that has? One very good reason is that IBM may be short these bills. Borrowing securities can be an expensive proposition, so IBM takes the safe road by buying back the bill that is about to be issued, and resets the short in the WI. Now they have another week to work the short before they have to think about borrowing the bills. IBM is willing to pay 1 basis point to do this, but SFR has done better for itself and won't concede anything to IBM. Who's right? It all depends on the next trade and where the market is going.

Bill rolls are the star of the show every Tuesday at 4:00 P.M., but today there are other people around the room who have no interest in the bill roll market. They are waiting for the announcement of the *auction results* for the three-year note. After the submission of bids, the most important moment in the auction procedure is the announcement of the results. It is even more important today because the three year is the first of a series of auctions, and how well the market receives this issue will set the tone for the rest of the week.

There are several determinants of how well an auction has been received. The first has to do with prices. Although the press and the general public focus their attention on the average price, the professionals are more interested in the lowest successful bid price, or the *stop*. Since competitive bidders are always trying to buy at the lowest successful bid price, or *hit the stop*, and since there is a great deal of discussion before the bidding closes about where the auction will stop, the most important relationship for the professional is between the *stop talk* and the actual stop. When an auction stops short of the stop talk, it is said to be a strong auction, and when it stops at a higher yield than the stop talk it is said to be a weak auction.

The second most important relationship is between the average bid and the stop. This spread is called the *tail*, and is thought to be a measure of how unified the market was in establishing a value for the securities. The tail varies with the issue's term to maturity, so longer issues normally have longer tails. A short tail normally means a strong auction, and vice versa, but a tail of two basis points for a three-year note may be moderately bullish, while the same tail for a thirty-year bond would be spectacularly bullish. In evaluating the tail, market participants will often look at several previous auctions of the same security for comparison.

There are other measures of success too. One is the size of the *non-competitive bids*, since these are thought to be a function of real retail interest in the issue. Another is the relationship of the total bids submitted to the total securities sold, or the *cover*. This is thought to be a measure of the total interest in the issue. Any cover above two times is usually a sign of strength, while a cover below 1.25 times is thought to be too close to the minimum for comfort. Last, *the amount awarded in New York* is viewed with interest, because New York bids are thought to be by dealers, as opposed to real investors. However, this is a lot less important than it used to be, because so many customers have taken to bidding through dealers.

So there is a lot to look for when the results are announced. And when the results for the three year are flashed across the Dow Jones ticker at 4:21 P.M., they are, as they often are, a mixed bag. The bid range was from 7.43% to 7.46%, with the average at 7.45%. There were $17.5 billion bids for the $10.3 billion in notes awarded. Non-competitive bids were about on target at $873 million. And the New York District won $8.85 billion of the $11.6 billion it bid for.

As soon as the results are announced, the trader and the manager huddle for a few moments. Their discussion is made a lot more pleasant by the fact that the WI is trading at 7.43% at the end of the day, but there is always the possibility that someone may read the auction poorly, and drive the price down after the announcement. In this case, however, prices seem to be holding, so they decide to feed some of their long position out over the next few days.

A Day in the Life of a Dealer

5:30 P.M. Eastern Time

The trading room is almost empty now, except for a few salespeople whose active West Coast accounts have just returned from lunch. Some of the traders are still in their seats, tidying up from the day's work and getting ready for tomorrow, or talking to their counterparts in the Tokyo office. After a strenuous day, no one has much energy for after-work partying.

As he was when we arrived this morning, the manager is in his office, on the speaker phone. This time, it is to the firm's Tokyo office manager, as he passes the book again.

"Well, Kitsu, we had a pretty good day, all things considered. We ended up long about $200 million of the WI, after we sold a bunch to retail. We saw plenty of follow-through after the auction, but not much after the results. We still have two more auctions to go, so I don't want to fall in love with anything. If you see buyers above 7.44%, I think you should let the WIs go."

"Okay, Larry, we'll get on the phones and see what we can do. Meanwhile, go home and relax. You have to do it all over again tomorrow."

"Thanks, buddy. See you later."

With that, the manager hangs up, turns out the lights in his office, grabs his suitcoat from the back of the door, and walks out past the cleaning crew.

CHAPTER THIRTEEN

Inside the Federal Reserve

As large as the government bond market is, as much as its slightest tremor registers all over the world, as diverse as its participants are, it is all tied together by the eminence that looms over it, the Federal Reserve. Every conversation in the market and about the market has, as its hidden subject, the Fed. Every morning at 11:30 the whole market stops to hear what the Fed has to say. Nowhere in the world does a market so large and so liquid depend so utterly upon a single government agency.

And yet, most of the market's participants, to say nothing of the rest of the world, know very little about how the Fed actually works. Everyone knows when the Open Market Trading Desk does a pass, and the whole world notices when the discount rate is raised, but not many people know why those things happen or how they are done. And the Fed is very happy to keep it that way.

A part of the Fed's murky image is due simply to the fact that it is a large and complex organization, but the major part is due to the Fed's penchant for secrecy. Operating on the premise that too much information, disseminated too soon, is bad for the market and its participants, the Fed has a long-standing policy of minimum disclosure. It never comments on the reasons for any of its open market operations. It never discloses the size of any open market transaction for the System Account. It never announces when it is intervening in the foreign exchange markets. And it delays the release of the minutes of Federal Open Market Committee meetings for 30 days.

Bad as that policy sounds, it used to be worse. In the 1960s, the Fed delayed releasing the minutes of the FOMC meetings for 90 days, not 30. Over the last ten years, the Fed chairman has been required to report regularly to Congress on the conduct of monetary policy, but those appearances have often been exercises in obfuscation. This is all part of a long tradition by which the Fed maintains its treasured independence from the political turmoil. In recent years, however, Congress and the public have taken the position that monetary policy and the Fed's other functions are too important to be carried on in the dark. All the signs are that more and more of the Fed's operations will be opened up to public scrutiny.

THE STRUCTURE OF THE FED

As we might expect of a large organization that has many functions, the Federal Reserve has several arms. And, as we might expect of an organization that has been in existence for seventy years, some of its parts make logical sense today, and some parts look out of date. Nevertheless it performs a variety of jobs with aplomb, often under difficult conditions.

At the apex of the Federal Reserve System is the Board of Governors, seven members appointed by the President, with the advice and consent of the Senate, for terms of fourteen years. The Federal Reserve Board shares with the Supreme Court the delicate position of being politically appointed but having an apolitical mission. The terms are staggered so that one expires every even-numbered year, giving each President the opportunity to appoint at least two Board members.

The Board is surrounded in Washington by a large staff of economists and bureaucrats, and throughout the country by the twelve Federal Reserve District Banks and their branches. Each Bank, which performs the entire gamut of commercial and investment banking functions, has the same kind of staff and management that we might expect in any bank. While the Board might tell you that the Banks act under its supervision, the Banks would probably tell you that they act under the Board's guidance. That is a fine distinction, to be sure, but it is important to the system, where independence is the watchword.

The third leg of the Fed's stool is the Federal Open Market Committee (FOMC). The FOMC is made up of twelve members—the seven Board members and a rotating five of the twelve Bank presidents. Unlike the other two parts of the triumvirate, which have many functions, the FOMC has only one function: the setting and implementation of monetary policy. The FOMC's schedule of meetings is not determined by statute but is set by the FOMC itself. Most recently, meetings have been held about eight times a year, and telephone conferences almost daily. (See Figure 13-1.)

THE FUNCTIONS OF THE FED

As important as the Fed is to the market, the market sees only a small part of what the Fed does. Because the market is concerned exclusively with its own world, it often concludes that everything the Fed does is market driven, but that is surely not the case. In fact, the Fed has six important functions, each of which is vital in its own eyes.

For example, in 1974, at height of the Arab oil embargo, Federal Funds suddenly rose to over 20%. Everyone concluded that the Fed had tightened monetary policy significantly, in the face of rapid inflation in oil prices. The reality was very different. At that time the Franklin National Bank was having severe financial problems, and was using the discount window to raise billions of dollars. Since those loans to the Franklin represented additions to the money supply, and since the Fed did not want to inflate the money supply at that time, the Open Market Desk responded by draining from the market what the Fed was adding to the Franklin. The market, however, was unaware of the reasons for these actions and drew the wrong conclusions. Obviously, in order to have any idea what the Fed is really doing at any time, we must understand its functions as:

1. Commercial and investment banker to the U.S. Treasury.
2. Primary U.S. market dealer for a list of official foreign investors.
3. Defender of our national currency.
4. Administrator of the government bond market.
5. Guardian and one of the regulators of the commercial banking system.
6. Source and implementer of the nation's monetary policy.

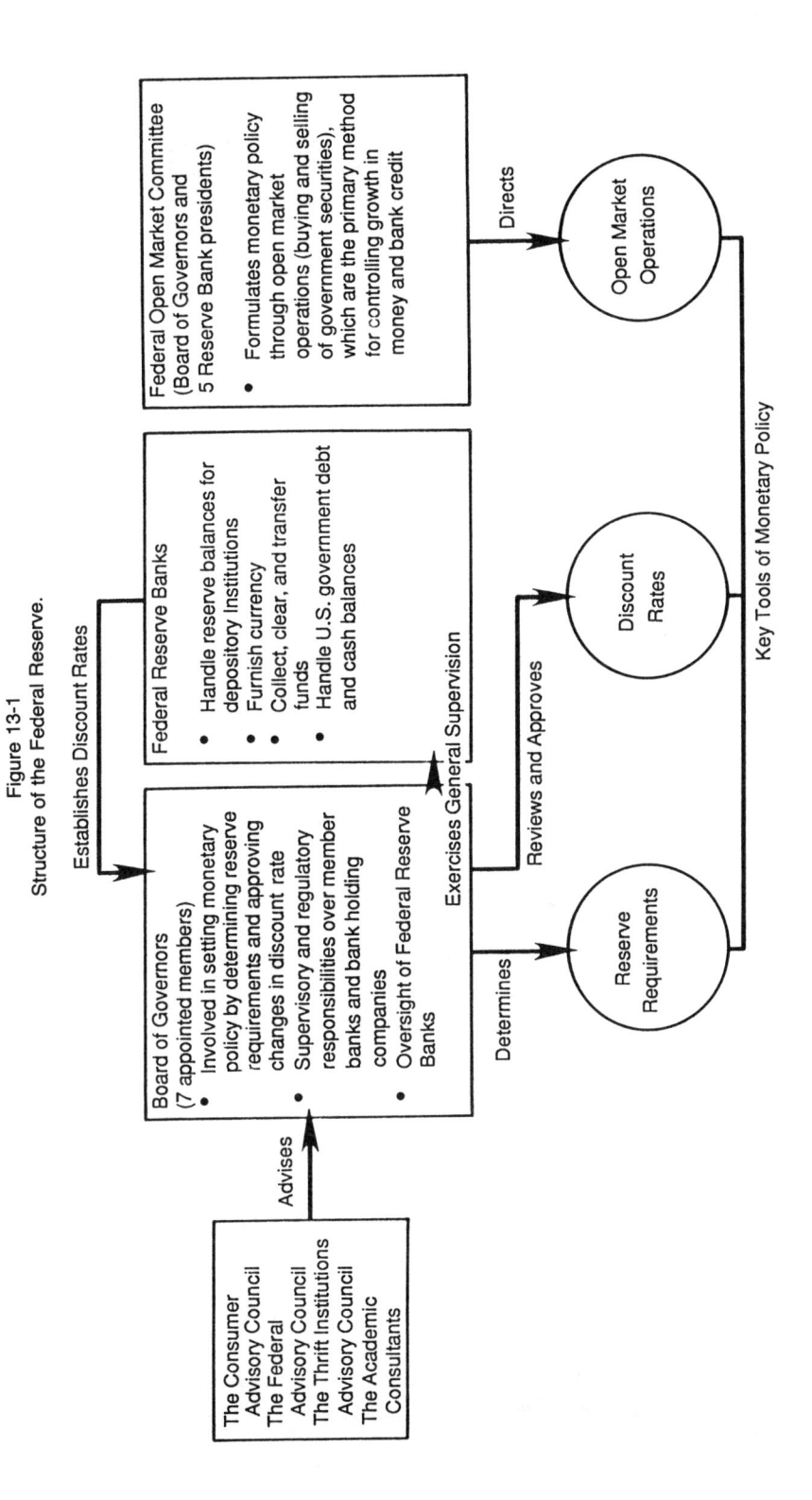

Figure 13-1
Structure of the Federal Reserve.

Federal Open Market Committee
(Board of Governors and
5 Reserve Bank presidents)

- Formulates monetary policy through open market operations (buying and selling of government securities), which are the primary method for controlling growth in money and bank credit

Federal Reserve Banks

- Handle reserve balances for depository Institutions
- Furnish currency
- Collect, clear, and transfer funds
- Handle U.S. government debt and cash balances

Board of Governors
(7 appointed members)

- Involved in setting monetary policy by determining reserve requirements and approving changes in discount rate
- Supervisory and regulatory responsibilities over member banks and bank holding companies
- Oversight of Federal Reserve Banks

- The Consumer Advisory Council
- The Federal Advisory Council
- The Thrift Institutions Advisory Council
- The Academic Consultants

Advises → Board of Governors

Establishes Discount Rates → Federal Reserve Banks

Exercises General Supervision

Reviews and Approves → Discount Rates

Determines → Reserve Requirements

Directs → Open Market Operations

Key Tools of Monetary Policy

217

Fulfilling its role in each of these six areas is a daily balancing act performed by the Fed. Needed actions in one area can have unwanted repercussions in another—while all the while, the market is reading its own interpretations, valid and invalid, into every course of action taken by the Fed.

Let's examine more closely how the Fed carries out each of its six functions.

*Commercial and Investment Banker
to the U.S. Treasury*

Every way in which the Treasury interacts with the financial markets, and every financial transaction the Treasury does, is handled by the Fed. The government's checking accounts are at the Fed, so every payment the government makes is in the form of a debit of a Fed account. All tax payments are made into accounts at the Fed, whether directly by taxpayers or through deposits to Treasury Tax and Loan Accounts (TT&L Accounts) at commercial banks, which the Fed draws down frequently.

Not only does the Fed act as the commercial banker, it acts as the investment banker as well. All securities issued by the Treasury are issued through the Fed. In auctions (the method of choice in the last few years), all tenders are received by the Federal Reserve Banks, and securities are delivered and paid for at the Banks. In other methods of issuance, the Fed plays an equally pivotal role. In subscription offerings, all subscriptions are received at the Banks, and in rights offerings (which haven't been used by the Treasury for years), maturing issues are tendered in exchange for refunding issues at the Banks.

The impact of this function is that the Fed is the financial engine of fiscal policy. When tax receipts fall significantly below outlays, the Fed is the organization actually pumping money into the system. When a new issue of Treasury securities is sold and delivered, the Fed is the organization that is draining reserves. The fact that these requirements may conflict with other jobs the Fed is doing is their worry.

*Primary U.S. Market Dealer for a List
of Foreign Investors*

One of the reasons that the dollar is the world's premier reserve currency is the deep and liquid market for Treasury securities. In order

Inside the Federal Reserve

to participate in that market, foreign central banks and other offshore sovereign holders of dollars often use the Federal Reserve Bank of New York's trading desk.

For many years, the New York FRB was the sole dealer for most foreign central banks, whose investment strategies were extremely conservative. In more recent times, however, the New York Fed's portion of these investors' business has steadily declined, until it now represents about half of all their investment activity. This decline in the Fed's importance is caused, in part, by the Fed's unwillingness to offer investment advice, largely because any advice the Fed might give could be construed to be based on the Fed's inside information on monetary policy.

The Fed still does a significant amount of business with foreign central banks, buying from and selling to them out of its own portfolio. These transactions occur every day in large amounts. But not all these transactions are between the Fed and its foreign customers. A few of them are accomplished directly with the Primary Dealers in the form of a pass. Which of these methods the Fed chooses has a significant impact on the level of bank reserves, because any transactions direct with the FRBNY add or drain reserves, while those done with dealers do not.

It is important to understand why this is true. All dollars held by foreigners are held in the form of commercial bank deposits, which means that they are part of the money supply and have reserves held against them. Funds held by the FRBNY are not considered part of the money supply. Thus, when a foreign central bank buys securities from the FRBNY, it pays for those securities with funds that have been part of the money supply, and are drained from the system when they are paid into the Fed. That same purchase of securities made from a dealer results in funds being transferred from one bank account to another, causing no change in the money supply.

Of course, a sale of securities by a foreigner to the FRBNY would result in the addition of funds to the money supply, while the same sale of securities made to a dealer has no impact on the money supply. The Fed is aware of the impact of its direct transactions with foreign central banks, and factors those transactions into its plans. When foreign central banks are supporting the dollar by buying in the market and thus have a lot of dollars to invest, those larger-than-usual investments could drain large amounts of money from the system. If other forces are also draining reserves, the Fed may have to add reserves, not because internal forces are at work, but because international forces are at work.

Defender of Our National Currency

For as long as there have been different countries, with different currencies, there has been the problem of foreign exchange rates. In essence, this problem has been one of determining how well your country does economically against other countries. The orthodox theory says that, if your country imports more goods than it exports, your currency will depreciate versus the currencies of your trading partners. As your currency falls in value, your products will become more competitive in foreign markets, and foreign goods less competitive in your markets. Thus the import-export imbalance will be corrected, and there will be an equilibrium exchange rate, which will relate to an equilibrium balance of trade.

Economic theory is great for classrooms, but it has less of a following in the marketplace. Somehow, the political realities of full employment and protectionism keep rearing their heads. Until after World War I, a gold standard kept everyone in line, at the expense of wracking economic cycles throughout the industrialized world. After World War II a system of fixed exchange rates was established in meetings held at Bretton Woods, New Hampshire; the system lasted until the explosive inflation of the 1970s. At that point, President Nixon abandoned fixed exchange rates altogether, and they have floated ever since.

Under any form of floating rates, the actions of each nation's central bank take on added significance. In the competition between nations to produce and sell goods, there are three variables to be juggled: domestic prices, the balance of trade, and exchange rates. The higher a nation's relative prices, given stable exchange rates, the worse its balance of trade. A nation that has high prices, and wants a good balance of trade, must face falling exchange rates. This would all be simple and unavoidable, except for the appearance of Eurocurrencies.

Eurocurrencies are currencies held outside their country of origin. Almost all Eurocurrencies are held as exchange reserves, against the time when they will be needed to buy that country's products. Eurocurrencies are more popular than gold for this purpose because they pay interest, while gold does not. The dollar is the most popular reserve currency in the world, because the market for dollar securities is so liquid. Until recently, this fact has allowed the United States to run substantial balance of payments deficits without seeing the exchange value of the dollar decline.

This fortuitous fact has overshadowed a very ominous side effect however. The accumulation of Eurodollar reserves has left the United States with a huge and volatile supply of its currency outside its borders. A modest swing in this pool of dollars could cause huge swings in the exchange value of the dollar, and substantial disruption in this country's trade with other nations. Thus the Fed (in conjunction with the Treasury) has a major job in keeping the dollar stable enough to remain the predominant reserve currency.

To do this job, the Fed has two choices: It can buy or sell dollars in the foreign exchange market, using up or adding to its reserves of other currencies—or it can adjust internal interest rates, thus making the dollar more or less attractive as a reserve currency. The higher our interest rates versus those in other countries, the more popular the dollar is as a reserve currency, and the less downward pressure on dollar exchange rates. Thus, a rate reduction action that might be called for by internal economics could be precluded by the fact that the dollar is under selling pressure in exchange markets.

Administrator of the Government Bond Market

Under the Securities Act of 1933, U.S. government and agency securities are exempt from the registration requirement placed upon corporations. Under the Securities Exchange Act of 1934, dealers who did business solely in securities exempt from the 1933 Act were themselves exempt from registration with exchanges, the NASD, or the SEC.

The government bond market was too large, too important, and too complex for it to be left entirely unsupervised. Since the Fed came into the most contact with the dealers in its other functions, it evolved into the day-to-day regulator of the market. Its regulatory style, however, is closer to the informal method used by the Bank of England than to the legalistic method used by the SEC. Since the FRBNY decides who gets and keeps its direct trading wire, and since the "Fed wire" is so important to government bond dealers, the Fed is able to exercise significant control over the Primary Dealers.

Among other things, Primary Dealers report a tremendous amount of information daily and weekly to the FRBNY, including their trading volume with other dealers, brokers, and customers, their securities positions, and how they are financed. When a Primary Dealer falls down on his job of providing liquidity to the universe of customers, the FRBNY calls the management in for a discussion of the problem.

Should the shortcoming not be corrected, the Fed can pull the wire, leaving the dealer out in the cold.

In the past, out in the cold is exactly where some government bond dealers preferred to be, since that put them outside the Fed's, and everyone else's, purview. Out of the mainstream, and out of the regulators' vision, these dealers were free to do things regulated dealers couldn't do, and to operate on much lower capital bases than regulated dealers needed. Eventually, the lack of regulation on these dealers led to a series of failures, capped by the collapse of ESM Securities in Boca Raton, Florida, and BBS Securities in Livingston, New Jersey. In both cases, the dealers had borrowed money from savings and loans and local banks under the auspices of a repurchase agreement, except that there was no collateral behind the loans.

The substantial losses suffered by unsophisticated financial institutions prompted Congress to pass a law requiring the registration of all companies that trade in government securities with the SEC. During the passage of that legislation in 1986, there was a lot of discussion about the impact of substituting the SEC's regulation for the Fed's, but the final impact of the legislation is that the SEC deferred, in the day-to-day regulation of the market, to the greater experience of the Fed.

One adjunct to its function as the regulator of the government securities market is the Fed's role as clearing agent for all government securities trades. Since government securities, for the most part, exist only on the Fed's computer, all trades must be settled on the Fed's computer. In this capacity, however, the Fed acts very differently from exchange clearing corporations. Where clearing corporations interpose themselves between contraparties, and become the contraparty to every position, the Fed does not. In fact, the Fed does not know anything about dealer positions or customer positions, only the gross positions of clearing banks. Still, the Fed plays a crucial role in the settlement of all government securities trades.

Guardian and One of the Regulators of the Commercial Banking System

This function is a primary reason the Fed was formed in 1913 and remains one of its most important jobs. Before 1913, banks had no reserve requirements against their deposits, so they could lend out the full amount they took in, with no cushion against sudden withdrawals. As a result, every so often banks would fail by the dozens, with financial panics and depressions following.

The Federal Reserve Act ended all that, by requiring all national banks to keep reserves against their deposits at the District Federal Reserve Bank nearest to their headquarters. In order to determine how large the reserves needed to be, member banks were required to report their levels of deposits regularly to the Fed.

The Bank Holding Company Act of 1958, the Bank Merger Act of 1960, and the Change in Bank Control Act of 1978 all solidified the Fed's control of certain aspects of the banking system. In particular, the Fed controls bank holding companies, whether they hold one bank or several, the branching and acquisition of banks or bank holding companies, and the levels of bank lending in certain areas like securities margin. By the 1980s, the Fed had the authority to examine all member banks and affiliates, but it had ceded the responsibility for examining national banks to the Comptroller of the Currency, retaining the responsibility for examining state-chartered member banks.

Finally, in its role as lender of last resort, the Fed has the responsibility of supporting the banking system in a crisis. Through the discount window, the Fed is prepared to lend funds to a bank or banks which are experiencing substantial outflows, as long as the banks can come up with sufficient collateral. When this need arises from a widespread run on the banking system, either real or imagined, the Fed generally makes its willingness to act as lender of last resort very public, in order to forestall any panic. If the need arises from the financial problems of one bank, the Fed will usually make its loans in secret, so the individual bank's problems do not escalate into a full-scale run. Either way, this function can get very much in the way of other functions.

Source and Implementer of the Nation's Monetary Policy

Orthodox economics holds that there are two ways in which a government can affect the level of economic activity: fiscal policy and monetary policy. Fiscal policy refers to the spending and revenue programs of the government, or whether there is a budget surplus or deficit. Monetary policy refers to the cost and availability of credit, or the general level of interest rates. Orthodox economics held that these two policy methods were entirely separate, and that one could be used one way while the other was used the opposite way. Orthodox economics has also held that, since the Fed is essentially an independent force, it has considerable freedom to exercise monetary policy in this country.

The reality is something quite different. In the first place, monetary and fiscal policy are inextricably intertwined, so that every change in fiscal policy has an enormous impact on monetary policy. In the second place, although the Fed purports to be independent of the political struggle, it cannot ignore the political implications of everything it does. And in the third place, the Fed has so many functions to perform that it seldom if ever gets a clean shot at monetary policy.

That being the case, the Federal Open Market Committee sets the monetary policy of the United States. That group, at its regular meetings, determines whether to make credit more or less available and whether to move interest rates higher or lower. In making those decisions, the FOMC weighs a myriad of concerns, encompassing all five of the Fed's other functions. One only has to read the FOMC meeting minutes to comprehend the complexity of its job.

Once the FOMC has set a policy, the open market implementation of that policy is the responsibility of the Open Market Account Manager, and is executed by the Open Market Trading Desk of the New York Fed. The choices the Fed has for implementing policy range from doing nothing to buying or selling large amounts of securities in the marketplace. The Fed can enter into financing transactions or outright purchases (or sales), and can do them on its own behalf or on behalf of the foreign central banks it trades with.

Although its options appear quite numerous, the Fed is constrained by the fact that the market perceives its choices in a very ritualistic way. Actions on behalf of customers are thought to be far less meaningful to monetary policy than actions for the System Account. Financing transactions are assumed to signify less important policy actions than outright buys and sells. Overnight repos and reverses are thought to signal a "rate protest" or displeasure with current rates, while multi-day financings do not. The Fed is perceived to have a "band" for Fed Funds, within which it is happy and outside of which it executes a "rate protest" transaction.

If the Fed is trying to "fine tune" the availability of reserves, perhaps because of unusual cash flows on the part of the Treasury, it may be severely limited in the actions it can take because of what the market may read into them. If the Fed is supporting the dollar by selling other currencies and absorbing dollars, the sellers of those dollars may need to sell government securities as well. If the Fed does not put the dollars it is absorbing back into the market, its currency support operation will have the effect of raising interest rates, which may go against the wishes of the FOMC.

THE BALANCING ACT

Thus we can see that the Fed is always balancing its many functions. Every day, various parts of the Federal Reserve System deal with a host of needs and problems. The Treasury is moving money in and out of the system and may also be announcing or auctioning new issues of securities. Commercial banks are buying and selling money in their own market and may be borrowing large sums at the discount window. The dollar may be falling in the foreign exchange markets, and foreign central banks may be adjusting downward their vast holdings of Eurodollars and government securities. The inventories of Primary Dealers may be extra heavy, due to a lack of investor interest in recent Treasury auctions, leaving the market without much support. Given all that, at 11:35 A.M., the Fed is expected to execute an open market operation that signals to the world the future of interest rates.

In that kind of environment, it is no wonder that the Fed prefers to operate somewhat behind a curtain, sometimes just to cover mistakes. In their candid moments, Fed officials will admit that they don't always balance everything just right and that they sometimes have to fly a little blind. Because the market watches the Fed so closely and reads so much into every little movement, a case can be made that so much secrecy breeds increased market volatility. If the Fed is shooting at a moving target and it misses a little, the markets are probably better off knowing that instead of thinking that the target has moved. Indeed, the Fed is substantially more forthcoming now than they were even five years ago, and will probably become even more so in the future.

In the meanwhile, the market will continue to operate in the shadow of 33 Liberty Street. "Fed watching" will continue to be a full-time occupation for a group of well-paid economists. No one will leave the trading floor after 11:30 in the morning. And the market will continue to provide the strength and liquidity that the world has come to expect. One can always find countless inefficiencies and quirks in the market, and one sometimes finds chaos, but the fact remains that one can also always find a bid or an offer for any amount of securities. For all its oddities and failings, the government bond market is still a genuine economic miracle.

Index

A

Accounts
  clearing account, 187
  customer account, 169
  reserve account, 44
  safekeeping account, 190
Accretion, 59
Accrual tranche, 94
Add-on, 34
Add week, 170
Adjustable rate mortgages (ARMs), 84
After-tax yield, 59
Agency mortgage-backed securities trading, 104–6
  average-life uncertainties, 105–6
  settlement, 104–5
  See also Mortgage-backed securities
Agency traders, 156–58
Agent, 13
All-or-none orders, 186
Arbitrage, 134, 136, 172, 179–82, 186
  auction arbitrage, 181
  kinds of, 180–82
  nature of, 179–82
Arbitrageurs, 65
ARMs, *See* Adjustable rate mortgages
At-the-money option, 132
Auction arbitrage, 181

Auctions, 49, 153, 206–8
  terminology of, 187–88
Average bids, 187
Average life, 108
  calculation of, 105–6
    constant prepayment rate (CPR), 105
    FHA method, 105
    PSA method, 106

B

Bankers' Acceptances (BAs), 113–14
  compared to CDs, 113
  issuance procedures, 114
Bank Holding Company Act of 1958, 223
Banking Act of 1933, 7
Bank instruments, 111–14
  Bankers' Acceptances (BAs), 113–14
  certificates of deposit (CDs), 112–13
  Federal Funds, 111–12
  See also specific topics
Banks for Cooperatives (COOPs), 9
Basis, 130
Basis traders, 156
Bids, 127, 184
  average, 187–88
  competitive bids, 187
  discounted bids, 88

Index

Bids (cont'd.)
  high bids, 187
  noncompetitive bids, 40, 44, 187, 212
  preparation of, 155
  stop, 187
"Big three" federal agencies, 72–87
  Federal Farm Credit Banks Funding Corporation (FFCB), 72–77
  Federal Home Loan Banks (FHLBs), 78–80
  Federal National Mortgage Association (FNMA), 83–87
Bill futures contract, 47
Bill pass, 187
Bills of lading, 33
Board of Governors, Federal Reserve System, 215
Bond authorization, 48
Bond market, 5
Book, *See* Trading position
Book-entry system, 44
Bounce, definition of, 192
Brokers, government securities, 18
Bull and bear spreads, 135
Butterfly yield curve, 180

C

Calendar spreads, 135
Call, 132
  call date, 68
  covered call, 135
  long call, 134
  money market call, 135
  short call, 135
Capital ratio, 73
Cash and carry trades, 130, 180
Cash secured put write, 135
Cash trades, 191
CBT bond futures contract, 65
Certificates of deposit (CDs), 112–13
  compared to other securities, 113
Change in Bank Control Act of 1978, 223
Chicago Board Options Exchange (CBOE), 136
  options market, 136–39
Chicago Board of Trade (CBT), 65, 125, 127–28, 139, 156
  bond futures contract, 65
  options market, 139–41
Clearing account, 44
Clearing agents, 127
Clearinghouse bank, 192
Clearinghouse funds, 192
Clerks, 127
Collateral, financing of customers' collateral, 120
Collateralized mortgage obligations (CMOs), 104, 159–60
Collateral swaps, 189
Combinations, 135–36
Commercial banks, 5, 16–18, 91, 162
Commercial paper (CP), 114–15
  issuers of, 115
Commission brokers, 126
Commitment, 146
Commodity futures contract, 65
Competitive bids, 187
Concession, 74
Consolidated financing, 56
Consolidated Systemwide Bonds, 73
Consolidated Systemwide Notes, 73
Constant prepayment rate (CPR), 105
Contract specifications, 127
Convergence, 108
Conversion factors, 128
Corporate tax payment date, 47
Corporate trades, 191
Cost of carry, 108
Cost of shorting, 131
Counter, 185
Coupon pass, 171, 187
Coupon rates, 74
Coupon securities, 32, 48
Cover, 188
  definition of, 212
Covered call, 135
Current coupon, 106
Current yield, 59
Customer account, 169
Customer information flow, 157
Customers
  government securities, 23–25
    common denominator for, 25
    definition of, 23–24
    leveraged investors, 24
    non-primary dealers, 24
    unleveraged investors, 24–25
Customer time, 192

Index

D

Day-to-day trading, Treasury bills, 150
Dealers, 5
  typical day of, 194–213
Dealer time, 192
Debt ceiling, 32
Deck, 126
Delivery
  delivery months, financial futures, 131
  delivery price, 128
  good delivery, 105
  partial delivery, 193, 210
Deltas, 133-34
Demand-driven inflation, 10
Derivative instruments, 123–41
  financial futures, 124–32
    delivery months, 131
    futures contract specifications, 127
    futures prices, 128
    futures versus forwards, 125
    inside a futures pit, 126
  option markets, 136
    CBOS options market, 136
    CBT options market, 139
  options, 132–36
    arbitrages, 136
    combinations, 135–36
    deltas, 133–34
    married positions, 135
    naked positions, 134–35
    options strategies, 134
    option valuation, 132–33
    understanding options, 132
Discount, 32, 33
Discounted bids, 88
Discount from par, 34
Discount rate, 168
Discount window, 168
Dollar roll, 190–91
Drain week, 170

E

Early call, 77
Economic backlash, 10
Economics department
  Primary Dealers, 166–71
    Federal Reserve System and, 168–71
    money market economist's job, 167–68

Eurocurrencies, 220–21
Exchange clearing corporation, 125
Expiration date, 132

F

Factor Book, 96, 99
  page from, 97–98
Fail, definition of, 192
Farm credit agencies, 71, 157
Farm Credit Association (FCA), 73
Farm Credit System, 72–73, 157
Federal agency securities, 7–11, 68
  individual agencies, 8
    Banks for Cooperatives (COOPs), 9
    Federal Farm Credit Banks (FFCB), 9
    Federal Home Loan Banks (FHLB), 9
    Federal Home Loan Mortgage Corporation (FHLMC), 9
    Federal Intermediate Credit Banks (FICBs), 9
    Federal Land Banks (FLBs), 8
    Federal National Mortgage Association (FNMA), 9
    Governmental National Mortgage Association (FNMA), 9
Federal Farm Credit Banks Corporation (FFCB), 72–77
  Farm Credit System, 72–73, 157
  issuance procedures, 73–74
  quote sheet of issues, 76
  Telerate screen of issues page, 75
  trading, 74–77
Federal Funds, 23, 111–12, 158, 191–92
  Federal Funds rate, 170
  Fed Fund trades, 191–92
  importance of market, 112
  trading periods, 112
Federal Home Loan Bank Board (FHLBB), 71, 78
  bonds, 78–80
  issuance procedures, 80–81
  quote sheet of issues, 82
  trading, 81–83
Federal Home Loan Banks (FHLBs), quote sheet of issues, 82
Federal Home Loan Mortgage Corporation (FHLMC), 26, 102–4, 158

Federal Home Loan Mortgage Corporation
    (FHLMC) *(cont'd.)*
  mortgage-backed securities, 103
  participation certificates (PCs), 102–3
    15-year certificates, 103
    30-year certificates, 103
  private collateralized mortgage obligations
      (CMOs), 104
Federal Housing Administration (FHA), 95
Federal Land Bank of Omaha, 71
Federal National Mortgage Association
    (FNMA), 26, 70, 83, 156–58
  history of, 83
  issuance procedures, 85
  quote sheet of issues, 86–87
  trading, 85–87
Federal Open Market Committee (FOMC),
    7, 224
Federal Reserve Act, 223
Federal Reserve System, 5, 27, 37, 111,
    191, 214–26
  Federal Open Market Committee (FOMC),
      224
  functions of, 216–25
    as administrator of government bond
        market, 221–22
    as commercial/investment banker to
        U.S. Treasury, 218
    as defender of national currency, 220–21
    as guardian/regulator of commercial
        banking system, 222–33
    as primary U.S. market dealer for foreign investors, 218–19
    as source/implementer of nations's monetary policy, 223–25
  minimum disclosure policy, 214–15
  open market operations, 168–69, 187
  structure of, 215–17
    Board of Governors, 215
    Federal Open Market Committee
        (FOMC), 214–16
    Federal Reserve District Banks, 215
Federal Savings and Loan Insurance Corporation (FSLIC), 71, 78, 80, 113
Fed time, definition of, 203
Fed watching, 127, 168, 225–26
Fed wire, 15, 221
FHA method, of calculating average life,
    105

Fifteen-year participation certificates, 103
Fill-or-kill order, 185–86
Financial forwards, 124
Financial futures, 124
  delivery months, 131
  futures contract specifications, 127
  futures prices, 128–30
  futures versus forwards, 125
  inside a futures pit, 126
Financial futures contract, 124
Financing, terminology of, 188–91
Financing market, 115–16
  repurchase agreements, 117–18
Firm, 185
Fiscal agent, 74
Five-year note, 56
Fixed term, 189
Floating rate notes (FRNs), 88–89
Foreign investors, 26–27
Formal regulation, 25
Forward contract, 123
Forward conversion, 136
Forward roll, 46
Four-year note, 56
Freddie Mac, *See* Federal Home Loan Mortgage Corporation (FHLMC)
Front month, 130
Front run, 207
Full faith and credit, 31
Full-service securities firm, 17
Fundamentals, trading on, 176–77
Futures contract, 125
  specifications, 127–28
Futures exchange, pit, 126–27

G

General collateral, 190
Ginnie Mae, *See* Government National Mortgage Association (GNMA)
Glass-Steagall Act, 17, 156
Gnomes, 103
Good delivery, 105
Government bond market, 5–7, 14–25
  development of, 5–7
  language of the market, 183–93
  organizational structure, 14
    Federal Reserve Bank of New York, 14
    Primary Dealers, 14
      customers, 23–25

Index

government bond brokers, 18
types of, 16–18
reading a broker's screen, 18–23
Primary Dealers
sales force/economics department, 161–71
trading desk, 145–60
trading, 172–82
Government National Mortgage Association (GNMA), 26, 83, 92, 125, 159
Factor Book, 96–98
Government quote sheet, 59
Government securities
brokers, 18
trading of, 172–82
arbitrage, 179–82
key to success, 173
methods, 177–78
trading styles, 173–77
Government Securities Dealer Group, 7

H

Haircut, 190
Hedge, 62, 164
Hedge ratio, *See* Deltas
High bids, 187
Higher Education Act, 88
Hit the stop, definition of, 211

I

Indications, definition of, 184
Inflation, 10
Information, as key to success, 173
Inter-American Development Bank (IADB), 89
Interest component, 34
Intermediate coupon traders, 153–55
Intermediate sector of market, sales force and, 163
International Bank for Reconstruction and Development, 89
In-the-money option, 132
Intrinsic value, 132–34
Issuance procedures
Bankers' Acceptance (BAs), 114
Federal Farm Credit Banks Corporation (FFCB), 73–74
Federal National Mortgage Association (FNMA), 85

minor agency securities, 88
Student Loan Marketing Association (SLMA), 88
Treasury bills, 37–44
Treasury bonds, 64–65
Treasury notes, 48
Issuer, 32
Issue size, 76–77

J

Japanese Ministry of International Trade and Industry (MITI), 69

L

Leveraged investors, 24
Life insurers, 65
Liquid markets, 15
Locals, 126
Long call, 134
Long coupon traders, 155–56
Long put, 134

M

Margin deposit, 190
Market, 184
background of, 3–11
federal agency securities, 7–11
government bond market, 5–7
national debt, 3–5
definition of, 12
intermediate sector, sales force and, 163
organizational structure, 12–27
government bond market, 14–25
over-the-counter (OTC) market, 12–14
recent/impending changes in, 25–27
overview of, 1–27
philosophies of, 176–77
recent changes in marketplace, 10–11
Market regulator, 7
Mark to the market, 190
Married positions, 135
Married put, 135
Matched book desk, 198
Matched book traders, 159–60
Matched sales, 169
Maturity at issuance, 32
MBS trades, 191

Method of interest payment, 32
Midgets, 101, 103
Minimum disclosure policy, Federal Reserve System, 214–15
Mini-refunding, 56
Minor agency securities, 87–89
  Student Loan Marketing Association (SLMA), 88
    issuance procedures, 88
    trading, 88–89
Modified passthrough securities, 92
Monetary policy, 123
Money market basis, 189
Money market call, 135
Money market demand accounts, 111
Money market economist, 166
  job of, 167–68
Money market instruments, 110–21
  bank instruments, 111–14
    Bankers' Acceptance (BAs), 113–14
    certificates of deposit (CDs), 112–13
    Federal Funds, 111–12
  commercial paper, 114–15
  financing securities, 115–16
  repurchase/reverse repurchase agreements, 116–20
Money market mutual funds, 110
Monthly auction, 153
Mortgage-backed securities, 90–109, 190
  Federal Home Loan Mortgage Corporation (FHLMC), 26
  GNMA passthroughs, 95–100
    GNMA graduated payment mortgages (GPMs), 101-2
    GNMA I 15 year (midgets), 101
    GNMA I 30 year, 101
    GNMA II 30 year, 101
    pool formation, 95–96
  market, 106–9
  multi-tranche collateralized mortgage obligations (CMOs), 93–94
  passthrough securities, 92–93
  Real Estate Mortgage Investment Conduit (REMIC), 94–95
  Telerate screen of securities page, 107
  See also Agency mortgage-backed securities trading
Mortgage-backed securities traders, 158–59
Mortgage banker, 91
Mortgage passthrough, 26

Multiple tenders, 56
Multi-tranche collateralized mortgage obligations (CMOs), 26, 93, 100

N

Naked positions, 134–35
Naked trading, 177–78
National debt, 6
  origins of, 3–5
Negative carry, 25
Net interest impact, 46
New York district, 188
New York Federal Reserve Bank (FRBNY), 219, 221
Non-competitive bids, 40, 44, 187, 212
Non-primary dealers, 24
No position, 186

O

Offer, 184
Off-the-run issues, 74, 85, 151
On special securities, 189
On-the-run issues, 22, 74, 85, 152
Open, 189
Open market operations, 168–69, 187
"Open mike" system, 196
Open repos, 119
Option markets, 136–41
  CBOE options market, 136–39
  CBT options market, 139–41
Options, 132–36
  arbitrages, 136
  combinations, 135–36
  deltas, 133–34
  married positions, 135
  naked positions, 134–35
  options strategies, 134
  option valuation, 132–33
  price volatility, 133–34
  understanding options, 132
Order, 185
Order flow trading, 173–74
Out-of-the-money option, 132
Overnight book, 160, 189
Overnight repo, 203
Overnight transactions, 119
Over-the-counter (OTC) market, 12–14, 136
Overvalued securities, 62

Index

P

Pair-off trades, 191
Partial delivery, 193, 210
Participation certificates (PCs), 102–3
　15-year certificates, 103
　30-year certificates, 103
Pass, 187
Passthrough securities, 92–93, 124–25
　GNMA passthroughs, 95–100
Pension funds, 65
Physical certificates, 48
Position trading, 174–75
Positive carry, 108, 130
Premium, 132
Price risk, 62
Price volatility, 62, 133
Pricing, Treasury bills, 33–37
Primary Dealer Association, 15, 106
Primary Dealers, 5, 7, 10, 145–60, 161–71
　areas of, 149–60
　　agency traders, 156
　　intermediate coupon traders, 153
　　long coupon traders, 155
　　matched book traders, 159
　　mortgage-baked securities traders, 158
　　short coupon traders, 152
　　trading desk, 150
　　treasury bill traders, 150
　　treasury coupon traders, 151
　definition of, 145–46
　duties of, 147–48
　economics department, 166–67
　　fed's impact on, 168–71
　　money market economist's job, 167–68
　Federal Reserve System and, 221–22
　sales force, 161–66
　　job of, 164–66
　　specialization in, 162–64
　structure of, 148–49
Principal, 13
PSA method, of calculating average life, 106
Public Securities Association (PSA), 15, 106, 146
Pull, 185
Put, 132
　long put, 134
　married put, 135
　short put, 135

Q

Quarterly refunding, 155
　Treasury notes, 48–56
Quote, 184–85

R

Rate
　definition of, 189
　rate change component, 34
　rate protest, 203
　rate volatility, 91
Real Estate Mortgage Investment Conduits (REMICs), 94, 100
Records, 197
Regular-way security, 186
Regular-way trades, 191
Repackagings, 26
Repricing, 190
Repurchase agreements (repos), 116–20, 188
　financing market, 117–18
　history of market, 116–17
　transactions, 119–20
　types of, 119–20
　　open repos, 119
　　repo to maturity, 119–20
　　term repos, 119
Reserve account, 44
Reserve ratios, 168
Reverse conversion, 136
Reverse repurchase agreements (reverse repos), 118–20, 169, 188
　reverse to maturity, 119–20
Reverse roll, 46, 186
Rights offering, 32, 48
Right of substitution, 189
Risk, 123
　effect of trading volume on, 123
　price risk, 62
Roll, 186
Run, 185
Runners, 127

S

Safekeeping account, 190
Safekeeping repo, 190
Sales force
　Primary Dealers, 161–66
　　job of, 164–66

Sales force
  Primary Dealers *(cont'd.)*
    specialization in, 162–64
Savings and loan associations, 78
Screens, 18
Securities Act of 1933, 221
Securities Exchange Act of 1934, 221
Securities and Exchange Commission (SEC), 25
Securities financing
  language of, 120–21
    financing customers' collateral, 120
    finding securities for dealers' delivery, 121
    putting customers' money to work, 120–21
Selling group, 73–74
Settlement, 88
  agency mortgage-backed securities, 104–5
  terminology of, 191–93
Seven-year note, 56
Shooting for the stop, 187
Short call, 135
Short coupon traders, 152–53
Short end of market, 162–63
Short put, 135
Short squeezes, 152–53
Skip day traders, 191
Special-purpose government securities, 17
Special repos, 119, 189–90
Special trader, 160
Spread, 88, 135, 177, 186
  bull and bear spreads, 135
  calendar spreads, 135
  spread trading, 178
  tail, 212
Stop bids, 187, 211
Stop talk, 40, 187, 212
Straddles, 136
Strangles, 136
Strike price, 132
Stripped issues, 26, 131
  Treasury bonds, 64
Student Loan Marketing Association (SLMA), 88
  issuance procedures, 88
  trading, 88–89
Subject, definition of, 185
Subscription offerings, 32
Swap trades, 172, 186
Synthetics, 136

T

Tail, 188, 212
T-bond contract, *See* Treasury bond contract
Technical action, 203
Technicals, trading on, 176–77
Telephonic network, 12
Tender form, 37–39
Ten-year note, 56
Term book, 160, 189
Term repos, 119, 162
Theoretical value, 133
Thirty-year participation certificates, 103
Three-year note, 56
Thrift institutions, 91
Time value, of options, 132–33
To maturity, definition of, 189
Traders, 150–60
  agency traders, 156–58
  basis traders, 156
  intermediate coupon traders, 153–55
  long coupon traders, 155–56
  matched book traders, 159–60
  mortgage-backed securities traders, 158–59
  short coupon traders, 152–53
  Treasury bill traders, 150–51
  Treasury coupon traders, 151–52
Trades
  cash and carry trades, 130, 180
  cash trades, 191
  corporate trades, 191
  skip day trades, 191
  swap trades, 172, 186
Trading
  Federal Farm Credit Banks Corporation (FFCB), 74–77
  Federal National Mortgage Association (FNMA), 85–87
  on fundamentals, 176–77
  government securities, 172–82
    key to success, 173
    methods, 177
    trading styles, 173
  minor agency securities, 87–89
  naked trading, 177–78
  order flow trading, 173–74
  position trading, 174–75
  spread trading, 178
  Student Loan Marketing Association (SLMA), 88–89

Index

on technicals, 176–77
terminology of, 184–87
Treasury bills, 44–47
Treasury bonds, 65–68
Treasury notes, 57–63
yield curve trading, 180
Trading desk, Primary Dealers, 145–60
Trading periods, Federal Funds, 112
Trading position, 26
Trading profit, 34
Trading rooms, 12
Trading volume, 146
Transaction balances, 110
Treasury bills, 33–47
 bill page, 45
 issuance procedures, 37–44
 prices, 35–36
 pricing, 33–37
 Telerate screen of auction results, 42–43
 tender for 3-month book-entry bills, 38–39, 41
 trading, 44–47
Treasury bill traders, 150–51
Treasury bond contract, 127–28
 delivery, 128–31
Treasury bonds, 63–68
 issuance procedures, 64–65
 stripped issues, 64
 Telerate screen of auction results, 66–67
 trading, 65–68
Treasury coupon traders, 151–52
Treasury notes, 47–63
 issuance procedures, 48
 other note issuances, 56–57
 quarterly refunding, 48–56
 Telerate screen of auction results, 54–55
 trading, 57–63
True yield, 34
Turn around, definition of, 192–93
Twelve-year life method, 105
Two-year note, 56

U

Underlying instrument, 132
Undervalued securities, 62

Underwriters, agency traders as, 157
Unleveraged investors, 24–25
Unsecured lenders, 190
U.S. government bonds, *See* Government bond market
U.S. Treasury, Treasury Tax and Loan Accounts (TT&L Accounts), 218
U.S. Treasury Department, 4
U.S. Treasury securities, 31–68
 price conversion table for, 21
 treasury bills, 33–47
 treasury bonds, 63–68
 treasury notes, 47–63
 See also specific topics

V

Veteran's Administration, 95
Victory Liberty Loan Act of 1919, 47

W

Wasting assets, 132
When-issued bill, 46
When-issued securities, 22, 153, 186
When-issued six-month, 46
Wireable securities, 158, 192
World Bank, 89
Writer, options, 132

Y

Yield
 after-tax, 59
 current yield, 59
 true yield, 34
 yield to maturity (YTM), 22, 59
Yield curve trading, 180

Z

Z tranche, 94